Books on comparative religion are mainly of three kinds: the informative, whose purpose is to review in more or less detail the beliefs and practices of various religious systems; the analytic, which presume on the information and go on to evaluate a number of living (or archaic) faiths according to certain normative principles; and the projective, where an author combines factual data and personal theory to anticipate what the future of man's religion may (or should) be like. Typical of the first category is the *Concise Encyclopedia of Living Faiths,* of the second, Joseph Kitagawa's *Religions of the East,* and of the third, Arnold Toynbee's *Christianity Among the Religions of the World.* Each type has its merits and limitations, and the growing output in this field suggests that among the limitations the most natural is the problem of space. There are too many religions with too much history and variety to make an adequate coverage of even the principal ones in a single volume.

The present book belongs to the first category of informative studies on the leading religions of mankind, currently practiced in the world and sufficiently known to allow some comparison of their faith and principles with those of other contemporary religious cultures.

As far as possible, the sources used were those published by representative writers within their own tradition, and always the main reliance was on the sacred books which the religions venerate as their special communication from the Deity or the sages of antiquity. In order to insure maximum accuracy and objectivity, the text of the different chapters was submitted for comment by those who have lived closely with the respective faiths, either as believers or as persons who know the religious persuasion by years of experience and study.

JOHN A. HARDON, S.J.

RELIGIONS
OF THE WORLD

·

VOLUME II

·

JOHN A. HARDON, S.J.

IMAGE BOOKS
A DIVISION OF DOUBLEDAY & COMPANY, INC.
GARDEN CITY, NEW YORK

Image Books edition: 1968
by special arrangement with The Newman Press

Image Books edition published March 1968

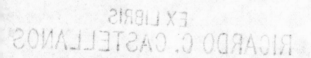

CONTENTS

VOLUME II

RELIGIONS OF JUDAIC ORIGIN

*To the Memory of Pope John XXIII
whose charity embraced all peoples
of every nation,
and whose wisdom saw the grace of God
active in all souls of every religious
persuasion*

EARLY CHRISTIANITY

Christianity is unique in the history of world religions. Its ancestry derives from almost two millenia of Judaism, whose prophets for centuries had foretold the coming of a great religious leader who would establish a new spiritual kingdom on earth; its origins are rooted in extensive historical facts, from the birth of Christ to His crucifixion and resurrection from the dead; its message centers around a core of doctrines which Christ revealed to His followers not as a philosophy of speculation nor even primarily as an ethic for self-conquest, but as mysteries whose inner essence lies beyond human reason, yet on whose acceptance would depend human salvation; its character from the beginning was social in the most comprehensive sense of that term, with a communal structure, a body of truths, rites and obligations that had for their purpose not merely the personal sanctification of those who believed, but their corporate unification and internal consolidation by the invisible Spirit of God.

MESSIANIC FULFILMENT

The great hope of the Jewish people nurtured by the prophets was the advent of a great leader whom they called "The Anointed," in Hebrew "The Messiah," whose kingdom would succeed the theocratic government of Israel and extend to all nations, races and classes of people. Membership in this kingdom carried the promise of order and peace in this world and of final beatitude in the next. The Messianic kingdom would be served by priests and teachers from all nations, dispensing an abundance of divine knowledge and a relish for things of the spirit; there would be one sacrifice, offering a clean oblation to the one true God throughout the world. Those who

belonged to it were assured the remission of their sins, sanctity
of life, justice among people and nations, and an outpouring
of divine benediction.

According to the prophets, this kingdom would be established by the Messias who was simultaneously priest, law-giver
and king, who would sacrifice himself for the redemption of
his people and institute a new order of society, beginning with
the Jews and then to be diffused to the ends of the earth.

What the prophets foretold in the Scriptures found reflection
in the extra-canonical writings of the Hebrews, like the *Testament of the Twelve Patriarchs,* in a passage that was written
two hundred years before the coming of Christ.

Then shall the Lord raise up a new priest.
And he shall execute a righteous judgment upon the earth for a
    multitude of days.
And his star shall rise in heaven as of a king,
Lighting up the light of knowledge as the sun the day,
And he shall be magnified in the world.
He shall shine forth as the sun of the earth,
And he shall remove all darkness from under heaven,
And there shall be peace in all the earth.
And the knowledge of the Lord shall be poured forth upon the
    earth, as the water of the seas.
And he shall give his majesty to his sons in truth for evermore.
And there shall be none succeed him for all generations for
    ever.
And in his priesthood the Gentiles shall be multiplied in knowledge
    upon the earth,
And enlightened through the grace of the Lord.[1]

Time and again Jesus proclaimed himself the Messias of
the prophets, but never more solemnly than when, in reply
to the woman at the well, "I know that the Messias is coming,"
He told her, "I who speak with you am he."[2] Already when
beginning His public ministry at Nazareth, He opened the
scroll of Isaias and read the Messianic text, "the Spirit of the
Lord is upon me, because He has anointed me," and added,
"today this Scripture has been fulfilled in your hearing."[3]

From the dawn of Christianity, the apostles and first leaders
of the Church were at pains to verify the origins of their faith

and how radically, therefore, the Christian religion differs from the mythology of pagan Greece and Rome. They were conscious of the strength of their position in having a historic center. "We do not utter idle tales," they told their contemporaries, "in declaring that God was born in form of man."

There never was a Mithra, the Romans were reminded; and he never slew the mystic bull. There never was a Great Mother of sorrows to wail over Attis and become a true mother to the suffering daughters of humanity. For all her beauty, Isis was only the idealized product of Egyptian zoolatry. The Logos of the Stoics was a pure abstraction, and of their ideal Wise Man, Plutarch wrote, "He is nowhere on earth, nor ever has been;" whereas for Christians "the Word was made flesh and dwelt among us."

The apostles staked their whole mission on this fact. Peter, writing from prison, assured the neophytes that "we were not following fictitious tales when we made known to you the power and coming of our Lord Jesus Christ, but we had been eyewitnesses of His grandeur."[4] Reproaching the Corinthians for their factious disputes, Paul appealed to historical continuity of his teaching with that of the first followers of Christ. "I delivered to you", he said, "what I also have received." Indeed the facts of Christ's life, death, and especially resurrection are so indispensable that without them the whole Christian faith is vain and "we are of all men the most to be pitied."[5]

Under pressure from their environment which was accustomed only to Greek speculation and Roman mythology, the early Christians were tempted to compromise, as many did in the Gnostic peril that faced the nascent Church. They were strengthened to resist by the aged apostle John, whose epistles seem almost strained in their effort to vindicate the foundations of the faith. "I write of what was from the beginning, what we have heard, what we have seen with our eyes, what we have looked upon and our hands have handled: of the Word of Life."[6]

In the same vein, Ignatius of Antioch stressed the need of watchfulness, not to give ear to those who would make of Christ only one of their aeons and something less than a real historical person. Christians must beware of the Docetae who denied the reality of Christ's human actions and therefore of His redemptive life and death.

> Stop your ears when anyone speaks to you that stands apart from Jesus Christ, from David to scion and Mary's son, who was really (*alethōs*) born and ate and drank, really (*alethōs*) persecuted by Pontius Pilate, really (*alethōs*) crucified and died while heaven and earth and the underworld looked on; who also really (*alethōs*) rose from the dead, since His Father raised Him up—His Father, who will also raise us who believe in Him through Jesus Christ, apart from whom we have no real life.[7]

Throughout his seven letters, written about 107 A.D., Ignatius returns to the same theme. He repeats the term *alethōs*, "really . . . truly . . . actually" the birth, life, death and resurrection of Christ took place, and therefore the faith of Christ is solidly established.

In the sub-apostolic and early patristic age, when the vested interest of the Roman Empire reacted against "the persons commonly called, who were hated for their enormities" (Tacitus), Christian apologists spent their energies proving the validity of the Gospel narrative of Christ. "Let us leave untouched," pleaded Polycarp of Smyrna (69–155 A.D.), "the useless speculations of the masses and their false doctrines, and turn to the teaching delivered to us in the beginning."[8] Not subjective theories but factual events were considered the mainstay of the Christian religion.

COMMUNITY OF FAITH AND WORSHIP

The facts of the Gospel narrative focus on the doctrines which Christ taught as the substance of His message and a condition for becoming His disciple. He proposed His divine Sonship and said He was one with the Father. When the Jews who were scandalized at this "blasphemy" picked up stones to kill Him, "He went forth out of their hands," but without retracting the claim.[9]

In much the same way He announced the Eucharist, telling the people that unless they ate the flesh of the Son of Man and drank His blood, they would not have life in them. As a consequence many of His disciples left Him, complaining that "this is a hard saying. Who can listen to it?" Yet instead of correcting a possible false impression or qualifying the mystery of faith, He turned to the Twelve and asked them, "Do you also wish to go away?"[10]

On the subject of marriage, He raised marital union to the sacramental level and added the precept of perfect monogamy, declaring that remarriage while the first spouse is living is wrong, no matter what concessions had been given to the ancient Jews. Again His followers, and this time the apostles themselves, were shocked at the severity of doctrine. Better not marry, they told Him, than to be so bound irrevocably for life. But there was no retraction; only a restatement to the effect that virginity, too, is possible with the grace of God.[11]

He proclaimed Himself the object of divine worship and demanded of His followers complete dedication. "If anyone loves father or mother, yes, and his own life also, more than me, he is not worthy of me."[12] Correspondingly He required that men pray to Him for all their needs, since "without me you can do nothing." But "whatever you ask in my name, that I will do."[13]

Implicit in all this teaching of Christ is the fact that He is communicating divine revelation to a chosen group of men, and bidding them transmit His message to all nations to the end of time. He is not expounding a purely natural philosophy or a system of ethics founded on human genius, but giving mankind a body of truths which "he who does not believe will be condemned" for rejecting.[14]

Besides uniformity of faith, Christ taught a community of worship and ritual as substantial elements of Christianity. His followers were indeed to believe in His teaching, but they had also to receive external baptism by water in the name of the Holy Trinity. He compared the effect of baptism to a new birth and emphasized in graphic language that just as in the natural order there is no life without physical birth, so in Christianity there is no life of grace "unless a man be born again of water and the Holy Spirit." In His parting commission to the apostles, He bade them "make disciples of all nations, (by) baptizing them in the name of the Father, and of the Son, and of the Holy Spirit," thus equating the initial following of Christ with ritual baptism according to a specified formula.

The early Christians stressed the consistency of the Old and New Covenants. Jesus said He did not come to destroy the law and the prophets but to fulfil them. Consequently where the Old Law had its ceremony of initiation in the rite of circumcision, membership in the society founded by Christ was to be effected uniquely through the sacrament of regeneration, which is the door of the Church and the basic external sign of every true Christian.

If baptism was the means for entering the kingdom of God on earth, the Eucharist became the normal condition for remaining in that kingdom. "He who eats my flesh and drinks my blood has life everlasting, and I will raise him up on the last day." No other mystery of faith more clearly identified Christianity as a visible society. "Take care," Ignatius of Antioch wrote to the Philadelphians, "to partake of one Eucharist; for one is the flesh of our Lord Jesus Christ, one the cup to unite us with His blood, and one altar, just as there is one bishop."[15]

In order to make the Eucharist a permanent institution and perpetuate the fruits of the Cross, Christ at the Last Supper gave His followers the power and duty to do what He had done, "in commemoration of me." When He ordained His chosen twelve, He was instituting those through whom the graces of the redemption were to flow from the Redeemer to the whole of mankind.

When pronouncing the words of His first consecration, Jesus spoke of "my blood of the New Covenant," to underscore the continuity between the two Laws and the perfection of the Christian over the Jewish dispensation. Among other early apologists, Justin the martyr argued from the Christian Eucharist to a fulfilment of the Messianic prophecies. The clean oblation foretold by Malachy, He said, is "the bread of the Eucharist and the chalice of the Eucharist." The ministry of Christ was to be open to all people, and not limited to the descendants of one family; it was to serve the welfare of all nations, and not only the sons of Abraham; it was to end the multiplicity of sacrifices among the Jews in favor of the one oblation of the Lamb of God offering Himself to the heavenly Father. This would give the Church of Christ a unity and universality that no other religion had ever enjoyed.

For the sins committed after baptism, Christ gave the Church power of remission that would further consolidate His Church as a society with tangible obligations on its members. Appearing to the Twelve the night of His resurrection, He told them, "As the Father has sent me, I also send you." And breathing on them in a gesture symbolic of the transmission of power, He said, "Receive the Holy Spirit; whose sins you shall forgive, they are forgiven them; and whose sins you shall retain, they are retained."[16]

KINGDOM AND AUTHORITY

The historical work of Christ during His visible stay on earth has a variety of aspects that range through the whole gamut of God's revelation of His nature and love for mankind, and of man's duty towards Him in order to return to God. Yet the master idea of Christ's message is epitomized in a single word that was most frequently on His lips, the *Basileia* of the evangelists, or the kingdom. All that He taught was somehow identified with the kingdom, from the opening of His public life when He began to preach repentance, "for the kingdom of heaven is at hand," to His dying profession before Pilate that "my kingdom is not of this world, my kingdom is not from here." Christ is reported to have used the word "Church" only twice in describing the society He founded. He spoke of His kingdom in almost every chapter of the Gospels, so that whatever concept they give us of the Church must be looked for in this notion of the kingdom.

Yet immediately a problem arises. The clear impression left by the evangelists is that Christ spoke of two kinds of kingdom, an earthly and a heavenly one. When He compared it to a grain of mustard seed that a man cast into his garden, and it grew and became a large tree, He was referring to an earthly kingdom that grows and develops in membership and influence. Or again, when He said that the kingdom is like a net cast into the sea and gathering in fish of every kind, the good and bad, which are later sorted out and the bad thrown away, this cannot mean the kingdom after death. The parable illustrates what will happen at the end of the world when the angels are sent to separate the wicked from the just and will cast the former into hell. On the other hand, Jesus also spoke of a kingdom that is not of this world, or a joy that awaits those who are poor in spirit, of the reward He will give on the last day to those who during life had fed the hungry and clothed the naked in His name.

These two kingdoms are mutually dependent. The heavenly kingdom is the goal and terminus of the earthly society, and the latter a means and condition for attaining the heavenly. It would be stressing the obvious to say that Christ preached the doctrine of a celestial kingdom that will never end and that God has in store for those who love Him. Even Mohammed, who did not accept the divinity of Christ and recognized Him only as a messenger of Allah, spoke of the "rich rewards for those who believe (in Jesus) and performed the works of virtue." They are promised after death a paradise "that is watered by rivers, and whose food and shade are perpetual."[17] What is less obvious is that Christ also founded an earthly society that would carry on His mission until the end of time.

Whenever a new society is being formed, the first stage calls for a "getting together" to lay plans for the prospective organization. This is true whether the original impulse to unite for a common purpose is something mutual or comes from a single individual who does the organizing. In the origins of Christianity this impulse came from Jesus of Nazareth.

John and Andrew, the disciples of John the Baptist, were first invited by Christ to "come and see" where He lived, to learn more about this man whom the Baptist had pointed out as the Lamb of God. Later on they were called to "Come follow me, and I will make you fishers of men." At once they left their nets and followed Jesus.

Meantime, Andrew found his brother Simon and said to him, "We have found the Messias." Jesus invited him by changing his name to Cephas, the Rock. Philip was invited with a simple, "Follow me," and passed the word on to his

brother Nathaniel, who responded by professing his faith in
Christ as "the Son of God and the King of Israel." Matthew
describes his vocation while sitting in the tax-collector's office.
On hearing these words, "Follow me," he arose and immediately followed the Master. In rapid succession six others were
called to join the apostles until the full complement of twelve
was filled, in imitation, we may suppose, of the leaders of the
twelve tribes of Israel.

They were all from Galilee, as suggested by the remark on
Pentecost Sunday, "are not all these men who are speaking
Galileans?" Their culture and ancestry were thoroughly Jewish. Even their names were Hebrew and Aramaic derivatives.
Nathaniel, "the gift of God"; John, "Yahweh is gracious";
Thomas, "the twin"; Matthew, "gift of Yahweh." The two
apparent exceptions, Andrew and Philip, likely had Jewish
names beside the Greek ones. In a word, everything about the
inner circle of Christ's original company was Jewish, in fulfilment of God's promise that in the seed of Abraham all
nations would be blessed, beginning with the Messias and the
first ambassadors of His kingdom.

Throughout the public life of Christ, the apostles were His
constant, chosen companions. Over thirty times in the Gospels
they are simply identified as "the Twelve." When the Master
preached to the multitudes, they were with Him, and not just
part of the crowd but near Him to receive the message that
was intended only for them. When He worked His miracles,
it seemed primarily for their benefit, from the first of His
signs at Cana where He manifested His glory "and His disciples believed in Him," to His resurrection from the dead when
He was most solicitous that all the apostles should be convinced, including the doubting Thomas who was favored with
a special visitation. At the Last Supper, the apostles alone
were chosen to share in the Savior's final testimony before the
passion, and to partake for the first time of the blood of the
new and eternal covenant. At the ascension, they received the
mandate to go into the whole world and preach the gospel
to every creature.

All the extant forms of Christianity consider themselves descended from the apostles and equally recite in the Nicene

Creed, "I believe in . . . the apostolic Church." They reflect on the teaching of St. Paul to tell the Ephesians, "you are no longer strangers and foreigners, but you are citizens with the saints and members of God's household: you are built upon the foundation of the apostles and prophets with Christ Jesus Himself as the chief cornerstone."

But while commonly recognizing their apostolic ancestry, Christians are not agreed on the transmission of Christ's authority through the apostles or even on the fact that such transmission had ever taken place. Catholics believe the Church's apostolicity was climaxed in the person of St. Peter, the "Prince of the Apostles," and continues unbroken in the visible headship of Peter's successor, the bishop of Rome. Eastern Orthodox prefer to invest the whole Church with apostolic authority, in such a way that every Christian shares the right to interpret the meaning of faith, and collectively the Mystical Body is the teaching and ruling organ of all the faithful. Protestants will have the Spirit of Christ in the heart of each believer guide him on the road to heaven, where no human person and no institution but only the Savior has the power to determine man's relationship with God.

PETRINE PRIMACY. According to Catholic tradition, Christ had the option of choosing any one of a number of structures for His Church. He might have made it a democracy, or an oligarchy, or an aristocracy. But then He would have established a different Church from the existing one, because the structure He chose was monarchial. From the opening scenes of His public life, it is pointed out, He selected one man to become the visible head of the Christian community.

At the first meeting with the Master at Capharnaum, Jesus looked upon Peter and told him that his name would be changed from Simon to Cephas (Rock) as a foreshadowing of his future leadership. Gradually He accustomed the jealous apostles to Peter's singular position among them. Even among the three who were nearest to the Savior, the sequence was always Peter, James and John; notwithstanding the fact that John was *par excellence* the beloved disciple.

Peter was regularly preferred for special instructions and

admonitions; he was trained above the others in humility, patience and trust in God; his faith was declared essential, in order to strengthen the others; he was recognized as the spokesman for the other apostles, not for any personal traits or natural gifts, but because the Lord had chosen him for leadership from the moment he was called to the apostolate.

Two events in the life of Christ stand out as the guarantee that Peter was intended to carry on the work of His Master with an authority that was shared by no other apostle. The first event took place in the midst of the public ministry and is recorded by the three synoptics, but especially by St. Matthew; the second occurred after the resurrection and is described only by St. John.

Shortly after the second miraculous feeding of the multitude, Jesus took His disciples to the neighborhood of Caesarea Philippi, on the extreme borders of the land of Israel. Secluded from the crowds of followers, in a territory that was now pagan, He put His apostles to the test, in order to clarify once and for all His position in their regard and determine their role in the work He had in store for them. He asked them, "Who do men say the Son of Man is?" They answered, "Some say, John the Baptist; and others Elias; and others Jeremias, or one of the prophets." When He asked them again, "But who do you say that I am?" Simon Peter answered, "Thou art the Christ, the Son of the Living God." Jesus then defined the new relationship between Peter and Himself.

> Blessed art thou, Simon Bar-Jona, for flesh and blood has not revealed this to thee, but my Father in heaven. And I say to thee, thou art Peter, and upon this rock I will build my Church, and the gates of hell shall not prevail against it. And I will give thee the keys of the kingdom of heaven; and whatever thou shalt bind on earth, shall be bound in heaven, and whatever thou shalt loose on earth shall be loosed in heaven.[18]

Set in paraphrase, the essential words of Christ, "Thou art Peter, and upon this rock I will build my Church," would read: I shall make you the foundation of the spiritual edifice I intend to build. Therefore what the foundation is to the building, its source of unity, strength and stability, you are going to be that in the Church which I am about to found. And since the unified strength and stability of any society derive from ultimate authority, I shall give you and your successors all the authority you will need to preserve my Church from harm, for all time, by confirming your judgment on earth with divine ratification in heaven.

This promise must be taken in conjunction with its actual conferral after the resurrection. In spite of Peter's denial of his Master, and the fact that humanly speaking he was anything but the rock on which to build an institution that could resist the powers of hell, Christ was faithful to what He had said a year before. Calling Peter aside on the shores of the sea of Tiberius, Jesus asked him, "Simon, son of John, do you love me more than these?" When Peter answered in the affirmative, Christ told him, "Feed my lambs." Then a second time, "Do you love me?" and the same answer, with the same commission. Finally a third time, to which Peter protested, "Lord, you know all things; you know that I love you," and the closing injunction, "Feed my sheep."

When Christ gave Peter the authority to govern the infant Church, His action was determined by the character of the society He was founding: a permanent institution with a body of religious truths to be kept unchanged as the instrument of salvation, whose members were to be united by the profession of a common faith and practice of a mutual love.

Knowing the need for external ultimate authority in any stable society, Christ desired nothing less for His Church. Accordingly Peter was only the first in the line of visible heads of the Church who, like Peter, would consolidate under Christ the institution whose basic principles were determined by the Savior before He returned to the Father.

By Catholic standards, such was the substantial judgment of believing Christians for ten centuries in the East and fifteen centuries in the West, and is still a cardinal dogma of Christianity. In the words of the first Vatican Council, it is "according to the institution of Christ our Lord Himself, that is, by divine law, that St. Peter has perpetual successors in the primacy over the whole Church," and, indeed, "the Roman Pontiff is the successor of St. Peter in the same primacy."[19]

SOBORNOST, KOINONIA, AND CONCILIARITY. The Churches in the Eastern Orthodox tradition find their ultimate authority in something less defined than the Roman primacy. For want of a better word, the English "conciliarity" has been coined to translate something of what the Russians mean by *sobornost* or the Greeks by *koinonia*. As explained by a contemporary Orthodox theologian, "conciliarity of government," or the mystical union of the faithful through love, is the true notion of the Church's authority.

While there is no official teaching of the Eastern Churches on the nature of *sobornost,* it is easily found in the stream of Orthodox history and frequently discussed in contemporary writings on the subject.

The classic idea of *koinonia* grew out of historical circumstances. For centuries the Church was faced with a series of theological crises, raised by those who denied the divinity of Christ, His consubstantiality with the Father, and the necessity of supernatural grace for salvation. With notable exception the crises were resolved, though under papal mandate or approval, mainly through conciliar action whether local, synodal, provincial or ecumenical. If there were many instances when the Popes intervened without the use of a council, the dominant impression in the East was that conciliar rule and teaching should be identified with the ordinary mode of governing the Church.

After the final breach with Rome in the eleventh century, the theory took hold that the first seven ecumenical councils are the final authority for instruction and government of the Church. Pronouncements from these assemblies, 325 to 787 A.D., are normative for the Christian faith and discipline.

Still held by many conservative Orthodox thinkers, the conciliar idea of Church authority has been modified in modern times to include a broader concept of the Church as basically Catholic in essence, yet not subject to Rome or any single visible head. All believers are joined in a mysterious bond of unity, which gives them collectively what is present only *in germine* in each individual. Sharing what each one has gives the body a new power that its separate members possess only inherently. Together they teach and govern, whereas individually they are only cells of the cosmic whole. In the last analysis, therefore, the government of the Church belongs to the body of the entire Church; so that even the decrees of a general council become valid only when universally approved by the faithful.

A variant explanation that has found wide acceptance in the United States and English-speaking countries begins with the postulate that the Bible and sacred Tradition are valid sources of the Church's doctrinal and governmental mind. The hierarchy has the privilege of applying these sources to contingent situations, since it has been so commissioned by Christ, but not speaking in its own name. Bishops are only delegates of the people and their external voice or mouthpiece for making explicit what resides implicitly in the hearts of all believers. They, and not the bishops, are the "court of last appeal" in matters of faith and morals.

Yet not the bishops alone nor the people of any territory alone enjoy this magisterial power. In the Orthodox view, each local church, headed by its bishop, is the Church of God, enjoying His gifts and forming not merely a part of the Body of Christ, but the whole of His Body in its sacramental reality. Yet no single church can live in isolation from the rest. Unity of origin and faith links the disparate churches together, so that the life of one passes on to the others by means of the episcopacy.

This concept of church authority is sometimes identified with a mysterious *sensus fidelium,* or "believers' consciousness," that varies with different interpreters but fundamentally precludes anything like obedience to visible, moral power vested in the papacy or episcopacy.

> The life of the Church is a miracle which cannot be subordinated to external law. The Church recognizes or does not recognize a given ecclesiastical assembly representing itself as a council: this is the simple historical fact.
> There are not and there cannot be external organs or

methods of testifying to the internal evidence of the Church; this must be admitted frankly and resolutely. Anyone who is troubled by this lack of external evidence for ecclesiastical truth does not believe in the Church and does not truly know it. . . . The ecclesiastical fetishism which seeks an oracle speaking in the name of the Holy Spirit and which finds it in the person of a supreme hierarch, or in the episcopal order and its assemblies—this fetishism is a terrible symptom of half-faith.[20]

In other words, in the Orthodox Church the final guardian of the purity of dogma is the Church itself, the Church people, and not any episcopal assembly. Eastern theologians who make the bishops representatives of the faithful may not require universal acceptance by the Church to validate episcopal decrees, but even they allow the people to call the bishops to task for what they teach and even depose their prelates when the Spirit of God so directs them.

SCRIPTURE AND THE SPIRIT. In the Protestant tradition, ecclesiastical authority vested in the Pope or bishops or council assemblies was replaced by the inspired word of God as found in the Scriptures, and by the indwelling Spirit which enlightens every man who comes into this world.

The groundwork on its theoretical side was laid by the Reformers who appealed against the Catholic position by arguing that where Baptism has been received there is no further need for ordination or consecration, or their correlative claims to a specially conferred juridical power from God. "Whoever has undergone Baptism," wrote Luther, "may boast that he has been consecrated priest, bishop, and pope, although it does not beseem everyone to exercise these offices. For since we are all priests alike, no man may put himself forward, or take upon himself without our consent and election, to do that which we all alike have power to do. If a thing is common to all, no man may take it upon himself without the wish and command of the community."[21]

Protestantism begins with the premise that Jesus Christ was a historical figure, and that therefore the paramount question for theology is posed by the historical gap between God's advent in the world two thousand years ago, and the sources of religious authenticity today. Catholic bodies, it is explained, fill the gap between Jesus Christ and the modern Christian by the authority of the Church and what it calls its *magisterium,* namely the official teaching body of the Church whose spokesman is the Pope. This position is said to be based on the supposition that Jesus Christ transferred His authority to the apostles and their ecclesiastically certified successors, the Bishops under the Roman Pontiff.

For its part, Protestantism in a sense admits that Christ conferred authority upon the apostles, but it believes that the apostles were unique. Their authority cannot be handed down to others.

On the crucial Petrine text in St. Matthew's Gospel, the growing Protestant stance is to concede that Christ's words, "You are Peter, and upon this Rock I will build my Church," refer to Peter himself and not merely to his faith. "When Jesus says that he will build his *ekklesia* upon this rock, he really means the person of Simon. Upon this disciple, who in the lifetime of Jesus possessed the specific advantages and the specific weaknesses of which the Gospels speak, upon him who was then their spokesman, their representative in good as well as in bad, and in this sense was the rock of the group of disciples—upon him is to be founded the Church, which after the death of Jesus will continue his work upon earth."[22] However, with Peter as with the other apostles, they received authority only for themselves, not authority to be passed on to their successors.

What, then, is the basis for the continuity of Christians today with the authoritative Jesus Christ? The written words of the Bible are the authority, conserving concretely the message of the Savior, and assured constant illumination from the same Savior's Spirit indwelling in the hearts of the faithful. Both facets are important. Implicit in the scriptural testimony is the promise that when the apostles, through their written record, remind the Church of God's presence in Jesus Christ, God will be present by the spirit of Christ. In the graphic words of the Reformers, the exterior spirit of the biblical clinker is reignited by the Holy Spirit to make it glow again interiorly in those who believe.

Among the Protestants who clarified these concepts, Kierkegaard was outstanding with his insistence that the authority of God does not require a person to be what he called "a disciple at second hand." Jesus Christ Himself lives again in the spirit of man through the equilibrium of the apostolic word and the invisible divine Spirit. What becomes in that process of the rebel in every man, of that part of man's nature which resents any imposition on its freedom? It does not submit, Kierkegaard would say, as though to a way of life alien to itself. It rather finds the basis of its rebellion, the true ground of its strivings which before were only a chaotic stream of ill-directed desires.

Accordingly faith itself takes on a different meaning than found in the Catholic Church. "Christians do not claim to have the truth. They are claimed by it." And Christian realities are spiritual, personal, historical things; they are not susceptible of dogmatic, in the sense of definitive and irreversible, verbal expression. Truths of faith are called possibilities, they are never necessities. In fact, any compulsion is a contradiction of faith.

> The highest truths are the truths which are spiritually discerned, and spiritual discernment, as the Bible says, always takes place in freedom. Christian authority is always consistent with assurance, never with certainty. A quest for certainty in the Christian life is an expression of bad faith. It is the antinomy of trust. The corollary of this is that the truth of the Christian faith does not inhere in propositions. Its propositions are always invocations. The proper response to an invocation is not, "I consent intellectually" or "I believe it to be true." It is *sursum corda*, a lifting up of the heart in willing response.[23]

In this estimate of faith, authority may seem to reside in human institutions or personalities, but its true presence is only in God. When a Christian submits in obedience to a higher power, he makes sure that his pledge is to no one less than God. Churches and synodical conferences may propose to him

what to believe and how to act, but they can never impose
upon him to follow their directives. He is ultimately responsible only to the Spirit within him, whom Christ promised to
send and by whom the believer is taught all that he needs.

13

ROMAN CATHOLICISM

Not the least difficulty in writing about Catholicism is the problem of isolating the subject. The history of the Catholic Church is so closely woven into Christian civilization that the one cannot be told fairly without the other, and to do justice by the Church would mean to retell the story of Christianity. Moreover not only Catholics claim the first millenium of Christian history as their own. The Orthodox and Protestants might therefore resent having all the centuries from Christ to Photius and Caerularius, or to Luther and Calvin, called Catholic instead of simply Christian.

Practically speaking, however, there is no choice except to treat the first thousand years in the East and fifteen hundred in the West under Roman Catholicism. The characteristic features of the latter today are imbedded in the Church's life before the Eastern Schism and the Reformation; Catholicism makes the claim of continuing these features and retaining them substantially unchanged through all the vicissitudes of time; and, most importantly, the institution of the papacy is a historical phenomenon that reaches back to the early centuries to give Christianity that cohesion which even the sharpest critics of Catholicism are willing to admit while they deplore, in Harnack's phrase, the lot of those who "have subjected their souls to the despotic orders of the Roman papal King."[1]

APOSTOLIC TIMES

The amount of authentic Christian literature from the first century after Christ's ascension is more extensive than most people who are not specialists suppose. Besides the Gospels, written between 50 A.D. for the Aramaic Matthew and 100 A.D. for St. John, we have the fourteen letters of St. Paul, seven

Catholic epistles, the Book of Revelations or Apocalypse and the Acts of the Apostles which Chrysostom called the "Gospel of the Holy Spirit," and Harnack "the manifestation in history of the power of the Spirit of Jesus in the apostles." Outside the New Testament are the *Didache,* written about the year 90 as a manual on the liturgy and Christian morals; the letter of Pope Clement I to the Corinthians (98 A.D.), the epistle of Barnabas of the same date, Polycarp's letter to the Philippians and the remarkable collection of seven epistles which St. Ignatius of Antioch wrote to seven churches while on his way to martyrdom in Rome (107 A.D.).

The first and strongest impression left us by these writings is the devotion of the early Christians to the person of Jesus. He dominates their thoughts, determines their ritual customs, inspires their daily practices and so completely enters every phase of their lives it is no wonder they were soon given the simple title of "Christians," as followers of one whom they called the Messias and on whom all their religion was centered.

According to Tacitus, the name was already current among the populace in Rome at the time of the Neronean persecution (A.D. 64) and soon became the official Roman designation for members of the new Church.[2] During times of persecution the confession or denial of this name was crucial, as reported by Pliny the Younger, proconsul of Bithynia in Asia Minor (A.D. 112). He described to the Emperor Trajan the method he used to ferret out the Christians.

> A placard was put up, without any signature, accusing a large number of persons by name. Those who denied they were, or had ever been, Christians, who repeated after me an invocation to the gods, and offered adoration, with wine and frankincense, to your image, which I had ordered brought for that purpose, together with those of the gods, and who finally cursed Christ—none of which acts, it is said, those who are really Christians can be forced to perform—these I thought proper to discharge.[3]

It is impossible to read a single letter of St. Paul without feeling that for him Christianity was Christ. He speaks of himself as "the servant of Jesus Christ," and of those to whom he is writing "called to be Jesus Christ's." His preoccupation with the Savior makes him say, "if any man does not love the Lord Jesus Christ, let him be anathema." In closing salutations, he writes, "My love is with you all in Christ Jesus." When necessary, he vindicates his authority, that he is an apostle, "sent not from men nor by man, but by Jesus Christ." In his suffering, he rejoices that "I bear the marks of the Lord Jesus Christ in my body," and in humility he prays, "God forbid that I should glory save in the cross of our Lord Jesus Christ."[4]

Paul's exhortations were not so much to virtue as to the following of Christ. "Have this mind in you which was also in Christ Jesus." His reproaches are less against vice than against those who "seek their own interests, not those of Jesus Christ." His great hope is to be dissolved, and to be with Christ. By comparison with this treasure, "I count everything loss because of the excellent knowledge of Jesus Christ my Lord. For His sake I have suffered the loss of all things." And in the apostrophe which summarizes his gospel, he sets the master idea that he learned from the Savior and that Christians in all times, and not only the converts in ancient Rome, have needed to remain loyal to the faith.

> Who shall separate us from the love of Christ? Shall tribulations, or distress, or persecution, or hunger, or nakedness, or danger, or the sword. Even as it is written, "For Thy sake we are put to death all the day long. We are regarded as sheep for the slaughter." But in all these things we overcome because of Him who has loved us. For I am sure that neither death, nor life, nor angels, nor principalities, nor things present, nor things to come, nor powers, nor heights, nor depth, nor any other creature will be able to separate us from the love of God, which is in Christ Jesus our Lord.[5]

Correlative with this dedication to the person of the Savior, early Christianity appears from the first as communal in character and under perceptible authority.

Shortly after the ascension of Christ, while the disciples in the company of Mary were awaiting the Holy Spirit, Peter stood up in the midst of the brethren and announced that another apostle should be chosen to replace the traitor Judas. He laid down the conditions of election, "of these men who have been with us from the time the Lord Jesus moved among us, from John's baptism till the day He was taken from us, of these one must become a witness with us of the resurrection."[6] Two candidates were put forward, Joseph called Barsabbas, and Matthias. After the assembly had asked the Lord to show "which of these two Thou hast chosen," lots were drawn and the choice fell upon Matthias, who was immediately numbered with the eleven apostles. Commenting on this first act of Peter's primacy, St. John Chrysostom remarked how spontaneously he was accepted as the shepherd of Christ's flock and the leader of the apostolic college.

When the Master commissioned His disciples to preach the Gospel, He also gave them power to work miracles in His name, to cast out demons, to heal the sick and even to raise the dead. These signs and wonders are part of the logic of revelation. If God demands faith in revealed mysteries, He makes them acceptable by integrating what exceeds human power in the realm of knowledge with phenomena that surpass human agency in the order of visible reality. Since the latter is certainly from God, the former must also come from Him. Consequently just as Christ went about simultaneously preaching His doctrine and confirming it with prodigies, so the apostles (beginning with Simon Peter) started the Christian catechesis with teaching what they had learned from Jesus and making His new-found society credible with signs and wonders that followed.

Soon after Pentecost Sunday, as Peter and John were going into the temple to pray, they met a certain man who was lame from his mother's womb. Instead of giving him the alms he begged, Peter gazed upon him and said, "Silver and gold I have none, but what I have I give thee. In the name of Jesus Christ of Nazareth, arise and walk." Immediately the man's feet and ankles became strong and "leaping up he began to walk."[7]

Illustrative of the ecclesiastical structure of Christianity in apostolic times, the authors of the New Testament outside the Gospels repeatedly speak of the Church (*ekklesia*) to describe the community of Christ's followers, as distinct from the synagogue of the Jews. The latter meant simply an existing religious gathering of people, the former the assembly of people called together by God. Also, where the term occurs in only two contexts in the Gospels, both in Matthew,[8] it is used over one hundred times in the Acts, Epistles, and Book of Revelation.

As the number of gentile converts increased, the ethnic nature of Christianity became correspondingly less Jewish. Members of the Palestinian Church who lived according to the pharisaic rule watched the development with regret and made every effort to keep the Church within the limits of Judaism. Its estrangement from Jewry, they believed, could be prevented or mitigated only when all the churches and their members agreed to observe the Mosaic law. The conflict which arose from this attitude provoked the most serious crisis in apostolic Christianity and was finally settled by the first ecumenical gathering of the Church, in which Peter presided and gave the decisive judgment. Once he declared that "We believe we are saved through the grace of the Lord Jesus, just as we are," and without the burden of the Mosaic code, "the whole meeting quieted down," and listened while Paul, the apostle of the Gentiles, and James, the venerable leader of the Judaeo-Christians, expressed their agreement.[9]

QUMRAN AND PRIMITIVE CHRISTIANITY

Since the discovery of the Dead Sea Scriptures from 1947 onwards, it is impossible to speak of Christian origins without taking stock of what some have called the most significant documents outside the Bible bearing on the foundations of Christianity.

Over sixty manuscripts and innumerable fragments have been excavated at the site of the ancient Qumran Community, located close to the Dead Sea in Palestine. The principal texts include a set of rules for the monastic community, namely *The Manual of Discipline, A Zadokite Document* (discovered earlier at Cairo) and a *Formulary of Blessings;* two collections of hymns, for the initiants and a psalm of thanksgiving; several commentaries, on the Books of Michaeas, Nahum and Habakkuk; a long oration of Moses which was a paraphrase of the Law; an epic on *The War of the Sons of Light and the Sons of Darkness;* and a manual for the future congregation of Israel, the so-called Messianic Banquet. Conservative scholarship holds that the scrolls were composed at various dates between 170 B.C. and 68 A.D.

The burning question on which a library is fast developing is the relation of this documentation to Christian beginnings. Some extremists have claimed that we have in these documents the rude clay of which the Christian Church was later molded, with the implication that the latter is not really unique but merely continuous with its Judaic predecessor among the ascetics at Qumran. Nothing could be further from the facts. There is in the Dead Sea scrolls no trace of any of the cardinal theological concepts of Christianity—the incarnation of the Son of God, original sin, redemption through the cross and the life of divine grace, the sacramental system or the universality of the Gospel *kerygma*.

On the other hand, there are numerous affinities which balanced scholarship has unearthed and which cast abundant light on the meaning of the Christian faith. The scrolls furnish a picture of the religious and cultural climate in which John the Baptist conducted his mission and in which Jesus of Nazareth was initially reared. They portray in vivid but authentic colors the spiritual environment whose language the Precursor and the Savior spoke, whose idea they used to teach their message of salvation, and whose sympathetic attitude they employed as the seedbed of the New Testament. They give the lie to over a century of rationalist criticism of the New Testament, that the ideals of the Gospels (notably St. John), and of the Pauline Epistles could not have come from Judaic sources but must have been imported from elsewhere, from Hellenism or from Gnostic lucubrations.

Among the affinities between the thought and language of the scrolls and that of the New Testament, the most prominent touches on the communal nature of the Qumran sect and the Christian community. The Qumran group had a variety of inspectors who were overseers and whose duty it was to admit new members, pass judgment on those in probation, direct the interests of the community and, when necessary, dismiss those who failed to live up to prescribed regulations. This spiritual leader is called "teacher" or "right-teacher." In the Gospel according to St. John, Jesus is hailed as the teacher sent by God, appointed by the Father to bring the light of truth to all nations.

In the *Manual of Discipline*, the community is promised to become a veritable "temple of God, a true holy of holies," provided it abides by the community regulations. This is more than superficially like the words of St. Paul to the Corinthians, "Do you not know that you are the temple of God and that the Spirit of God dwells in you? If anyone destroys the temple of God, him will God destroy; for holy is the temple of God, and this temple you are."[10]

Members of the Qumran body styled themselves "the elect" or "the elect of God," with an accent that is familiar in the writings of St. Paul, who spoke of himself as an apostle of Jesus Christ, "according to the faith of God's elect," and in St. Peter who said he was an apostle of Jesus Christ "to the elect who are sojourners of the dispersion."[11] In both sources, the Qumran and Christian, the faithful declared that they stand in the eternal congregation of God, hold direct converse with Him, and "share the lot of the holy beings." They enjoyed a community of goods, practiced obedience to superiors, and were told to abstain from divorce with the right to remarry. Thus in the *Zadokite Document* we read, "One of the traps is fornication, by marrying two women at the same time, even though the principle of creation is, male and female He created them."[12] And in Mark we read, "Because of the hardness of your heart he (Moses) wrote you that precept (allowing a bill of divorce to put away one's wife). But from the beginning of creation God made them male and female."[13] Some commentators have been so struck by the similarity they rushed to conclude that the *Zadokite Document* is Judaeo-Christian.

Comparable to the Christian emphasis on the struggle between light and darkness is the theme of the Qumran manuscripts that speak at length of the two spirits, the Prince of Light and the Angel of Darkness, with constant opposition between them. While the idea is a commonplace of ancient Iranian and later Jewish thought, it suggests a development that became part of the structure of Christianity. It should be noted, however, that the New Testament subjected this doctrine to an essential change by contraposing the Angel of Darkness not with an Angel of Light but with Christ or the Holy Spirit, with never a suspicion that the two were equally matched.

Even more striking is the parallel between the meal of the Palestinian monastery and the Lord's Supper. There was no transformation of the elements in the Dead Sea documents, but otherwise the two ceremonies were quite similar. Speaking of communal duties, the Qumran members were told that "when they prepare the table to eat and wine to drink, the priest must be the first to extend his hand to bless the first portions of the bread. And if wine is being drunk, the priest must be the first to extend his hand to bless the first portion of the bread and wine."[14] So, too, in describing the Messianic banquet, "When they gather around the table to eat or to drink wine, and the common board has been spread and the wine mixed, no one is to stretch out his hand for the first portion of bread and wine before the priest. For it is he who is to bless the first portion of bread and wine, and the first to stretch out his hand to the bread. After that the Messias of Israel will place his hands on the bread."[15]

In spite of these and similar analogies, the early Church was aeons removed from the Judaic community which some have identified with the Essenes and others, with more caution, describe as the Dead Sea Covenanters. The Jewish ascetics were legalistic in the extreme, attached to externals, and at the opposite pole to the injunctions of Christ for internal faith, purity of heart and detachment from the things of this world. Their observance of the Sabbath was more demanding, if possible, than the burdens laid down by the Pharisees. They were a closed sect, socially, psychologically and even physically; and forbidden association with others at the risk of being excommunicated for consorting with outsiders. Their whole thought and practice was steeped in the Old Testament, with no hint of a new communication from on High, and combined with a rigid determinism that comes closer to the predestination passages in the Koran than to anything found in the New Testament.

Future research may reveal new correlations between Qumran and the Church of the Apostles, at least in heightening the spiritual idealism of the Jewish people at the time of Christ. It will also show that, while Christianity appealed to the best in human nature and made demands on generosity beyond anything hitherto suspected in Judaism, its inspiration did not come from the Law or the Prophets alone but from a new dispensation which fulfilled and superseded the old.

FATHERS AND EARLY COUNCILS

From earliest times, the title *Pater* (Father) was applied to bishops of the Church as witnesses to the Christian tradition. But from the close of the fourth century it was used in a more restricted sense of a more or less clearly defined group of ecclesiastical writers of the past whose authority on doctrinal matters carried special weight. St. Basil (330–379) and St. Gregory of Nazianzen (329–389) are among the first to prove the orthodoxy of their teaching by appealing to the agreement of the Fathers, technically the *consensus Patrum,* in support of their position.

By the end of the fifth century the term "Father" was also applied to teachers who were not bishops, like St. Jerome (342–420), and even the layman, St. Prosper of Aquitaine (390–463). According to the commonly accepted teaching, the Fathers were characterized by orthodoxy of doctrine, holiness of life, approval by the Church and antiquity. The patristic period is generally held to close with St. Isidore of Seville (560–636) in the West, and St. John Damascene (675–749) in the East.

The significance of the Fathers in the history of Catholicism lies in their witness to the apostolic tradition, of which they were the faithful transmitters and their deference to the Church as final interpreter of Christian revelation. Quantitatively their testimony is monumental (upwards of four hundred volumes in the Migne edition), and qualitatively their function has been that of reservoirs from which subsequent generations may safely draw on the deposit of faith. Even popes and general councils, while standing above the Fathers as final judges, depended on their wisdom and insight to define the Church's mind.

For seven hundred years, the patristic teaching, periodically stabilized by ecumenical councils, was the mainstay of Christianity. Yet the Fathers were not self-made but created by a series of crises which threatened the Church at every turn in her history.

In the second and third centuries arose the peril of Gnosticism, a complex religious movement which denied the historical validity of the Gospels. Essentially a claim to the possession of "higher knowledge," independently of the stream of apostolic tradition, Gnosticism already plagued the Church before 100 A.D. Among the reasons which led St. John to write his Gospel was the refutation of the Gnostic Cerinthus and the Nicolaites. At the turn of the century, Ignatius of Antioch stressed the reality of Christ's earthly life, death and resurrection against the Gnostic perversion of these facts.

However this was only a prelude to the inundation that broke over the Church in the middle of the second century. The last survivors of the apostolic age felt they were faced with a new and powerful enemy that came out into the open. Now that the apostles were gone, Oriental zealots began to preach and organize religious sects. Other factors were also operative, like the rapid growth of the Church and her penetration into the world of philosophy and letters, where the simple faith of the people was exposed to Hellenic speculation and an attempt to engraft Asiatic fancies on the body of Christian revelation.

Christ, they said, was not the Deity in human form but only an aeon, or intermediary, who was apparently endowed with human nature. Accordingly salvation was not to be obtained through the merits of Christ, but through the *Gnosis* or superior knowledge which was manifested in Him and discovered by the Gnostics. Christ, therefore, was not really born, nor did He actually live and die or rise from the grave. The events described in the Gospels were not historically but only symbolically true. Spiritual insight, possessed by the Gnostics, and not the reported words and deeds of Christ demonstrable by history, furnished Christianity with the religious truths of salvation.

The sequence of Fathers who combated Gnosticism reads like a roster of the Christian writers before the Edict of Constantine, but the outstanding among them was St. Ireneus (130–200), Bishop of Lyons, who forms in thought and action an important link between the East and West. His chief work, *Against the Heresies,* is a detailed exposé of Gnosticism.

Ireneus was the first great Catholic theologian. Unlike the Fathers in the East, he opposed Gnosticism not by setting up a rival Christian speculation, but by emphasizing the traditional elements in the Church, notably the papacy, the episcopate, the canon of Scripture and religious tradition. At every point in his writing he is conscious of the chasm that separates the Oriental concept of God and religion, inherited from the Hindus and Parsis, from the Christian message preached by Christ and handed down by His disciples. Christians have only one God, infinite Creator of all things; their revelation comes from this same Deity, especially in the person of Jesus of Nazareth, "Savior, King and God." Their faith is founded on His preaching and on the teaching of His Church, whose seed has been sown to the ends of the earth; and preserved by the bishops "who were instituted by the apostles," as the apostles were by Christ.

To discover Christian truth, therefore, and sift it from error, we have only to see what the bishops have taught since the time of Christ.

> But as it would take too long to transcribe here the successions of bishops of all the churches, we will consider the greatest and ancient, known by all, founded and established by the two glorious apostles, Peter and Paul. We will show that the tradition which it received from the apostles and the faith it has preached to men have come down to us through the succession of bishops. We will thus confound those who, in whatever way, through self-satisfaction, vain-glory, blindness or error, gather in a way other than they should.
>
> For with this Church, on account of its preeminent authority, every church must be in agreement, that is, the faithful

everywhere, among whom the tradition of the apostles has been continuously preserved by those everywhere.[16]

Even before the Gnostic danger had passed, another problem arose, in the form of Arianism, which denied the uniquely divine nature of Jesus Christ. Its author was Arius (256–336), a priest of Alexandria, who in 318 began to teach that there were not three distinct persons in God, coeternal and equal in all things, but only one person, the Father. The Son is only a creature, made out of nothing like other created beings. He may be called God, but only by an extension of language, as the first and greatest person chosen to be divine intermediary in the creation and redemption of the world.

Boldly anti-trinitarian, Arianism struck at the foundations of Christianity by reducing the Incarnation to a figure of speech. If the Logos, the Word of God, was created and not divine, God did not become man nor redeem the world and all the consequent mysteries are dissolved. In Arianism we see the first major challenge of the non-Christian world to the premises of the Christian faith. Philo among the Jewish Hellenists and Plotinus among the Neo-Platonists contributed the theory of an agglomerate of ideas as the first mediator between God and the world; Gnosticism furnished the notion of aeons or lesser deities, so familiar in Zoroastrian and Hindu thought.

The Council of Nicea was convoked in 325 to meet this challenge. Since the signature texts are defective, the exact number of prelates who attended this first ecumenical gathering is not known. However, at least two hundred and twenty bishops, mostly from the East, but also from Africa, Spain, Gaul and Italy, signed the creed which affirmed the divinity of Christ. "We believe," the formula read, "in one God, the Father Almighty, Creator of all things visible and invisible. And in one Lord Jesus Christ, the Son of God, the only-begotten of the Father, that is, of the substance of the Father; God from God, light from light, true God from true God; begotten, not created, consubstantial (*homo-ousion*) with the Father."[17]

The soul of the council was St. Athanasius (296–373), Bishop of Alexandria, whose resolute character and theological clarity were the main obstacle to the triumph of Arianism in the East.

About thirty years after Nicea, some Arian bishops began to teach that the Holy Spirit is also not divine. Called *Pneumatomachi* (enemies of the Spirit), they were answered by St. Basil and the two Gregories, of Nyssa and Nazianzen, and condemned in 381 by the second general council at Constantinople, which reaffirmed the Nicene Creed and clearly defined the divinity of the Holy Spirit. The present Nicene Creed, used at Mass in the Catholic Church on feast days, dates from this council. The interpolation *Filioque*, "and the Son," was added, to its dogmatic formula to express a Double Procession of the Holy Spirit, in the next century and has since become a symbol of tension between Roman Catholicism and Eastern Orthodoxy.

Closely connected with Arianism was the theory of Nestorius (died 451), a Syrian monk who preached against the expression *Theotokos* (Mother of God), applied to the Blessed Virgin. The principal defender of Mary's honor was St. Cyril of Alexandria (died 444), whose efforts were crowned with success at the Council of Ephesus (431).

During the next century and a half, the Church underwent the interior trial of purification at the hands of Pelagius and his followers, who claimed that a man does not need supernatural grace to be saved.

Pelagius was a lay monk, born in England about 354, who came to Rome at the end of the fourth century. Having heard a bishop quote St. Augustine with relation to chastity, "Grant what You command, O Lord, and command what You will," he attacked the doctrine on the ground that the whole moral law was imperilled. If a man were not responsible for his good and evil deeds, there was nothing to restrain him from indulgence in sin. He was moreover so alarmed by the low morality of the day that he felt it could only be reformed by concentrating on man's personal responsibility for his actions. Together with his disciple Celestius, he began teaching that the only real grace we possess is free will, which alone, without any elevation or assistance from God, can lead us to heaven.

St. Jerome wrote that the world woke up one day and

found itself Pelagian. He and Augustine spent themselves vindicating the traditional doctrine that free will is indeed a gift of nature, but in addition we need supernatural light and strength and, above all, infusion of sanctifying grace in order to be saved.

So numerous were the Church's pronouncements in defense of the supernatural life that by the end of the fifth century a catalogue had to be made for easy reference. Known as the *Indiculus* (short index), it re-stated the teaching of Christ, "without me you can do nothing," and closed every avenue of escape for a naturalistic interpretation of man's relations with God. "No one," it declared, "not even the person who has been renewed by the grace of baptism, has sufficient strength to overcome the snares of the devil, and conquer the passions of the flesh, unless he obtains help from God each day to persevere in a good life."[18]

One more trial plagued the Church before the end of the patristic age. Under suasion from Manichaean tendencies, inherited from the Zoroastrians, and pressure from Islam, certain Christian emperors in the East opposed the use of images in divine worship. One of their reasons was that icons are a grave obstacle to the conversion of Moslems and Jews, who outlaw sacred images on principle.

St. John Damascene, chief representative of the Christians to the Caliph, became protagonist for the believers against the Iconoclasts (image breakers) and wrote three discourses on the subject. He barely escaped martyrdom for his zeal. The second Council of Nicea (787), and the last accepted by the Eastern Orthodox, settled the issue on dogmatic grounds, but left untouched the crucial problem that three centuries later led to the separation of the East from Rome.

Caesaro-papism, or the theory of absolute control of the Church by a civil ruler, showed itself with increasing clarity during the iconoclast struggle. Started by the intervention of the State in religious matters, the conflict encountered less and less resistance in the Greek Church, especially among the secular clergy, while it was viewed by the popes with growing apprehension. The unity achieved by Imperial decree in 787 and again in 843 proved artificial, and with the restoration of

the Empire by the Franks and the development of the temporal power of the popes, the ground was ready for the final
separation between the Church of Rome and the state-
dominated Church of the Byzantine Empire.

CHURCH AND STATE RELATIONS

With the disintegration of Charlemagne's empire in the
tenth century and the inroads of the Northmen, Magyars and
Saracens, political and moral values fell into decay and the
Church herself was deeply affected by the return to "semi-
barbarism." When feudalism emerged as a reaction to the
crisis, ecclesiastical authority came under the sway of feudal
lords and princes.

A reforming tendency inside the Church had started as a
monastic movement in France (Cluny) and in Germany (Lor-
raine). After the deposition in 1046 of the anti-pope, Sylvester
III (created by a Roman political party), a series of high-
minded pontiffs ascended the papal throne, culminating in the
pontificate of Gregory VII (1073–1085), who had served as
secretary and adviser to his five predecessors.

The two principal objects of Gregory's reform were clerical
celibacy and lay investiture, with the prior importance attached to the second as a contributing cause of the first. By
controlling the elections of bishops, lay princes had been able
to name their own creatures or relatives and even to sell
bishoprics to the highest bidder. And after a bishop's consecration, they further assumed the power of "vesting" the prelate ostensibly with temporal assets like property and buildings
but actually (as symbolized in the ring and pastoral staff used
for investiture) by claiming also to give him ecclesiastical jurisdiction in the diocese. As a result, bishops considered themselves quite independent of the pope. Simony, incontinence and
clerical abuses remained unchecked and were fostered by the
political overlords.

A year after his election, Gregory held a synod in Rome,
which renewed old legislation against simony and violations of
celibacy. This was followed by another synod against the custom of lay investiture, with the result that at Worms in 1076

the Emperor Henry IV forced the bishops to repudiate the authority of the pope. Gregory thereupon excommunicated two German archbishops and the emperor, and then absolved Henry's subjects from all their allegiance—the first recorded papal deposition of a civil monarch.

Henry made his submission and was absolved at Canossa in 1077; but as soon as he had regained power, he renewed the opposition and was again deposed and excommunicated. But this time, the pope went beyond the first sentence. Not only was Henry dethroned but the royal power was granted by the pope to the Duke Rudolf of Suabia. In concluding the sentence, Gregory prayed that Henry "be confounded until he makes penance in order that his soul be safe at the day of the Lord."

This time the king retaliated by marching into Italy with an army, seizing Rome and setting up an antipope, Clement III. Gregory received protection from the Normans but had to retire to Salerno, where he passed away in 1085 as the greatest reformer in the history of the papacy. His last words were, "I have loved justice and hated iniquity, therefore I die in exile." Victor III, who succeeded him, excommunicated Clement III and continued the policy of Gregory, which even non-Catholic writers admit was the salvation of the Roman primacy.

The most controversial figure in the history of Church and State relations was Pope Boniface VIII (1234–1303), and his Bull, *Unam Sanctam*, issued in 1302, was the high point of the controversy.

In order to appreciate the full import of Pope Boniface's legislation, we should recall the circumstances under which it was enacted. Political rivalry among the Hapsburgs prevented the coronation of a Western Emperor for half a century in the late 1200's, with the result that during this time the Roman Pontiffs became the acknowledged visible heads of Catholic Christianity to a degree unparalleled in papal history. When Boniface VIII, a professional jurist, ascended the throne of Peter, he decided to embody in a general enactment the legal position of the Roman See, as it had crystallized during the thirteenth century. His instrument was the Bull, *Unam Sanc-*

tam, which subsequently became part of the Church's Canon Law.

The immediate occasion of the Bull was a long and heated conflict between the pope and the king of France, Philip IV, called "The Fair." Philip insisted on deriving his authority in the tradition of Charlemagne and was reluctant to admit any principle of subordination to the papacy in secular matters. When the king imposed a heavy taxation on the French clergy without previous agreement with Rome, Boniface took this as an infringement of ecclesiastical rights and after protracted study of the principles involved, published the document that was to sum up the plenitude of papal power over all the Christian community, including France and her king. Some have wrongly considered the *Unam Sanctam* an angry rejoinder of the pope, composed in a fit of revenge. Actually it was the deliberate pronouncement of a synod, headed by the pope, in which there were (besides others) thirty-nine French archbishops and bishops. Nor is it a document which the Holy See has ever retracted. In fact it was solemnly confirmed by the Fifth Lateran Council in 1513; and the very point in its teaching to which exception has been taken, is reaffirmed in the Syllabus of Errors of Pius IX.

After declaring there is only one Holy, Catholic and Apostolic Church, over which Christ placed only one head, "not two heads as if it were a monster," Boniface explained the relation of the secular power to the spiritual. "We are taught by the words of the Gospel that in this Church and in its power there are two swords, namely, a spiritual and a temporal. It is necessary that one sword should be under the other, and that temporal authority be subjected to the spiritual. For, the truth bearing witness, the spiritual power should instruct the temporal power and judge it, if it be not good. Hence We declare, affirm, and define and pronounce that it is altogether necessary for the salvation of every creature to be subject to the Roman Pontiff."[19]

At the outset we must distinguish between defined doctrine and ordinary papal teaching. Only the final sentence was solemnly defined and clearly represents traditional Catholic dogma on the Church's necessity for salvation.

But how are we to understand the preceding statements on the subordination of State to Church. We cannot interpret Boniface to mean that the whole sphere of temporal jurisdiction is directly subject to the Church; an injustice against which he protested shortly after the Bull was published. Followers of Philip the Fair inserted into the document the spurious phrase, "We wish you (the king) to know that you hold your kingdom from Us," adding that anyone who denied the proposition was a heretic. In a solemn consistory, Boniface denounced the forgery. "For forty years We have studied law, and We know that there are two powers appointed by God. Who should, then, or can, believe that We entertain, or have entertained, such stupid absurdity? We declare that in no way do We wish to usurp the jurisdiction of the king. And yet, neither the king nor any one else of the faithful can deny that he is subject to Us where a question of sin is involved (*ratione peccati*)."[20]

The pope's phrase *"ratione peccati,"* has since become the Church's norm to judge when and to what extent she may use her spiritual power to intervene in the secular affairs of State. She may do so when, in her judgment, an otherwise temporal affair (like civil legislation) affects the religious interests of the faithful by placing unwarranted burden on their conscience, exposing them to sin or otherwise conflicting with that spiritual welfare over which the Church believes she alone has ultimate jurisdiction by the mandate of her Founder.

THE MIDDLE AGES

The period from the beginning of the twelfth to the end of the fifteenth century, spanning about four hundred years of European culture, has been called the Middle Ages. Once viewed as a sterile interlude between the age of barbarism and modern times, it has come to be regarded as one of the most creative and fruitful periods in the world's history. For the historian of Catholicism it has special interest as the age which approached most nearly the ideal of Christendom as a religious unity.

Superficially it might seem that the source of this unity was an external agency, namely, the despotic control by an absolute papacy. Actually it was the fruit of interior solidarity of faith, which ten centuries of conflict had purified and that, in spite of sporadic upheavals, remained substantially intact until the dawn of the Reformation. The papacy was created by the faith, not vice versa; and as long as Christians believed substantially the same truths, Western Christianity remained one.

At the heart of the medieval faith was a conviction that the Church was a visible society, guided invisibly by its divine Founder but visibly directed by the successors of Peter in the apostolic see. Saints and mystics, scholars and the ordinary faithful commonly recognized this principle.

According to Paul Sabatier, Francis of Assisi (1181–1226) had been "expected, desired, longed for and prepared for by the sigh of Christian humanity. He drew from the Gospel a new spirit, a new soul, he vivified these by humility, love and submission." Yet his message and program were simple: to follow Christ in perfect poverty. Stirred by the words of the Master, "Do not possess gold nor silver," he gave away all that he had and soon gathered around him a group of like-minded companions.

True to the spirit of his age, Francis went to Rome to secure approval for his project. He had three audiences with Innocent III, whose pontificate is said to climax the medieval papacy. In the first he told the *poverello* to "go and pray God to manifest His will; when we know it we shall be able to answer you in all security." In the second he listened to Francis address him as "Holy Father" and tell the parable of the king, the poor woman and her children, personifying Christ, himself and the begging mendicants whom he wished to organize. Finally after the third interview Innocent verbally approved the Franciscan Rule. As he explained, he saw in this humble man, who asked only the authority to live by the Gospel, one who would redress the great Church of God and put it back into equilibrium.

It was no coincidence that among the provisions of the rule was this short one on Orthodoxy. "Let the Brethren on pain of being expelled from the fraternity behave themselves always as good Catholics; let them follow the usage and doctrine of the Roman Church."[21]

Excited by the reformers of the epoch, some Christians professed contempt for the sacraments administered by incontinent or simoniacal priests. Some refused to assist at Mass celebrated by them; others trod under foot the sacred species they had consecrated. One of these people approached Francis, who answered his questions with candor. "The hands of this priest may be such as you know, I know nothing about it. But even if they be so they cannot change the virtue of the sacraments. By these hands God bestows on His people a multitude of graces. I kiss those hands in honor of the benefits they dispense and of Him whose sacraments they are."[22] Francis himself was not a priest, but he knew the distinction on which the Catholic doctrine of the sacraments rests: that their efficacy is not dependent on the sanctity of the one who ministers them.

The greatest theological light of his day, St. Thomas Aquinas (1225–1274) professed the same faith. His *Summa Theologiae* has been compared to a great cathedral, built of the elements that twelve centuries of Christian wisdom had accumulated but never synthesized. "He combined, without confusing philosophy and theology, State and Church, civic and Christian virtues, natural and divine law, Christ and culture."[23] He also believed the Church of Christ was a divine creation, solid as a house built on massive foundations.

> The principal foundation is Christ Himself, for other foundation no man can lay but that which is Christ Jesus. Secondary foundations are the apostles and apostolic teaching; hence the Church is called apostolic. Its strength is signified by Peter, or Rock, who is its crown. A building is strong when it can never be overthrown though it may be shaken. The Church can never be brought down. Indeed it grows under persecution, and those who attack it are destroyed.
>
> Only the Church of Peter, to whose lot fell Italy when the disciples were sent out to preach, has always stood fast in the faith. While the faith has disappeared or has partly decayed in other regions, the Church of Peter still flourishes in the faith and free from heresy. This is not to be wondered at, for our Lord said to Peter, "I have prayed for you that your faith fail not, and you, when you are converted, confirm your brethren."[24]

St. Thomas was no idle theorist. He singled out for special mention the dangers to the Church from within in her unholy churchmen. He could recall that John XII (955–964) was elected Bishop of Rome at the age of eighteen and in less than a decade proved so unworthy that a synod, ordered by the emperor, tried and deposed him on charges of sacrilege, simony, perjury, murder and incest; that Benedict IX (1032–1048) was driven out of Rome because of his wicked life.

Although the popes, as a class, have been men of high integrity, there were tragic exceptions. And what even Aquinas had not experienced, came to pass within a century of his death, when the low morality of Catholic prelates and the weakness of several Pontiffs brought on the Western Schism (1378–1417), of which de Maistre asked, "What human institution could have withstood the ordeal?"

The schism broke over the harsh methods that Urban VI (1318–1389) used to try to reform the college of cardinals. Though Urban had been validly elected, the malcontents proceeded to choose one of their own number, Clement VII, as antipope, and until the Council of Constance settled the dispute by electing Martin V, there were three lines of rival claimants: the Roman started by Urban VI, the French under Clement VII, and the Pisan begun by Alexander V in an effort to solve the previous rupture.

Theologians, canonists and saints were divided in their allegiance, St. Catherine of Siena recognizing Urban VI and St. Vincent Ferrer Clement VII. True, the Great Schism was not schismatic in the ordinary sense because all parties upheld the supremacy of the Holy See. The problem was: which of the two or three claimants was legitimate pope? In spite of this trial, the Church grew in strength and vitality. Gregorovius, an impartial observer, remarked that the Schism "raised the papacy from decadence to a new eminence, and showed the world once again how the mystical faith of the people endows the pontiffs with powers that can rise to glory even when apparently dead."[25]

A dramatic proof of this mystical faith was the conduct of St. Catherine of Siena (1333–1380), Dominican tertiary and contemplative. Her extant correspondence with Gregory XI and his successor Urban VI reveals the spirit of Catholicism that acknowledges the Vicar of Christ while mercilessly rebuking his human failings.

Addressing Gregory as "sweet Christ on earth, on behalf of Christ in heaven" she censures his self-love which condoned the three vices then plaguing the Bride of Christ: impurity, avarice and swollen pride. "Human wretchedness!" she exclaims. "Blind is the sick man who does not know his own need, and blind the shepherd physician, who has regard to nothing but his own advantage. Such men do as Christ says: for if one blind man guide the other, both fall into the ditch. Sick man and physician fall into hell." In another letter, she begs his pardon for her boldness, explaining it was "the great love which I bear your salvation, and my great grief when I see the contrary, that makes me speak so." Then she adds, "Take care that I do not have to complain about you to Jesus crucified. There is no one else I can complain to, for you have no superior on earth."[26]

Catherine was equally explicit with Urban VI, at once recognizing his supreme authority and his human failings. "You are father and lord of the universal body of the Christian religion; we are all under the wings of your holiness. As to authority, you can do everything, but as to seeing, you can do no more than one man."[27]

It would be naive to assume that papal authority was uncontested during the Middle Ages. A theory of conciliarism, which claimed that a general council was above the pope, had been current in France since the thirteenth century. It reached its climax in the fifteenth, at the Council of Constance (sixteenth ecumenical) that put an end to the Western Schism by electing Martin V.

Among its published decrees were statements that contradicted papal supremacy and personal infallibility. Speaking of itself, the council declared that "it holds authority immediately from Christ, and all persons, of whatever authority, even the pope himself, are bound to obey the council in all that regards the faith, the healing of schism, and the reformation of the Church of God in her head and members. Anyone who disobeys this or any other general council, even the pope himself, shall, unless they repent, suffer the punishment they deserve."[28]

In approving the Council of Constance, Martin V excluded these sentiments from his approbation, and the restriction was accepted by the Church. Under his successor, Eugenius IV, the Council of Florence (1438–1445) removed the last vestige of doubt by solemnly proclaiming "that the holy, Apostolic See and the Roman Pontiff have the primacy over the whole world, and that the Roman Pontiff is the successor of St. Peter, the Prince of the Apostles, and the true vicar of Christ, the head of the whole Church, father and teacher of all Christians."[29]

Florence came at the end of a great schism in the West and was convoked to heal the centuries-old schism in the East. Among its most celebrated members were the Greek Emperor, John VIII Palaeologus, and Joseph, Patriarch of Constantinople. A decree of union between the East and West, based on the Roman primacy and beginning with the words *"Laetentur Coeli"* (may the heavens rejoice), was signed by all but one of the Eastern delegates. Political pressure in the East prevented the union from taking permanent effect.

There is something pathetic about the Council of Florence in trying, unsuccessfully, to heal the Eastern Schism and yet taking no cognizance of the still greater rift in Christendom about to take place in the next generation.

By the close of the Middle Ages, the Church had become involved in a turmoil of change. The rise of the modern secular State created a new rival to the Church's authority and a strong competitor for allegiance from citizens who were also Catholic Christians. Contact with the culture of the Islamic East, inspired by the Crusades, opened new horizons of knowledge that were a challenge to European and, by association, to Catholic forms of thought. Discovery of the Greek and Roman classics stimulated research in the ancient languages, and produced a critical attitude towards the Scriptures and a desire to have the inspired word of God, in or from the original.

The same sort of conflict appeared on the social and religious planes. Invention of printing multiplied the diffusion of ideas by geometric proportion, and where before 1440 men like Waldo, Aquinas and Huss could affect only a small number in restricted areas, by the end of the fifteenth century dynamic concepts and personalities had influence on numberless thousands in all parts of the Christian world. For the Church this was an opportunity and a threat, depending on whose ideas became prevalent and whether the new instrument was used to support or question ecclesiastical authority.

An accurate calculation shows that ninety saints and blessed from the fifteenth century were raised to the honors of the altar, men and women whose virtues during life were so outstanding they merited to be called heroic. At the same time, the contrast with the immorality and avarice in high places, including high churchmen, was so startling that the very term "Reformation" was coined to describe the reform of the Church "in head and members" demanded on all sides. It is symptomatic of the age that one of the purest flowers of Christian sanctity, St. Joan of Arc (1412–1431), was burned to death through the connivance of a corrupt ecclesiastical court. Her words, under trial, when asked to recant, "Let all the things I have said and done be reported to Rome, to our Holy Father, the Pope, to whom, after God, I refer them," only emphasize the struggle that men had to remain faithful to their Church under grave provocation."[30]

In one of the most remarkable documents of religious history, Adrian VI (1522–1523), the last non-Italian pope of modern times, held nothing back in describing the state of affairs on the eve of the Reformation, which he called a persecution.

> We frankly acknowledge that God permits this persecution of the Church on account of the sins of men, and especially of prelates and clergy. Of a surety the Lord's arm is not shortened that He cannot save us, but our sins separate us from Him, so that He does not hear. Holy Scripture declares aloud that the sins of the people are the outcome of the sins of the priesthood. We know well that for many years things deserving of abhorrence have gathered around the Holy See; sacred things have been misused, ordinances transgressed, so that in everything there has been a change for the worse. Thus it is

not surprising that the malady has crept down from the head to the members, from the Popes to the hierarchy.

We shall use all diligence to reform before all things the Roman Curia, whence, perhaps, all these evils have had their origin. Thus healing will begin at the source of sickness. We deem this to be all the more our duty, as the whole world is longing for reform.[31]

Adrian has been blamed for Teutonic bluntness in making this open confession of sins. But he was too clear-sighted a theologian not to distinguish between admission of moral guilt and acceptance of divinely-instituted authority. The latter he professed with courage and humility. "We desire," he said, "to wield our power not as seeking dominion or means for enriching our kindred, but in order to restore to Christ's bride, the Church, her former beauty, to give help to the oppressed, to uplift men of virtue and learning and, above all, to do all that beseems a good shepherd and successor of the blessed Peter."[32]

All the evidence shows that the original intention of the Reformers was to reform the Church and not to separate from papal authority which they at first recognized as the bulwark of Christian unity. Among the extant writings of Martin Luther is a sermon he preached in 1516 on the feast of St. Peter in Chains. It would have done credit to Adrian himself as a testimony to the papacy. "If Christ had not entrusted all power to one man," he told the audience, "the Church would not have been perfect because there would have been no order, and each one would have been able to say he was led by the Holy Spirit." Since the invisible head of the faithful desires that "all may be assembled in one unity, Christ wills that His power be exercised by one man, to whom also He has committed it. He has made this power so strong that He permits all the forces of hell to be let loose against it without injury."[33] Clearly, as a Catholic, Luther had no misgivings about Church authority or whether a Reformation of morals was possible without a revolution of doctrine.

REFORMATION TO MODERN TIMES

The immediate effect of the Reformation on Roman Catholicism was theological. The Protestant emphasis on the Bible and rejection of the Roman primacy stimulated theologians to investigate more closely the sources of revelation in Scripture and Tradition, and establish the grounds for a rational apologetic in support of the Catholic claims. The first need was met by developing a system of positive theology, whereby the truths professed by Catholic Christianity were shown to be found in the deposit of faith. The Jesuits, led by St. Robert Bellarmine (1542–1621), became the main expositors of this system, as they also laid the groundwork for fundamental theology, which proves from history and philosophy the credibility of the Christian religion.

Speculative theology also began a new era, occasioned by the challenges of Protestantism on almost every portion of the Catholic Church. During the twenty years of the Council of Trent (1545–1565), the combined intelligence of Roman Catholicism concentrated its efforts on so defining the nature of grace and justification, the Sacrifice of the Mass and the priesthood, the sacramental system and ecclesiastical authority, that insights were gained on which post-Tridentine writers have built an imposing theological structure.

But the fruits of the Counter-Reformation were more than theological. Since the Council of Trent, the Catholic Church has entered on a new phase of existence. The dogmatic bases were not changed, but their implications broadened; the very need of defending her claim to autonomy made the Church more than ever conscious of her corporate character; and the loss of large segments of membership (or practical disappearance under political pressure in England and Scandinavia), was made up by a new devotedness among those who remained faithful to the Church of Rome. "We must put aside all judgment of our own," wrote St. Ignatius Loyola (1491–1556), "and keep the mind ever ready and prompt to obey in all things the true Spouse of Christ, our Lord, our holy Mother, the hierarchical Church."[34]

This was no pious rhetoric. Catholics throughout Europe rallied to the defense of their common Mother and, as in England and Ireland, laid down their lives in her cause. "I am a Catholic man and a priest," Edmund Campion told the judge who condemned him. "In that faith have I lived and in that faith I intend to die."

The trials of purification during the sixteenth century were a blessing in disguise. Though at a terrible price, the Church bought a lease on her spiritual life that had no counterpart in previous history. There was a growth in the personal sanctity of her leaders and people, an expansion of zeal in missionary enterprise, a development of religious education, a deepening sense of solidarity among the laity, and a rising influence of Catholic principles on the world at large.

Holiness is an elusive concept. The title "saint" has been applied to such varied individuals as Savonarola, John Wesley, and Mahatma Gandhi. In the Catholic Church, however, only those are called saints who were either martyrs or who during life practiced the moral virtues over a long period of time, under severe trial and temptation, and to a degree that clearly exceeds the native capacity of the human will. All the virtues were comprehended, but especially charity, fortitude and temperance, including chastity. Several thousand men and women, in every walk of life, have been raised to the honors of the altar (saints and blessed) in the past four hundred years, almost seven hundred since Pius XI, as a living witness to the Church's capacity for uniting the soul with God.

Coupled with the miraculous sanctity of a small number has been a raising of demands on the conscience of all Catholics in modern times that were practically unknown in the "ages of faith." In pluralistic societies, the pressures from an alien environment, the tendency to moral conformity, the urge to follow prevalent standards in marriage, business and the professions, the example of well-meaning persons whose religious principles are foreign to the Catholic way of life, have placed clergy and laity in the dilemma of choosing between compromise or often near-heroism in remaining true to their own convictions. Mere respectability is swept along with the stream; only a strong faith and more than normal courage have been able to withstand the tide. Yet the Church has grown, from an estimated world membership of a hundred million at the turn of the century to over half a billion in the sixties.

Foreign missions outside Europe were few and sporadic until the sixteenth century. The Counter Reformation brought a rebirth of missionary zeal, comparable only to the evangelization in apostolic or early medieval times. Some have called it an effort to counteract the losses in north-western Europe. More accurately it was a spontaneous result of the change of interior life among the Catholic peoples who had for so long taken their faith for granted. A letter of St. Francis Xavier, written from Cochin to Rome in 1543, illustrates the spirit of the Gospel to which he could appeal and be heard by so many volunteers they had to be restrained from following him to the Indies.

> There is now in these parts a very large number who have only one reason for not becoming Christian, and that is because there is no one to make them Christians. It often comes to my mind to go around to all the universities of Europe, and especially that of Paris, crying out everywhere like a madman, and saying to all learned men there whose learning is so much greater than their charity, "What a multitude of souls is through your fault shut out of heaven and falling into hell."[35]

Missionary enthusiasm has continued unabated through the centuries, in spite of obstacles from rapacious or near-sighted political rulers, indifference or savage reprisal among the natives, domestic and foreign wars, and all the inclemencies of learning a strange tongue and living in an atmosphere devoid of Christian principles and customs. A current annual increase of more than one million Catholics in the Far East, where Communism has become dominant, indicates the established character of the Church's missions.

Since the liberation of Christianity under Constantine, the Church had conducted an immense variety of schools and institutions in every branch of learning. In the Middle Ages, a home of study was attached to the monasteries, convents and cathedral chapters scattered throughout Europe. Chantry endowments were normally associated with giving free instructions to the children of the surrounding country-side. After some two thousand chantries were suppressed in England during the sixteenth century, there was no English grammar school for the next two hundred years which had not previously been a chantry. Universities were spread over the continent and in Great Britain, always by the initiative and under the protection of the Holy See.

If anything, Catholic education has been intensified in modern times, and in countries like the United States, where freedom of religion is enjoyed, it has reached a scope and degree of intensity unknown in previous history. Catholic education in Catholic schools for Catholic youth was the ideal proposed by Pius XI, where "all the teaching and the whole organization of the school, its teachers, syllabus, and textbooks in every branch are regulated by the Christian spirit."

In many countries, e.g., England, France, Scotland, Canada, and the Netherlands, the State contributes to the support of church-affiliated institutions, on the principle that "the school plays a vital part in the child's attitudes and sense of values. If the school gives little place to religious teaching, then the child quite naturally assumes that religion is not an integral part of his mental development."[36] The judgment on the need for religion-centered education, originally professed by the Church, is now shared by many educators in the western world.

Cultivating a sense of unity among widely scattered peoples is a difficult process, and one contributing factor to the breakdown of solidarity in the sixteenth century was that so little was done to make the faithful conscious of their common heritage and their bond of union under the See of Rome. A great deal has happened since then. The very option that Catholics were forced to make, between acceptance or rejection of the pope, resulted in strengthening the ties of membership in the Catholic Church.

But that was only the beginning. The modern world has become smaller than ever before. Mass media for the exchange of ideas and rapid transportation have made neighbors of once-distant nations and joined whole continents closer than formerly were towns of the same province. All of this has affected the Catholic Church whose inner structure is already based on a principle of inter-relationship that no other body enjoys. Where in the Middle Ages the pope was for most people only a distant figure, he is now as near (or nearer) to the average Catholic anywhere on the globe as the local parish priest; papal statements and attitudes become in a few hours the common property of all nations. The happenings and misfortunes of Catholic people in once remote places in Asia or Africa are made known to their co-religionists in America overnight.

The sense of fellowship thus created between church leaders and the laity, and among the laity themselves is a matter of experience, and heightens the faith-accepted idea that Catholics are more than members of a juridical society, that they belong to a mystical organization whose principle of unity is the Spirit of God.

Bound in with the foregoing and rising out of the Church's sense of mission, is the influence which Catholicism exercises in modern times beyond anything previously known. The Catholic Church believes itself to be in full possession of revealed truth, and divinely qualified to interpret and transmit this revelation to its own members and, indeed, to the whole world. Among the crucial areas on which it believes the human mind is naturally incapable of complete and accurate knowledge is the moral law, involving such basic responsibilities as the precepts of the Decalogue.

With the growing secularization of Western society, the call for enlightening the people, once Christian in their religious duties to God and neighbor, has increased enormously. On one side the grave need, and on the other the Church's felt duty to answer the need, have given Catholicism a role to play in "teaching the nations" that some of its worst critics are willing to respect.

It is not only papal encyclicals on the social order, like *Rerum Novarum* of Leo XIII or *Mater et Magistra* of John XXIII, but the whole gamut of natural religion founded on belief in a personal God, that passes from the Church into every phase of human society. At the first Vatican Council, when atheism and rationalism were scored as denials of man's nature and insults to God, principles were set forth that have penetrated wherever the faithful live and affect those with whom they come into contact. An issue like artificial contraception, for example, has been raised as a moral problem mainly because of the Church's stand on the intrinsic dignity of womanhood and the sacred character of sex relations in marriage.

At the opening of the Second Vatican Council, Pope John XXIII stressed a new dimension in the Church's outreach to the world at large. Where previous ecumenical councils had been convoked to stem the rise of some error or clarify a disputed area of revealed doctrine, this one was met for a different purpose. "Nowadays," the Pope said, "the spouse of Christ prefers to make use of the medicine of mercy rather than that of severity. She considers that she meets the needs of the present day by demonstrating the validity of her teaching rather than by condemnations." Behind this attitude is the conviction that no other way is more effective to promote unity among Christians and, indeed, among all men than the practice of charity, particularly of that supernatural love which seeks to communicate to others the graces it has received from God.

> Such is the aim of the Second Vatican Ecumenical Council, which, while bringing together the Church's best energies and striving to have men welcome more favorably the good tidings of salvation, prepares, as it were, and consolidates the path toward that unity of mankind which is required as a necessary foundation in order that the earthly city may be brought to the resemblance of that heavenly city where truth reigns, charity is the law, and whose extent is eternity.[37]

Active participation of Protestant and Orthodox delegates at the Second Vatican Council has made history. It also demonstrated the new spirit which people in every communion sense has entered the Christian world.

MEANING OF CATHOLICISM

The term "Catholic" was first applied to the Church by Ignatius of Antioch in his letter to the Smyrneans, to whom he said that "wherever the bishop appears, let the congregation be present; just as wherever Jesus Christ is, there is the Catholic Church."[38] No doubt Ignatius used the adjective to distinguish the universal Church from particular churches in different countries. Yet the emphasis he placed on unity of doctrine suggests that already at the beginning of the second century the word "Catholic" had something of the connotation it soon acquired, of an institution that claimed to remain true to the teachings of its Founder in contrast with other Christian systems and modes of thought.

Along with the profession of fidelity there developed the idea of universality, which the early apologists were quick to exploit in their defense of Christianity. "There is not one single race of men, whether barbarians, or Greeks, or whatever they may be called, among whom prayers and giving of thanks (the Eucharist) are not offered through the name of the crucified Jesus."[39] Thus wrote Justin the Martyr around 150 A.D. But the classic expositor of what "Catholic" means was St. Ireneus, Bishop of Lyons, writing at the end of the second century in his controversy with the Gnostics.

> Though scattered throughout the whole world (*kath' olēs tēs oikoumenēs*) to the ends of the earth, the Church received from the Apostles this teaching and this faith. . . . The Church carefully guards this faith, as though it dwelt in a single house; this doctrine it believes as though it had one soul and heart; this creed it teaches and communicates as if it possessed one mouth.
>
> Although there are many different languages in the world, there is one and the same power of tradition. The churches founded in Germany teach no different doctrine from those in Spain or the surrounding Celtic countries; those in the East, or those in Egypt, do not differ from those in North Africa. Just as the sun, the creature of God, is one and the same in the whole world, so also is the preaching of the truth,

the light that shines everywhere and illumines all men who
wish to come to a knowledge of the truth.

Different doctrines are not taught by more cultured and able
among the leading churches, nor is tradition diminished by
those who are weak in controversy. For, since there is one and
the same faith, it is neither added to by the effective speaker
nor diminished by the one less skilled.[40]

Here is the essence of Catholicism as its adherents understand their faith: a universality pervading all nations and
languages, races and social structures.

Yet, even as they identify catholicity with universality, Catholics believe their religion is more than a broadly diffused
form of Christianity. They see their Church as an extension
of the Incarnation and view it as participating in the twofold
nature of Christ, who was at once true man and the Son of
the living God. According to one view, therefore, the visible
phase as a juridical institution is stressed—corresponding to
the humanity of Jesus; and according to another aspect are
emphasized the internal qualities of a spiritual entity whose
cohesive force is the invisible grace of God—comparable to
Christ's divinity.

JURIDICAL SOCIETY. The clearest exponent of the Church as
a visible institution was St. Robert Bellarmine, contemporary
of Luther, Calvin, and the early Reformers. To meet their
challenge of a new concept of Christianity as a purely invisible
society composed of all the believers, or all the just, or all the
predestined, he described the Catholic Church as "the assembly of men, bound together by the profession of the same
Christian faith, and by the communion of the same sacraments, under the rule of rightful pastors, and in particular of
the one Vicar of Christ on earth, the Roman Pontiff."[41] The
purpose of this definition was mainly functional, to determine
who are members of the Catholic Church and who are not.
To make sure his meaning was not misunderstood, Bellarmine
added: "the Church is an assembly of men, as visible and
palpable as the gathering of the Roman people, or the Kingdom of France, or the Republic of Venice."[42]

Each of three different elements set down the conditions for membership in this juridical body. Since profession of faith is the first requisite, only those who accept all that the Church infallibly proposes for belief actually belong to the Catholic Church. They may not be aware of the whole corpus of required doctrine, or may be subjectively mistaken in their understanding of what is taught, but they accept whatever is part of the Church's official teaching.

Behind this condition for Church affiliation is the premise that God came to earth in the person of Jesus Christ to teach people the way to salvation—how to live in this world in order to attain heaven in the next. If this is true, it is argued, then Christ would not have left the door of salvation opened for His own times only. He wanted His saving teachings to remain available to mankind until the end of time. Yet this availability would have been less than sterile if He had not provided a living authority to explain and interpret His doctrine as found in the Gospels. Is divorce with remarriage moral? Was Christ born of a virgin and did He rise in bodily form after death? Does the Church in her priests have the power of forgiving sins, and will impenitent sinners be punished eternally in hell? Without a sure court of appeal, Catholicism says, moral and theological disintegration seem inevitable. It was therefore to avert such disintegration that Christ established the Church to be His authoritative interpreter on earth, to be His one completely competent spokesman for adjudicating between truth and error on life and death matters.

Sharing in the same sacraments is also necessary for Catholic membership, on the postulate that those who belong to the Church must be united not only by profession of the same faith but in the manifestation of the same forms of divine worship. The Sacrifice of the Mass in particular is considered the mainstay of ritual solidarity, wherein the same High Priest who offered Himself on the Cross for the Redemption of the world offers Himself in an unbloody manner every time the Eucharistic oblation is repeated.

Up to this point, all Christians participate in some of these conditions, and a few (among the Orthodox and Episcopalians) subscribe to practically everything. But the third element, obedience to the Roman Pontiff as Vicar of Christ, is uniquely Catholic. It explains why the term "Roman" is commonly added to "Catholic Church" in popular terminology.

In accepting papal authority, the Catholic Church understands that the Roman Pontiff has more than just the highest office of inspection as a kind of superintendent or director. He is believed to have received from Christ the full and supreme power of jurisdiction over the universal Church, not only in matters of faith and morals, but also in things relating to the discipline and government of the Church throughout the world. Consequently, the pope is held to possess not merely the principal part but the fulness of this supreme power. His authority is not merely occasional or delegated, but ordinary and immediate over each and all the churches and over all the pastors of the faithful.

In Bellarmine's ecclesiology, the external phase was emphasized to bring out the Church's visibility and sense perceptibility. It is a definite society, he explained, not of angels or spirits but of men. It must then be bound together by external and visible signs, so that those who belong to it can recognize one another as members and thereby share in their common and distinctive possessions.

SACRAMENTAL AGENT. There is another, more profound concept of the Church, which the late Pius XII traced to the writings of St. Paul and the early Fathers. "If we would define and describe the true Church of Jesus Christ," he said, "which is the one, holy, Catholic, apostolic Roman Church—we shall find nothing more noble, more sublime, or more divine than the expression 'the Mystical Body of Jesus Christ.' "[43]

The term "mystical" has a variety of meanings in theological parlance, but when applied to the Church it describes the mysterious presence of Christ which Catholics believe is the Incarnation extended into history and destined to be consummated in heaven after the last day. Once the word "mystical" is seen to be the same as "sacramental," the full import of how Catholicism understands itself becomes clearer. In a broad sense anything spiritual conveyed through bodily means partakes of the nature of a sacrament. There are seven sacraments properly so-called in the Catholic Church, containing the grace they signify and conferring that grace from the rite itself (*ex opere operato*) on those who place no obstacle in the way. However, by analogy the Church itself may be considered sacramental, and the two concepts together afford the deepest insight into the meaning of Catholic Christianity.

As explained by St. Thomas, who borrowed his ideas from the patristic tradition, the body with which St. Paul identified the Church is a living entity, and like every organism requires suitable means to enter into life, to grow and mature according to its nature. Similarly Christ has provided for His Mystical Body by endowing it with the sacraments, to give its members access to powerful channels of grace, from birth to death, and to provide for the social needs of the society He founded.

Leading this sacramental series is baptism, called the door of the Church because it is the only way a person can become an actual member of the Catholic Church. At the Council of Florence, which sought the reunion of the Eastern Orthodox, "holy Baptism" was said to "hold the first place among all the sacraments because it is the door of the spiritual life. By it we are made members of Christ and of His Body the Church. And since through the first man death has come to all men, unless we are reborn of water and the Holy Spirit we cannot enter into the kingdom of heaven."[44]

Having entered the Church, a Catholic is held by divine law to give profession of his belief in Christ, at no matter what cost and under penalty of eternal loss of his soul. When explaining this injunction, Canon Law refers to the precept of Christ: "Everyone who acknowledges me before men, him will the Son of Man also acknowledge before the angels of God. But whoever disowns me before men will be disowned before the angels of God." Since the precept is universal and may at times require extraordinary courage to fulfil, the faithful receive the sacrament of Confirmation by which they are given additional strength to protect and defend the Church, their Mother, and the faith she has given them.

Confirmation, therefore, has a double aspect: to safeguard not only one's own faith but also to defend the Church from whom the faith was received. Its function is not only negative, to shelter the faith and the Church, but openly to defend both against the forces of opposition.

Likewise, in the sacrament of Penance or Confession, the benefit is considered both individual and social. Here the Church is seen as providing a salutary remedy for those who have fallen into sin, and at the same time removing from other members of the Mystical Body the danger of contagion—besides giving them an incentive and example for the practice of virtue. As sin is removed from one cell of the Body, the rest of the Church profits accordingly, much as the removal of a diseased organ or limb benefits the whole person. What happens is not merely the checking of bad influence, in this case the effects of sin, but the transmission of new vitality in the form of grace from one part of the Church's body to all the others.

The Eucharist is pre-eminently the sacrament of Catholicism. It is a dramatic symbol of the unity of the Church, about which St. Augustine and other ancients wrote their homilies, and illustrated in the liturgical prayers of the Mass, like the oration from the *Didache,* dated in the first century of the Christian era: "As this broken Bread was scattered over the hills and then, when gathered together became one mass, so may Your Church be gathered from the ends of the earth into Your Kingdom. For Yours is the glory and the power through Jesus Christ forevermore."[45]

Moreover in the Eucharist Catholics believe they receive the very Author of grace and the Head of the Mystical Body, and through Him an increase of charity towards God and of love for others for the sake of God. Thus the Eucharist is an aliment of the Church, wherein Christ nourishes Christ, Head to members, and they in turn become more unified with one another through Him.

In a category by itself is the Sacrifice of the Mass, which the popes down the centuries have said is the central act of worship in the Church, and the main single source of grace for mankind, benefiting people in the Church and out of it, whether in the friendship of God or estranged from Him by sin.

The Eucharist is not only a sacrament but also a sacrifice. As a sacrament it has effect upon living beings, where life is required to make a sacrament effective. But as a sacrifice it is effective on others besides the living, for whom it is offered, who are not actually but only potentially living in grace. Consequently, as long as they are properly disposed, the Mass will obtain grace for such people in virtue of that true Sacrifice (of the Cross) from which all grace is poured into us. So that grave sins are deleted in these sinners by the Mass, not as a proximate cause but insofar as the Mass infallibly obtains for them the grace of sorrow for their sins.[46]

Extreme Unction is the sacrament of passage from the Mystical Body on earth to the Mystical Body in heaven. Where the other sacraments help the faithful to remain steadfast during life, anointing with the *oleum infirmorum* gives the promise of strength to resist the evil spirit at the hour of death. There are two effects proper to this sacrament and both are related to the Mystical Body. Its main purpose is to remove the vestiges of sin and strengthen the soul in its departure from this world, thus facilitating its entrance into the Church Triumphant, which is the Mystical Body in heavenly consummation. An important secondary effect, however, is to remove the guilt and punishment due to sin, whether grave or venial, thus restoring (if need be) life to a dead member of the Church and making possible, besides accelerating, his admission to celestial glory.

Two sacraments of the Church are conceived as providing directly for the social needs of the Mystical Body. In Matrimony the husband and wife are ministers of grace to each other. Since they are not only man and woman but also belong to a supernatural society, the procreation of children for them means more than just conserving the human race and providing for its orderly development; it means the duty of preserving and increasing membership of the Mystical Body. All the laws that nature has implanted in the two sexes to insure the welfare of mankind are sublimated by grace in the faithful for the common benefit of the Church. Where natural instinct makes the two sexes mutually attractive, grace provides for a similar attraction on a higher level, so that children will be not only physically brought into the world but also spiritually reborn in Baptism, educated and nurtured into vital cells of the Body of Christ.

It is this concept of Matrimony that makes the Catholic Church so adamant in its stand on divorce and contraception. Marriage between Christians is indissoluble because it should reflect that most perfect union which exists between Christ and the Church which is perpetual. One of the most frequent causes of estrangement from the Church of his Baptism and his deepest loyalties on the part of a Catholic is a marriage attempted after a divorce. He is reminded that "the whole of eternity is gambled against the fascination of human companionship," that men are ultimately made not for earthly happiness but for heavenly joy. "Hence, if there is loneliness and a longing for companionship, let these be looked upon not as a warrant to contravene divine law, but as a challenge to Christian fortitude."[47]

The same with contraception. "Since the conjugal act is destined primarily by nature for the begetting of children, those who in exercising it deliberately frustrate its natural power and purpose sin against nature and commit a deed which is shameful and intrinsically vicious."[48] If this applies to all married persons, it is specially pertinent to Catholics who would thus frustrate not only the natural function of sexual intercourse but the connatural way in which Christ intends His Church to increase and multiply in the supernatural order.

By the sacrament of Ordination the Church is provided with the means of nourishing the life of the faithful through the Mass and the sacraments and, in a true sense, with the juridical power to govern by legitimate authority and proclaim the word of God. Except for the sacraments of Baptism and Matrimony, which do not require ordination to be administered, all the others depend on the power of priestly orders.

Here is a crucial difference between Catholic and other forms of Christianity. In Catholic thought, the priestly powers communicated by Christ through the apostles and their successors are intimately bound up with the power of jurisdiction. In practical terms, the authority which the pope and bishops exercise in the Church derives from their ordination and consecration. No doubt a single person, say a bishop-elect, may be invested with jurisdictional powers before his consecration. But considering the Church as a whole, the power of jurisdiction requires the power of orders necessarily and absolutely. If there were no power of orders at all, there could be no ecclesiastical authority in the accepted Catholic meaning of that term.

Viewed in this light, the Catholic Church's claim to apostolic lineage is more than a simple assertion of fidelity to the teaching of the apostles. It is a claim to historical continuity from Christ, through the apostles, to all the members of the hierarchy and from them to all priests: that when Christ ordained the first ministers of the Gospel, He gave them delegated power to communicate to others what they had received, in literal and direct succession until the end of time.

However, the Catholic Church professes to more than having a sacramental system, from Baptism to Holy Orders. It claims to be itself the great Sacrament of the New Law. The logic behind this profession stems from the general principle that although God can perform by His own power all that is effected by created natures, nevertheless in the counsels of His providence He has preferred to help men by the instru-mentality of other men's work; so also He makes use of human aid for that which lies beyond the limits of nature, for the salvation and sanctification of souls.

It is assumed that the divine mission committed to Him by His Father was not to end with Christ's death but continue after his ascension through the Church which He founded. Consequently as Catholics view their Church, it is undoubtedly spiritual if we consider the chief purpose of the Church, which is to make men holy, and the immediate cause of holiness, which is supernatural grace in its various forms. But as re-gards the persons who constitute the Body of Christ and the means which lead to these spiritual gifts, the Church is external and its very external elements are the instruments for com-municating the internal life of God to souls.

This fusion of visible and invisible elements is not coinci-dental; it is causally interdependent. Comparable to what oc-

curs in one area of the Church's operation in the sacramental
system is perennially taking place in the Church as a whole.
External unity among the members and stability in doctrine
and discipline are the sign of a deeper solidarity which comes
from the animating Spirit of God. Conversely, doctrine and
discipline, and the juridical forms which govern the faithful
carry the assurance of an invisible efficacy which for Catholics
as far transcends the material instruments used as the raising
of Lazarus exceeded the sound of Christ's voice or the conversion of the Mediterranean world was beyond the capacity
of a dozen Jews.

The Body of Christ is said to be mystical, then, because it
is sacramental, not only in the functional sense of an external
action signifying the conferral of interior grace, but on the
cosmic level of a visible entity whose Body, in all its amplitude,
is a manifestation of God's presence on earth, begun at the
Incarnation and extended into human history. Those who
benefit from this communication are first of all the actual
members of the Mystical Body, who receive these gifts as by a
special privilege. But also outside the Body, whoever is eventually saved is told to credit his salvation to the instrumentality
of the Church, whose invisible Head is the fountain of all
life and holiness; and of whose fulness anyone who is sancti-
fied must have received.

Although the main lines of this concept of Catholicism are
clear enough, its full implication is open to wide development,
as Pope Paul told the Second Vatican Council. "It is necessary," he said, "to elucidate the teaching regarding the different components of the visible and Mystical Body, the pilgrim,
militant Church on earth, that is, priests, religious, the faithful, and also the separated brethren who are also called to
adhere to it more fully and completely."[49]

For the first time since the Reformation, the term "separated brethren" has taken on a new and profound meaning, in
which the Catholic Church sees other Christians as related to
herself spiritually by the three-fold bond of baptism, faith and
devotion to the person of Jesus Christ.

14

ISLAM

To most Christians, Mohammedanism is only a vague religious movement that somehow gave rise to the Crusades and that presently affects the culture and political aspirations of certain people in North Africa, the Near East and Pakistan. Actually Mohammedanism is the most powerful force among the living religions outside of Christianity, and to many observers its greatest competitor for the spiritual domination of the world.

The correct name of Mohammedanism is Islam, which Mohammed himself adopted as a description of the faith he proclaimed. Grammatically Islam is the infinitive of a verb that means to resign, submit, or surrender, by implication oneself or one's person to God. Those who profess it are called Muslims, of which the Western form is Moslems, meaning "believers" who offered themselves to God, as distinct from Kafirs or Mushriks, "the rejectors" of the divine message of salvation. Moslems dislike the word Mohammedan because it suggests the worship of Mohammed, even as the term Christian implies the worship of Jesus Christ.

HISTORICAL ORIGINS

A balanced study of Islamic origins must take into account the religious and ethnic conditions in Arabia before the rise of Mohammed. In ancient times Arabia remained quite outside the threshold of the great civilizations. Its inhabitants never really bowed to a foreign master. The tribal and political divisions of the people combined with the rough terrain to foil attempted conquests by alien powers.

While the early history of the Arab race is veiled in obscurity, historical tradition agrees in assigning Ishmael, the

son of Abraham by Agar, as one of the important early ancestors of the race. In any case, the Semitic people who
formed the permanent population of Arabia were joined several centuries before Mohammed by colonies of immigrants,
chiefly Jews but also Christians, who settled among the native
population. Thus three religious currents ran through pre-
Islamic Arabia: the native Arabian, the Jewish and the
Christian.

Idolatry combined with elements of Biblical tradition to
form the religion of the native Arab. Derived from a primitive
form of animism, it consisted largely in the worship of the
heavenly bodies. Though he seems to have believed in one
God, the early Arab found little difficulty combining his weak
monotheism with adoration of the fixed stars and planets, or
at least with offering sacrifice to the angels who were believed
to dwell in these stellar bodies. The title "goddesses" or
"daughters of God" was given not only to the intelligences
but to their images as well, which the Arabs looked upon as
either animated by the spirits or graced by their presence with
the power of special protection.

Mohammed, the founder of Islam, was born into this environment at Mecca, about 600 miles south of Jerusalem, some
time between 570 and 580 of the Christian era. His father,
Abd Allâh, died on a journey to Medina, before Mohammed
was born; the mother, *Aminah bint Wahb,* died ten years
later. The young *Muhammad* (as spelled in Arabic) was first
brought up by his paternal grandfather, and after the latter's
death by his uncle *Abû Tâlib.* Except for a pathetic reference
in the Koran to his hardships as an orphan, most of the early
life of Mohammed before his vocation is either legendary or
difficult to verify.

It is certain that he engaged in the caravan trade, became
commercial agent to a widow *Khadija,* married her and had
children, of whom four daughters survived. What pious tradition suggests, that he showed prophetic insight already in his
youth, should be set aside. More important and surely authentic is the series of conflicts to which Mohammed was subject and which deeply affected his later experiences. His or-
phaned background deprived him of external care and

security, and encouraged a sense of dependence on the preter-
natural; the evidence of idolatry among the Arabs contrasted
strongly with the monotheistic religion of the immigrant Jews
and, mostly Nestorian, Christians; his deep sensibility responded as by instinct to the social injustice he saw all around
him at Mecca, with its extremes of wealth and poverty, and
its underworld of slaves, thieves and vagabonds.

When he finally emerged about the age of forty (610–
612 A.D.) as the prophet of a new revelation, the immediate
object of reform and castigation was the prosperity-sodden
Mecca, whose inhabitants he faced with the message of repentance because the judgment of God was at hand.

Mohammed's message to the Meccans was simple and forthright. He proclaimed the existence of one only absolute Lord
and Creator, whose name Allah was known but almost buried
in the Arabic pantheon. This God was sole master of mankind,
whose final judgment would be a terrible vengeance on the
ungodly. Man's only hope before the Deity was a blind
abandonment (Islam) to the divine will, and a life of prayer
and resistance to one's sinful inclinations.

But the leading people of Mecca would not listen. Religious
leaders were too entrenched in their polytheism and the
wealthy merchants in secular affairs to take Mohammed seriously. Gradually he made some converts, beginning with his
wife, and mostly among the slaves and foreigners. Opposition
arose when the impact of his ideas became more evident.
Occasionally there were riots and always a hidden persecution
in the form of social boycott.

For ten years Mohammed struggled to make a headway
with only minimal success until the autumn of 622, when he
fled secretly from Mecca, escaped his pursuers, and established
himself at Medina, about two hundred miles north. The city
had been suffering from a fratricidal war, and feared lest its
weakness be exploited by the Jewish tribes under municipal
control. So the people invited Mohammed to come to Medina
as arbitrator and peace-maker.

This migration of Mohammed and his followers is known
as the *hijrah* (departure) and marks the year *one* of the Moslem era. Moslem years are counted A.H., or after the *hijrah*.

The flight to Medina changed not only the scene but the actor and the drama in Islamic history. In Mecca the prophet had been simply a religious leader, concerned for the social morals of his people and zealous to share his revealed convictions; at Medina he suddenly became a political and military figure, whose new role is clearly indicated by a sudden transition in the Koran.

Three important battles, provoked by Mohammed, mark the period of a slow conquest of Mecca, finally accomplished in 630. An attempted raid on a Meccan caravan was first repulsed by armed soldiers, who were then roundly defeated by the Moslems at Badr (624). The following year in a pitched battle at Uhud, the Meccans won a partial victory which they did not follow up. In the Battle of the Ditch (627), Mohammed successfully resisted a siege of Medina by digging large trenches before the unprotected entrances to the city. Three years later he determined to attack his native city with an army of ten thousand men. He took possession without a struggle, broke down the pagan idols of the Kaaba, rebuilt the sacred temple and into its foundation set the same black stone which Arabian animists had kissed for centuries as part of their pilgrimage ritual. Probably a meteorite, the stone came to be worshiped by the Semitic tribesmen as "of heavenly" origin. Islam's tradition explains the present black color of the stone as a result of contact with the sins and impurity of the pagan world.

For a moment his Medinian companions feared that Mohammed would leave them now in favor of Mecca, but they were promptly reassured. Within a few months after his entrance into Mecca, he broke the final resistance of the Bedouin tribes at the battle of Hunajn and returned to Medina to establish that city as the political capital of a new Moslem state. Here he received delegates from the Arabian chieftains who vowed their submission, and from here sent out his last military expeditions, including one against the Byzantine power which failed indeed but foreshadowed the vast expansion of the Islamic empire of the future.

From Medina, in 631, the prophet issued his definitive norms excluding idolaters from the pilgrimage which had become entirely Islamized, and in 632 Mohammed made the pilgrimage himself for the first and last time. An estimated forty thousand people made the journey with him. It was a pilgrimage of farewell. His mission was complete: paganism had been crushed, the new faith was solidly established, and a young generation of ardent followers was ready to carry the prophet's message to the far reaches of Asia and Northern Africa. Scholars dispute as to whether Mohammed personally ambitioned this conquest. There is not a syllable in the Koran suggesting a mission of Islam outside of Arabia, or of a conscious universalism such as we find in the New Testament. Yet expansion was inevitable—given the Moslem abomination of pagan idolatry, the claim to superseding Judaism and Christianity, the charge of polytheism against the Christian dogma of the Trinity, and Mohammed's insistence on a zealous prosecution of the enemies of Allah.

On his return to Medina after the pilgrimage, Mohammed was seized by a violent fever which caused his death at the age of sixty-three, in the eleventh year of the *Hijrah* and the year 632 (June 8) of the Christian era.

THE KORAN

The Bible of Islam is the Koran or *Qur'an*. It consists of those revelations which Mohammed claimed to have received from Allah, yet not directly but through the mediation of the angel Gabriel. According to Islamic tradition, the book is not a new creation but exists in archetype in heaven, fixed in the very essence of God and delivered piecemeal to the prophet. The word Koran means "recitation," and suggests its primary function of being recited during religious ceremonies.

Mohammed memorized his own utterances and taught his followers to do the same, but no single disciple knew the whole Koranic revelation. When the prophet died, the oracles were found on scattered bits of leather, ribs of palm leaf, and even on stones. These were gathered together, put into a chest and entrusted to the keeping of Haphsa, one of Mohammed's wives. During the reign of the first Caliph, Abu Bekr, a hurried edition of the Koran was made by Zaid of Medina, Mohammed's secretary, relying on oral tradition and scattered writings. But variant texts soon appeared, which alarmed the prophet's followers and prompted the third Caliph, Othman, to order all variants burned and have a canonical edition published by Zaid and three members of the Koraish tribe. Thus the text of the Koran was finally settled within thirty years of Mohammed's death, and in its present form is universally accepted by Moslems as authentic.

In English translation, the Koran is a book of some two-hundred thousand words, divided into one hundred fourteen chapters, called Surahs, arranged roughly in descending order of length, with some of the final chapters as short as a single paragraph. Surahs are further divided into verses, totalling about six thousand, and numbered as in the Christian Bible.

The Surahs are not numbered in the manuscripts, but are headed by titles taken from a particular matter treated, a person mentioned, or generally from the first significant words. Typical titles are: Women, Abraham, Mary, the Angels, Divorce, Small Kindnesses, and the Disbelievers.

Moslems universally recognize the language of the Koran as elegant in the extreme. "The Koran," they say, "cannot be translated." Nothing can duplicate "that inimitable symphony, the very sounds of which move men to tears and ecstasy." It is admittedly the standard of the Arabic tongue, and as the book itself teaches, beyond the capacity of any human pen. This, they claim, is a permanent miracle, greater than raising the dead and alone sufficient to convince the world of its divine original.

No satisfactory theory explains either the time or sequence of the purported revelations. Most likely the shortest Surahs were the earliest, and references to current events within the text may indicate when some of the statements were made.

Heading many of the Surahs is the declaration, "Revealed at Al-Madinah" or "Revealed at Mecca"; where no place is given, the locale of revelation is uncertain. Also at the beginning of each chapter, with the exception of the ninth, occurs the phrase, "In the name of Allah, the Beneficent, the Merciful."

Only the most uncritical Moslem holds that the Koran is

wholly original. Mohammed wove into his discourse large quantities of tribal tradition, popular sayings, legends beloved by the people, and much that he had gathered from his contact with the Jews and Christians, although the latter was mainly apocryphal, and the Jewish was more rabbinical interpretation than Old Testament content.

DOCTRINE AND WORSHIP IN THE KORAN

Islam is a glomeration of sects and traditions that bewilder the Western mind. Yet after thirteen centuries, the followers of Mohammed are somehow united and their unity traceable to a common devotion to the Koran. It is the duty of every Moslem, man, woman, or child, to read the Koran and understand it according to his capacity. There runs through the book a consistent body of doctrine and of practical obligations which has remained in all ages the inspiration of the Muslim religion.

Unexpectedly, the famous *Shahada* or profession of faith, "There is but one God, and Mohammed is the Apostle of God," nowhere occurs as such in the Koran. The nearest equivalent, often called the Islamic Credo, is found in the Surah of Women: "You who believe, believe in God and His apostle, and the Book which He revealed to His apostle, and the Book which he revealed to those before him. Whoever denies God and His angels and His books and His apostle and the day of judgment has strayed far away from the truth."[1]

While the Koran itself is central, three other sources of Islamic doctrine and practice are recognized by orthodox Moslems: tradition or *Qunnah,* community agreement or *igmah,* and the principle of analogy called *gijas.*

Tradition as a source of revelation is co-equal with the Koran in binding power and authority. It consists of all the sayings, explicit or implicit, of Mohammed, which he did not personally set down in the Koran.

Consensus of believers is more difficult to define and has occasioned endless dispute and schism. But in theory it means that whenever a sizeable portion of the Moslem faithful agrees on some cardinal issue of doctrine or ritual, this becomes part of the creedal structure of Islam.

The method of analogy finds special application in the field of morals and conduct, where a new situation is evaluated by comparison with a similar one in the past. Understandably the principle of *gijas* lends itself to arbitrary interpretation and, in fact, has been the cause of grave tension and conflict in Moslem jurisprudence.

GOD. The Arabic word for God is Allah, an abbreviation for *al-ilah,* "the God," to distinguish the supreme Deity from the numerous lesser divinities that were worshiped in Arabia in Mohammed's time. Koranic attributes of God are rich and varied. He is called the Hearer, Seer, Bestower, Reckoner, Pardoner, Keeper and Guide; and the epithets applied to Him have been gathered together into the ninety-nine "most beautiful names of God."

Among the most impressive descriptions of the Deity is the eloquent Throne-verse in the second Surah:

> God, there is no god but He—the Living, the Self-subsisting, Eternal. No slumber can seize Him nor sleep. His are all things in the heavens and on earth. Who is there can intercede in His presence except as He permits? He knows what appears to His creatures as before and after or behind them. Nor shall they compass any of His knowledge except as He will. His throne extends over the heavens and the earth, and He feels no fatigue in guarding and preserving them, for He is the Most High, the Supreme in glory.[2]

In the Koran the essential element of true belief is an uncompromising monotheism. Mohammed rejected the legends of contemporary Arabs that Allah had daughters who were goddesses, and on the same grounds opposed the worship of Christianity as based on human invention. Loving faith requires *ikhlas,* or surrender of oneself completely to God alone, and the basic error is *shirk,* when companions are ascribed to the Creator and creatures are worshiped as God. This is the one monstrous sin: "God forgives not that partners should be set up with Him. But He forgives everything else, to whom

He pleases. To set up partners with God is to devise a most heinous sin."[3]

God's unity, therefore, is absolute, and allows no filiation, which would be an outrage, or even association in the making or government of the world. He is complete Master of the universe and by His will determines all things, whether good or bad. He has predestined mankind according to eternal decrees, yet Koranic teaching does not clearly reduce man's lot to a crude fatalism, which some Moslem interpreters have since found in their scriptures.

There are two strains of thought on human liberty in the Koran. When speaking speculatively, man's absolute dependence and even induction into sin by God are taught for "Allah sends astray whom He wills, and whom He wills He guides."[4] But when the context is moral exhortation, the existence of freedom and the need for making a right choice are emphasized. In the first verse of the Koran, these two elements are combined, at once recognizing Allah as Lord of the universe and invoking His mercy against the day of judgment for sins ostensibly committed by an abuse of free will.

> In the name of the One God, the Compassionate One, the Merciful.
> Praise be to God, the Lord of the Universe—the Compassionate One, the Merciful.
> The Ruler on the Day of Judgment.
> You do we worship, and from you do we seek aid.
> Guide us into the straight path—the path of those to whom you have shown mercy.
> Not to those who have incurred your anger, nor those who go astray.[5]

God is not only one and inimitable, but He is also the primal and unique cause of everything outside Himself. Although some passages obscurely suggest the pre-existence of matter co-extensively with God, elsewhere the Koran is perfectly clear on creation out of nothing. "The Originator of the heavens and the earth! When He decrees a thing, He says to it only: Be! and it is."[6] And again, "Lo! Your Lord is Allah who created the heavens and the earth in six days, then He established Himself upon the throne, directing all things."[7]

With regard to the divine moral attributes, there is confusion of thought which later gave rise to such contrary Islamic theologies as the pantheism of the Persian Sufis and the orthodoxy of a modern Koranic commentator who says "the attributes of God are so different from anything we know in our present world that we have to be content with understanding that the only fit word by which we can name Him is 'He.' (Yet) the pantheist places the wrong accent when he says that everything is He. The truth is better expressed when we say that everything is 'His.' "[8] Often the Koran presents God as a magnified Arab chief or Sheikh, who is ready to forgive, who desires the salvation of men, and sends them prophets and the Book to guide them. Elsewhere He appears to act arbitrarily and through caprice. "He forgives whom He wills and He punishes whom He wills."[9]

CHRIST AND MARY. Consistent with denying any filiation in God, Christ appears in the Koran as only a messenger of Allah, His servant and prophet, but nothing more. The Blessed Virgin, therefore, although respectfully treated is only the Mother of Jesus. She is called Maryam, and the name occurs thirty-four times in the Koran, always referring to the Mother of Christ, except in three passages where she seems to be identified with Mariam, the sister of Moses and Aaron. Her virtue is of a high character, which many commentators interpret as absolute sinlessness from birth and even conception. According to Abu Huraira, Mohammed had said, "No child comes into this world without being at the time of his birth touched by Satan, and because of this touch the child utters a cry. Mary and her Son have been exempted from this touch."[10]

The privilege of the virgin birth of Christ is unique in the history of mankind. Appearing to Mary at the Annunciation, the angels spoke to her in words reminiscent of the Gospel of St. Luke. "O Mary," they said, "truly God has chosen you and purified you, and chosen you above the women of all nations. God gives you glad tidings of a word from Him. His name will be Christ Jesus, the Son of Mary, held in honor in this world and in the hereafter." When Mary objected, "How

shall I have a son, when no man has touched me?" one of
the angels assures her, "Even so, God created what He willed.
When He has decreed a plan, He merely says to it, 'Be,' and
it is. Your Lord says, It is easy for me. And it will take place
that We may make of him a revelation for mankind and a
mercy from Us, and it is a thing ordained." Whereupon "she
conceived the child, and withdrew him to a far place."[11]

After His birth, when Mary brought the infant to her people
they rebuked her for infamy. She referred them to the new-
born babe for an explanation. "How can we speak to one
who is in the cradle?" they asked. Whereupon the child spoke
in defense of His mother, "Behold I am the servant of Allah.
He has given me the Scripture, has made me a prophet."[12]
To which Mohammed was careful to add, "It was not befitting
the majesty of God that He should take unto Himself a son"
—thus exalting Christ to the dignity of a prophet like Moses
but insisting that He was only a man.

God performed miracles to confirm the teaching and mission of Christ, who also gathered to His company a number
of apostles. "When Jesus perceived unbelief" among the Jews
to whom He was preaching, He inquired, "Who are my helpers in the cause of Allah? The disciples replied, 'We will be
Allah's helpers. We believe in Allah, and do you bear witness
that we have surrendered unto Him.'"[13] After finishing His
mission, Jesus returned to Allah who spoke in uncompromising
terms against those who should reject the Christian message.
"I should punish them with a violent punishment in this world
and in the next, and they shall have no aid. But as for those
who believe and do good works, He will repay them their
wages in full."[14]

The religion of Jesus, like that of Moses, was at first
equated with his own revelation. Later on, however, when
Mohammed tried and failed to reconcile the three communities, he reversed his earlier approval of Christianity. Although
Jesus resembled Mohammed by receiving the Scriptures, being declared a prophet and confirmed by signs, later Surahs
declare the Christians unbelievers and fit only to burn after
the day of judgment. "Allah! There is no God save Him, the
Alive, the Eternal. He has revealed unto you (Mohammed)

the Scripture with truth, confirming that which went before it, even as He revealed the Torah and the Gospel previously as a guide to mankind. . . . He it is who revealed to you (Mohammed) the Scriptures which are clear revelations. . . . Those who reject this faith, neither their possessions nor their progeny will avail them against Allah. They are but fuel for the fire. Say to those who disbelieve: You shall be overcome and gathered into hell, an evil resting place."[15] Centuries of Mohammedan history testify to the seriousness of this anathema.

Following the doctrine of the Docetists, the Koran denies that Christ was slain by the Jews. Yet God will punish the Jews rejecting Mohammed, slandering Mary's virginity and claiming to have crucified Jesus. "Allah has set a seal upon them because of their disbelief, and of their speaking against Mary a terrible calumny, and because of their saying, 'We slew the Messiah, Jesus son of Mary, Allah's messenger.' They did not slay nor crucify him, but so it appeared to them. For Allah took him up unto Himself."[16] Inconsistently, however, in another passage the Koran explicitly affirms Christ's death and resurrection, as in the prophetic statement of the Christ Child shortly after His birth, when He miraculously announced, "Peace on me the day I was born, and the day I died, and the day on which I shall be raised alive."[17]

Woven into the Koran as a Christological theme is the repeated denial that God could have a son and therefore that Jesus could be one with Allah. "Jesus in Allah's eyes is in the same position as Adam. He created him of dust, and then said to him, 'Be,' and he is." This is the truth from the Lord, and "whosoever disputes with you concerning him, we will summon our sons, and your sons, and our women and your women, and we will pray humbly and solemnly invoke the curse of Allah upon those who lie."[18] In one eloquent passage, Mohammed consigns all Trinitarian Christians to eternal doom.

> They surely disbelieve who say, "Behold, Allah is the Messiah, son of Mary." The Messiah himself said, "Children of Israel, worship Allah, my Lord and your God." Whoever

ascribes partners unto Allah, for him Allah has forbidden
Paradise. His abode is the Fire. For evildoers there will be no
relief.

They surely disbelieve who say, "Behold Allah is the third
of three," when there is no god save the One God. If they
desist not from so saying, a painful doom will fall on those
who disbelieve.

The Messiah, son of Mary, was no other than a messenger.
Many were the messengers that passed away before him. See
how God makes his signs clear to them (the Christians); yet
see how they are deluded away from the truth.[19]

This studied reduction of Christ to the status of mere man is
part of a larger Koranic message, that Moses and Christ and
Mohammed are equally prophets of Allah, except that Mohammed is the last of the prophetic line. Moslems are told
that "Mohammed is not the father of any man among you,
but he is the messenger of Allah and the Seal of the Prophets."[20] When a document is sealed, it is complete, and there
can be no further addition. Mohammed therefore closes the
long line of prophets. God's teaching will always be continuous, but there has been and there will be no prophet after
Mohammed. As Moses prepared the way for Christ, so Christ
was the precursor of Mohammed. This is not an arbitrary
matter. In Islamic tradition it is a decree full of knowledge
and wisdom and irrevocable with the immutability of Allah
Himself.

Less familiar than the denial of Christ's divinity, is the positive concept of the Trinity suggested by the Koran and further
elaborated by its commentators. According to Mohammed, on
the day of resurrection God will ask Christ the following
question, "Jesus, son of Mary, did you say to mankind: Take
me and your mother for two gods beside Allah?"—to which
Christ will give the answer, "Be glorified! It was not mine to
utter that to which I had no right. If I used to say it, then You
knew it. You know what is on my mind. Behold, You only
are the knower of things hidden."[21]

Mohammed was adamant in denying the Trinity. "Believe
in God and His messengers," he told the people, "and do not
say, three. Cease, it is better for you. Allah is only one God.

Far is it from His transcendent majesty that He should have a son. His is all that is in the heavens and all that is in the earth. And Allah is sufficient as defender. The Christ will never scorn to be a slave unto Allah, nor will the favored angels. Whoever scorns His service and is proud, all such will He assemble unto Him (and) will punish them with a painful doom."[22]

Yet the Koranic conception of the Trinity is a bizarre notion that is hard to find anywhere in contemporary religious literature. Mohammed quite literally believed that Christians professed a divine triad of Allah, Jesus of Nazareth and Mary. He is clear in asserting that the Messias was not divine, and equally (though less forthrightly) clear that the Holy Spirit is not God but only a special, mysterious power issuing from Him, or, perhaps an angel, whom commentators identify with the Angel Gabriel who spoke to Mohammed.

Islamic exegetes confirm this judgment in their interpretation of the term, "Three," of the fourth Surah. Some say bluntly that the three in question are "Allah and Jesus and his Mother." Others are more precise and more crude. Allah, Christ and Mary are three gods and the Messias is the child, "in the flesh" (*walad' Ullah*) of Allah from Mary. Still others repeat the same Islamic tradition but prudently add that this may not be the explanation which Christians accept, since according to them, "Three means that God is three persons, the Father, the Son and the Holy Spirit. They understand by Father the essence, by the Son the knowledge, and by the Holy Spirit the life" of Allah. While still erroneous, the latter at least offers an alternative to the traditional Mohammedan concept of the Trinity which was condemned as blasphemous.

ANGELS. For a religion as notoriously earth-bound as Islam, the spiritual world is remarkably prominent. Some thirty Surahs speak of the angels, and another dozen of the *jinn* who are created like men but of fire instead of earth. In the imagery of the Koran, angels appear to be messengers of God: to bear up His throne, descend to earth with His decrees, record men's actions, receive their souls when they die, witness for or against them at the last judgment, and stand guard over the gates of hell.

Besides the angels, there are devils, whom the Koran represents not as fallen spirits but rebellious *jinn,* also called *shaitans* who lead men astray, oppose the prophets, and try to overhear what goes on in heaven but are driven away by shooting stars. They teach people sorcery and will finally go to hell along with wicked men on the day of final resurrection.

REVELATION AND PROPHETS. Next to unity of God, the doctrine of the prophets or apostles is the central dogma of the Koran. God has at all times and to all peoples, including the *jinn,* sent His messengers to preach the unity of Allah and warn men of the judgment to come. Most of them were rejected and as a consequence brought divine punishment on the nations that refused to listen. Among the more prominent mentioned in the Koran are Adam, Noah and Abraham, Moses and Jesus the son of Mary. Unlike his predecessors, Mohammed is God's apostle to all mankind and not only to one people or time. While only implicit in the Koran, this broad universalism later on became a cardinal principle of Islam.

All told, twenty-eight prophets are named, including four obscure Arabians and eighteen Old Testament figures. Their doctrine is entirely consistent, except that each succeeding apostle adds to and clarifies the preceding, until Mohammed in the Koran not only confirms earlier Scriptures, but, as the final revelation, clears up all uncertainties and is the repository of perfect truth. In fact, Mohammed's coming was foretold by Jesus under the name of *Ahmad,* which the Jews and Christians seek to conceal by misquoting the Bible and even wilfully perverting its meaning.

ESCHATOLOGY. The last day is always present to the author of the Koran, almost to the point of obsession. It will be a cataclysmic event to come suddenly at a time known only to God. Some of the most beautiful poetry in Koranic literature deals with this theme. Whole Surahs are devoted to the same, as the eighty-second, entitled "The Cleaving," revealed at

Mecca and referrable either to the judgment at death or to the final day of reckoning.

> In the name of God, most Gracious and most Merciful
> When the heaven is cleft asunder.
> When the stars are scattered abroad.
> When the seas are allowed to burst forth.
> And the graves are overturned.
> Then shall each soul know what it has sent before it
> and what has been left behind.
> O man! What has seduced you from your most
> beautiful Lord?
> Who created you, fashioned you in due proportion,
> and gave you a first balance.
> Into whatever form He will, He puts you together.
> Yet, men reject right and judgment.
> But over you are appointed angels to protect you, kind
> and honorable, writing down your deeds. They
> know and understand all that you do.
> As for the righteous, they will be in delight.
> And the wicked will be in the fire, which they will enter
> on the day of judgment, and will not be absent
> thence.
> Who will explain to you what the day of judgment is;
> again who will tell you what the day of judgment
> is!
> A day when no soul shall have power to keep
> another, for the command on that day will be
> wholly with God.[23]

While modified in minor details, Koranic eschatology has remained substantially unchanged in modern Islam. After death, when the body is buried, each person is judged by two angels, Munkar and Nakir, on his faith and good works. Unbelievers and Moslem sinners will suffer "the torments of the grave," whereas prophets and martyrs enter heaven immediately. Ambiguity on the resurrection has produced two opposing theories: either that the soul dies and later rises with the body, or that it continues to live and will later be re-embodied.

Preludes of the general judgment include universal discord among nations, the appearance of a mysterious "beast of earth" and the coming of Antichrist. Jesus will return to earth, only to be slain. At the first sound of the trumpet, the world will come to an end, at the second the dead will rise and assemble on the plain of judgment. God will appear between angels, and Mohammed will intercede for the souls. Each man's guardian spirit will bear witness to his record, weighed in the balance, and his book will be placed in his right hand, if blessed, otherwise in the left. The souls will then start crossing a bridge as narrow as the blade of a knife, spanning the fires of hell, into which the wicked fall but the good, with help received from the prophet, will safely enter Paradise.

Hell is described as a valley of smoke, where the damned suffer eternal hunger, burning and chains. They are fed with boiling water and the fruit of the cursed *zaggum,* resembling the heads of demons and like molten brass in the belly. Words fail to convey the horrors implied in such dire predictions as "The word of the Lord has been fulfilled, 'Verily I shall fill hell with the *jinn* and mankind together,'" or the observation, "One day we shall ask hell, 'Are you filled to the full?' It will answer, 'Are there any more to come?'"[24]

Paradise, on the other hand, is a haven of gardens and meadows, flowing with brooks of water and streams of honey, milk and wine. Spreading lotus trees cast their cooling shade. The blessed, attired in rich garments and jewels, recline on silken divans covered with cushions and tapestry. They eat and drink to satiety, and never feel any pain. For companions they have dark-eyed maidens and wives of recurring virginity. Their only spiritual joy is a mysterious presence of God.

PRAYER. Ritual prayer, *salah,* was first prescribed by the Koran and further defined by the earliest tradition or *sunnah.* All Moslems are obligated to its prescriptions, once they reach puberty and as long as they are in good health. The aged, infirm, travelers and others are excused only as long as it is impossible to fulfil the ritual demands.

The rite consists of a series of seven movements or postures, joined to appropriate recitations, collectively termed a "bowing" *rakah,* and each *salah* is made up of a fixed number of bows. In sequence the *rakah* begins with the recitation of the phrase, "God is most great," while the hands are open on each side of the face; then the recitation of the *fatihah*, or opening *surah* of the Koran, and another passage or passages while standing upright; bowing from the hips; straightening up; falling on the knees and a first prostration with face to the ground; sitting back on the haunches; and a second prostration with face to the ground.

Only the first *rakah* in the day requires the opening salutation. Second and subsequent rites begin with the recitation of the first Koranic *surah*, and at the end of each pair of *rakahs* and the conclusion of the day the worshiper recites the *Shahada*, "There is but one Allah, Mohammed is Allah's apostle" together with ritual salutations. Then he sits up and with upraised finger makes his private prayers.

Set times for prayer are at daybreak (two rakahs), noon (four rakahs), mid-afternoon (four rakahs), after sunset (three rakahs), and in the early part of night (four rakahs). Prayers may be said in private or, preferably, together with the congregation in a mosque. When said publicly the worshipers stand in rows behind the prayer-leader, *imam*, all facing in the direction, *quibla*, of the sacred mosque at Mecca, marked by a niche in the wall of the mosque. Private recitation should be on clean ground or on a rug, in the direction of Mecca. Additional prayers, especially at night, are recommended but not prescribed.

Fridays at noon is held the main ritual service of the week, and consists of a formal address in two parts: invocations of the prophet, Moslem leaders, and the political ruler of the state; and a sermon delivered by a preacher. Similar major functions are held on the two principal feast days of the year: the day of the Breaking of the Fast after the fast of Ramadan, and the feast of the Sacrifice at the Pilgrimage.

Hours of prayer are announced by a caller, *muezzin*, from the minaret of the mosque, following the formula, "God is most great, God is most great. I bear witness that there is no god except the One God. I bear witness that Mohammed is the prophet of God. Come to prayer. Come to the Good. Prayer is better than sleep. God is most great. God is most great. There is no god but the One God."

Elaborate provisions require cleansing before prayer, whether in public or private, as prescribed in the Koran, "When you rise up to prayer, wash your faces, and your hands, and arms to the elbows, and wipe your heads and your feet to the ankles." Another, "greater ablution" must be performed after major pollutions. The purification should be done with water if available, otherwise with clean sand. Curiously the rite of circumcision, though generally binding on Moslems, is not prescribed in the Koran.

LEGAL ALMSGIVING. Two forms of ritual donation are mentioned in the Koran: freewill offerings and mandatory contribution. The latter, *zakah,* is gravely prescriptive as an outward sign of piety and a means of salvation. In juridical theory, the *zakah* is exacted on grain, fruits, livestock, silver, gold and merchandise, and amounts to about one-fortieth of the annual revenues. Though not called a tax, it is required of all who, whether voluntarily or otherwise, enter the brotherhood of Islam. As stated in the Koran, the beneficiaries of these alms are the poor, the needy, those employed in collection, persons engaged in propagating religion, slaves and prisoners, insoluble debtors, fighters for the faith and travelers.

In Moslem countries the *zakah* becomes formal taxation and applies as well to those outside the fold. Freewill offerings are also encouraged beyond the call of duty, notably in favor of religious enterprises not directly under control of the State.

FASTING. In its earliest form, fasting was prescribed by Mohammed at Medina in the same form and on the same day as for the Jews. Moslem commentators observe that until a mitigation was revealed, Moslems used to fast completely from the evening meal of one day until the evening meal of the next, and if they fell asleep before they had taken their meal, they had considered it their duty to abstain, with the result that men fainted and came near to death. Intercourse with their wives had been similarly restricted.

Given the revelation, however, which was occasioned by estrangement from the Jews and the growth of Islamic autonomy, the former fast became optional and the ninth lunar month each year, called *Ramadan,* was made a period of strict observance. It affects all Moslems in sound health who have reached maturity. The old, the sick, travelers, and women in certain conditions are exempt. But the exemption lasts only as long as the disability, and the fast must be made up later on. Breaking the fast is punishable by fines of expiation, of different quantity, depending on the gravity of the sin. The fast consists in complete abstention from food and drink, tobacco and perfumes, and sexual intercourse, from sunrise to sunset of each day of Ramadan. There are no prohibitions for the nights. Other fasts, of greater or less intensity, are also part of Islamic custom, for example, to expiate certain offences.

PILGRIMAGE TO MECCA. Much as fasting is the result of contact with the Jews, so the pilgrimage (*Hajj*) to Mecca became part of the Moslem religion through relations with the pagans. Indeed the pilgrim ritual has been largely taken over from pre-Islamic paganism, but now directed to the worship of a single deity.

At least once in a lifetime every Moslem is expected to go on a pilgrimage to the sacred mosque at Mecca, in the twelfth month of the lunar year. Physical strength for the journey and the necessary financial means are assumed to make the precept strictly binding.

The immediate object of the pilgrimage is to kiss the famous Black Stone that Arabian polytheists had worshiped for centuries before Mohammed came on the scene. Other ritual ceremonies are stoning of the pillars which represent the devil in the vicinity of Mina, offering sacrifices of sheep and camels on the way back from Mina, visiting the mosque and going seven times around the *Kaaba* (former pagan animist shrine), running between two small elevations outside the sanctuary (*Safa* and *Marwa*), and visiting the prophet's mosque at Medina. Essential to the pilgrimage are the afternoon services held at the hill of Arafa, about twelve miles east of Mecca.

Elaborate ritual purifications are required before entering the territory of Mecca. Men shave their heads, discard their ordinary clothing and put on two plain unsewn sheets, leaving face and head uncovered. Women keep their head covered. No fasting is prescribed, but the use of perfumes and sexual relations are forbidden.

The most telling effect of the pilgrimage has been to consolidate the Moslem community and give the pilgrim a new sense of belonging to the elect. The title he acquires, *Hajji*, on returning home adds to his prestige and assurance of final salvation.

HOLY WAR. Not the least embarrassing provisions of the Koran for Moslem commentators are those advocating a Holy War, *Jihad*, against pagans, Jews and Christians. Yet these prescriptions are historically most significant to explain the propagation of Islam for upwards of a thousand years. Three passages are classic and deserve to be quoted in full.

First is a duty stated in general terms, in the same context with pilgrimages and fasting. Its language recalls the situation that Mohammed faced in his conflict with the recalcitrant Meccans who resisted his revelations.

> Fight in the way of Allah against those who fight against you, but do not transgress limits, for Allah loves not transgressors. Slay them whenever you find them and drive them from whence they have expelled you, for tumult and oppression are worse than slaughter. Fight them on until sedition is no more and allegiance is rendered to God alone. But if they desist, then make no aggression except against evildoers.[25]

The foregoing was not merely directive but prescriptive, and not only for the early period of Moslem origins but for all its subsequent history. Yet it does not so directly touch the grave issue of ordering the sword for the extension and not only for the preservation of Islam. Two other passages do so overtly and have for centuries been understood to refer to Jews and Christians, besides the pagan polytheists.

> When the Sacred Months (of truce) are over, kill those who ascribe partners to God, wheresoever you find them. Seize them, encompass them, and ambush them. Then if they repent and observe the prayer, and pay the alms, let them go their way.

Fight against those who believe not in Allah, nor in the last day, who prohibit not what God and His prophet have forbidden, and who refuse allegiance to the True Faith—until they pay the tribute readily after being brought low. The Jews say, "Ezra is the son of Allah," and the Christians say, "Christ is the son of Allah;" that is their saying with their mouth. They imitate the saying of those who disbelieved of old. Allah Himself fights against them. How perverse they are![26]

This duty of waging a Holy War against unbelievers is a collective obligation, not an individual one. According to Islamic tradition, the world is divided into subjugated zones and regions not yet under Moslem control. To conquer the latter is an apostolic venture and those who die in the cause are not dead. "They are living. With their Lord they have provision, rejoicing because of that which Allah has bestowed upon them of His bounty."

While it is impossible to find a complete consensus of Moslem opinion on the subject, modern Islamic commentators fairly agree on certain general facts and interpretations about the Holy War. Next to their attitude toward women, they feel that Moslems have been most misinterpreted in their attitude toward the use of force.

Apologists for the more liberal view, who are in the majority, admit that the Koran teaches the *jihad*, but they insist this should be balanced by other verses where toleration is proclaimed.

There is no compulsion in religion. The right direction is henceforth distinct from error.

For each one We have appointed a divine law and traced out a way. Had Allah willed, He could have made you one community. But that He may try you by that which He has given you (He has made you as you are), wherefore press forward in good works. Unto Allah you will all return, and He will then tell you concerning that wherein you disagree.

Say: O disbelievers! I worship not that which you worship; nor do you worship that which I worship. And I shall not worship that which you worship, nor will you worship that which I worship. Unto you your religion, and unto me my religion.[27]

When reflecting on their record in history, Moslems admit to the widespread use of force, but make the countercharge that every religion at some stages in its career has been used by its professors to mask aggressions and Islam is no exception. They make three basic denials in this area: that Islam's record of intolerance is greater than that of other major religions, that Western histories have been fair to Islam in their accounts of its use of force, and that blots on their history are due to the principles of their faith.

ECCLESIOLOGY. According to an edict promulgated by Mohammed at Medina, the concept of the Islamic community is carefully defined. He substituted faith for the bond of tribal unity, and thus made believers a family of equals under the direct supervision of Allah.

In this organizational theory, the teaching authority is immediately centered in God but channeled through the Koran. Consequently Islam has no provision for divinely authorized institutions either to guard the deposit of faith, or apply its teaching to existential situations; still less has it the right to define infallibly on matters of doctrine or morals. There are only interpreters of the divine *magisterium,* the learned *Ulama,* who are laymen without clerical orders or special privileges of caste. Yet the *Ulama* have acquired quasi-clerical status by reason of the respect they enjoy as custodians of the law. Often in practice, if not in theory, their casuistic solutions become the accepted standard of Islamic morality.

The ministry reflects a similar condition. There is no organized priesthood, as there are no sacraments to administer. An oriental nomism, where the religious basis of conduct derives from external observance of law, has become so inveterate in classic Islam that the internal forum or conscience of believers is practically ignored in questions of moral judgment.

In place of a sacerdotal hierarchy, orthodox Islam has ever looked to the political sovereign for the direction of Moslem affairs, not excluding imposition of sanctions for breach of Koranic precepts and interpreting these precepts by civil decree.

MARRIAGE, DIVORCE AND POLYGAMY. In the long years of its history, Islam has undergone many changes in its attitude on sex and marriage, notably emancipating women in such countries as India and Pakistan and recognizing the impracticality of polygamy on a large scale in modern society. Yet basically the principles enunciated in the Koran still remain in effect and, as more than one historian has pointed out, most clearly distinguish Moslem culture from its Christian counterpart.

The Koran is extremely detailed on the subject of women's modesty or, more accurately, of their complete subservience and obscuration. They are bidden always to "lower their gaze" and "not display their beauty" except to husbands, fathers and a restricted clientele of relatives and friends. Covering their faces with a veil was a practical carrying out of this injunction.

A father has the right to give a virgin daughter in marriage to whomsoever he pleases. In all marriages the formal contracting parties are not the bride and groom but their fathers or other responsible male relatives. Indeed the marriage of a woman without the intervention of a qualified male relative is invalid, and where no such relative exists, his office is filled by the *gadi*. Moslem men may marry a Christian or Jewish woman but Moslem women do not enjoy the same liberty.

First marriages do not debar a man from further unions, since polygamy is legal. Also outside the married state, a husband may cohabit with an unlimited number of concubines. Their children have the same status as those of wedded wives. Mohammed formally approved polygamy. He had several wives—nine according to one tradition, and fourteen according to another. But for his followers he limited the number to four, as stated in the Koran. "Marry of the women who seem good to you, two, or three, or four." Tradition has therefore set the limit for ordinary believers to four wives, but authorizes Caliphs and Sultans, as successors of the prophet, to have nine.

Concubinage seems not to be anywhere directly sanctioned in the Koran, and the stringent Koranic laws against adultery intimate that the custom developed after Mohammed. In any case, polygamy is a costly luxury, so that only the rich can afford to practice it. For one thing, the legitimate wives cannot live together; each must have a separate apartment and domestics. Men of moderate means usually have only one wife.

Divorce by the husband's repudiation of his wife is a privilege granted in the Koran. No intervention of any judicial authority is necessary, nor any assignment of reasons or justification; but a "certificate of divorce" must be given the wife. However the husband must wait four months before actually dismissing his spouse, meantime not cohabiting with her. After a first repudiation the wife may not remarry for at least three months, during which time she may be taken back without a further contract. The same holds after a second repudiation. But a third repudiation is irrevocable, unless the woman has in the meantime married and been divorced by another man. An ancient custom allows a triple repudiation to be made at one and the same time, with corresponding effects on its irrevocability.

A woman's right to divorce her husband is highly restricted. She cannot repudiate her partner by declaration. One option is to reach an agreement with him that the marriage should be dissolved on payment of compensation, which usually means the return of her dowry. Some Moslem jurists claim that compensation is void if the reason for dissolving the marriage is cruelty by her husband. Another way open for the wife is to appeal to the courts for annulment, *faskh,* on such grounds as a husband's incurable disease or failure to support. Anticipating difficulties, Moslem women nowadays often insert a clause in the marriage contract, laying down certain stipulations which, when broken, obligate the husband to grant his wife a divorce or annulment. For centuries the stipulation that a husband should not marry another wife was held to be invalid, since it contradicted the Koran. But more recently such contracts have been considered binding.

ISLAMIC ASCETICISM

Mohammedanism as a religious culture is not naturally ascetical. Its condemnation of celibacy, absence of a priesthood with spiritual functions, sanction of divorce and polygamy, and, with emphasis, a liaison with the political and military power to exploit its aims, argue to a religion that is nothing if not this-worldly and material minded. Add to this a strong legalism and concern with external forms, and one has what seems the antithesis of asceticism and the interior life.

Yet this very preoccupation with secular values produced a reaction within a century of the *Hijra*. Popular preachers and acetics arose who were at once depressed by the materialism so prevalent in Islam and attracted by the ideals of Christian solitaries, Gnostic and Neo-Platonist philosophers, and Oriental *sannyasis*. Among these elements, the function of Christianity was paramount. Often operating through filtered and heterodox channels, the principles of Islamic asceticism are mainly of Christian ancestry, whether present by implication in the Koran, or later explicitated by the followers of Mohammed.

Already in the time of the prophet, two of his companions, Abu Darr and Hudajfah, were known for their condemnation of Moslem rulers as sinners and for their detailed precepts on the spiritual life. Some of their disciples became public preachers, others preferred retirement. In general the dominant feature of this first phase was a fear of God's punishments, based on the Koranic threats of an imminent last judgment.

Rising out of this tradition was the earliest figure in Moslem spirituality, al-Hasan of Basra (643–728), an eloquent preacher on the interior life. By the second century of the *Hijra* appeared the name of Sufist, etymologically connected with the wearing of undyed garments of wool (*suf*). Ascetically the concept of fear became clarified into a notion of love for God, expressed in the famous verses of the woman ascetic Rabia al-Adawiya (died 801):

> I love Thee with two loves, love of my happiness,
> And perfect love, to love Thee as Thy due.
> My selfish love is that I do nothing
> But I think of Thee, excluding all beside;
> But that purest love, which is Thy due,
> Is that the veils which hide Thee fall, and I gaze on Thee,
> No praise to me in either this or that,
> No, Thine the praise for both that love and this.[28]

During the third century of the Moslem era, Sufism took on those popular features which made it suspect to religious leaders. Though firmly based on the Koran, their simplicist appeal to the rank and file and their reaction against the impersonal teachings of the orthodox, brought the Sufis into conflict with authorities. Some attempts were made to silence them, and when these failed, an example was made of their most prominent member, Mansur al-Hallaj, who was crucified at Bagdad in 922 for claiming he was God. However, repression proved futile, and the Sufite spirit entered Moslem tradition so deeply that scholars believe it has actually determined the type of Islam known at the present day.

Soon the Sufi leaders organized into congregations and instead of a bare recitation of the Koran introduced liturgical ceremonies, the singing of litanies and other practices frowned upon by orthodox theologians. The issue between the two was deeper than appeared on the surface. It concerned the ultimacy of Islamic religion: whether, as the orthodox said, there is only one way to know God, by means of rational dialectic (*ilm*) upon the Koran, or, as the Sufis maintained, by direct and personal experience (*marifa*), culminating in periodic union and absorption into God.

Among other tensions which developed was the unheard-of praise of celibacy. "Marry those among you," is the clear directive of the Koran. Yet Christians for centuries had praised the virginal state. Gradually the influence was felt. Where in the third century A.H. practically all *Sufis* were married, by the fifth we find one of their great exponents declaring, "It is the unanimous opinion of the leaders of this doctrine that the best and most distinguished *Sufis* are the unmarried, if their hearts are unstained and their minds free from sin and lust."[29]

Parallel with a stress on celibacy was the respect which Sufi disciples paid their masters during life and the worship they gave them after death. Nothing could be more alien to ancient Islam than to have saints and intercessors with God. Yet again popular Sufism prevailed. "Know," says the same early authority, "that the principle and foundation of Sufism and knowledge of God rests on Saintship." The highpoint of Moslem hagiology was reached in the development of an elaborate hierarchy of demiurges, culminating in the *Quth*, whose function is to superintend the universe, under Allah, as the Pole of the universe.

The revolution in Islamic thought which Sufism provoked was finally crystallized in the life and writing of al-Ghazali (1058–1111), whom historians rank with Augustine in religious insight and Moslems venerate as a saint. Ghazali broke the stronghold of the sceptic philosophers and hairsplitting theologians and reintroduced a wholesome respect for the word of God in the Koran and in the traditions of the Moslem faithful. He did not disdain philosophy, but sought to place it at the service of the faith, and above all, to make it intelligible to the people. His re-emphasis on hell and the need of fear brought a welcome balance to the rationalism of men like Avicenna (980–1037), and the near pantheism of many Sufis.

What Ghazali did not foresee, however, was that once Sufism became orthodox, and private communion with God was a valid source of religious knowledge, not only Islamic theology but Islam itself was in danger of being submerged. Moslem leaders, the Ulama or "learned," took strong measures to meet the challenge. They gained control of education, largely through institutions of theological study (*madrasas*) with official status, salaried teachers, and a prestige that by the thirteenth century practically solidified orthodoxy in the upper classes of Moslem society.

But Sufism remained alive, in the aspirations of millions of believers and in countless traditions which have become co-essentials of the Koranic creed.

RELIGIOUS FRATERNITIES

Not the least impress of Sufism on Islamic culture is the development of what correspond to religious orders or congregations in the Christian tradition. Their general characteristics are pliability in religious beliefs, ranging from pantheism to close imitations of Christianity and, with notable exceptions, a tendency towards extremism in practice and ritual.

Typical of a conservative order are the *Qadiri*, whose members are distinguished for their piety, philanthropy and aversion to fanaticism. One of their customary prayers, to be recited a hundred times daily is, "I ask pardon of the mighty God. Glorified be God. May God bless our Master Mohammed and his household and his Companions. There is no God but Allah." Founded in the eleventh century by the jurist Gilani, credited with having forty-nine children, its members are divided into provincial congregations, with headquarters in Baghdad.

An offshoot of the Qadiri, however, is definitely fanatical. Organized by Gilani's nephew, the *Rifaiya* indulge in extreme self-mortification and thaumaturgical exercises such as glass eating, fire-walking and playing with serpents. They are found in Turkey, Syria and Egypt.

The *Mawlawyya* were founded by the Persian mystic poet, Jami, whose pantheistic effusions left no room for individual personality. "The universe," he taught, "is the outward visible expression of the Real, and the Real is the inner unseen reality of the Universe. The Universe before it was evolved to outward view was identical with the Real, and the Real after this evaluation is identical with the Universe." Jami's followers are best known for their dervish dancing. While singing their liturgical chants they gyrate in continuous circles to the sound of accompanying music. In the old Ottoman Empire, their chief had the privilege of buckling the sword on the new Sultan when he assumed office.

Among the syncretist groups, the outstanding are the *Bektashis*, fully established in the fifteenth century as a strange mixture of Islam, Gnosticism and Christianity. They honor Ali, cousin of Mohammed and husband of Fatimah his daughter, Mohammed, and Allah as a kind of Trinity. In place of the traditional Moslem ceremony, they have a sort of communion service of bread, wine and cheese. They also confess their sins to the superior, who gives them absolution. Women participate in the ceremonies without veils. Those who take a vow of chastity wear pendants on their ears as a sign of this dedication. They acquired notoriety through their association with the Janissaries, Christian youths taken captive and brought up as leading Moslem soldiers, whom the *Bektashis* indoctrinated and exploited in the promotion of Islam. They are centered in the Balkans, especially Albania, and Egypt.

One of the most recent orders, the *Sunusiya*, was organized by the Algerian, Mohammed Ali al-Sunusi (died 1859). Deeply religious and bent on converting the surrounding people from paganism, Sunusi carried on a life-long propaganda in Egypt and Syria to the point of establishing a quasi-state that took active part in both World Wars on the side of Turkey in the first and of England in the second. They contributed heavily to the growth of Pan-Islamism in North Africa and Asia Minor.

NON-CONFORMISTS

In the absence of ecclesiastical authority or infallible doctrine, dissident factions in Islam were inevitable, and began within a few years of Mohammed's death. While the number and variety of Moslem sectarians are beyond calculation, three principal heterodox movements may be clearly distinguished. Others are either subsidiary to these or qualify in spirit under the main classes.

The *Mutazilites* (dissidents) are often described as Rationalists or Freethinkers who abandoned faith in Mohammed and the Koran and constructed a religion of reason in their place, after the fashion of Ernest Renan and David Strauss in their Lives of Christ. Actually their position is more complex, and for Western readers far more significant in view of the contact they effected with classic Greek philosophy.

Mutazilism began at the end of the first century A.H. as an opposition movement to two extremists, the ethical laxists (*Murjites*) who were willing to barter moral principle for the sake of political gain, and the pragmatists (*Kharjites*) who claimed that religion must be propagated in season and out of season, if need be at the cost of life itself. Well intentioned but radical, the Mutazilites flourished for centuries until they began to force Moslem doctrines into the mold of Greek concepts and derive their theology speculatively from Greek metaphysics instead of the Koran. They passed out of corporate existence as a sect but left in Islamic tradition a worship of reason and a suspicion of Koranic faith that cultured Moslems the world over consider their special possession.

Comparable to the golden age in Christian scholastic theology, which produced Peter Lombard, Albertus Magnus, Bonaventure and Thomas Aquinas, the Arabs had Avicenna, Avempace and Averroes, all in the eleventh and twelfth centuries, whose works in religious philosophy are among the glories of Islamic civilization. Yet the master ideas of these men were alien to Moslem orthodoxy, and advanced such extreme views as the existence of only one soul in all men (Averroes), and the principle of pure potentiality independent of God (Avicenna). It is said that Avicenna knew the Koran by heart at the age of ten, and other Moslem philosophers were also, if less fervently, attached to their faith. But the solvent of rationalism which they inherited from the Mutazilites and passed on to their followers has permanently entered the religion of Islam.

Best known representative of this Moslem deism is Omar Khayyam (died 1123), philosopher and freethinker, whose *Rubaiyat* in Fitzgerald's eloquent translation symbolizes the pessimism of a culture that has lost its hold on revelation. Omar tells of listening to doctor and saint, and hearing great argument on the purpose of life, but sadly concludes, "With them the seed of wisdom did sow, and with mine own hand wrought to make it grow; and this was all the Harvest that I reaped—'I came like water, and like wind I go.'" Or again, "I sent my Soul through the Invisible some letter of that afterlife to spell; and by and by my Soul returned to me, and answered, 'I myself am Heaven and Hell.'"

Unlike the Mutazilites, who were mainly theorists, the *Shiahs* came into being as a group of faithful who disapproved the election of Abu Bakr, Omar, and Othman as caliphs to succeed Mohammed. They maintained that Ali, the prophet's cousin, and his line were legitimate successors. Gradually political reasons were colored by doctrinal and ritual differences to solidify the breach between the Shiahs, "partisans" of Ali, and the Sunnis, followers of the Sunna or "tradition." Drawing on all sorts of old oriental beliefs, Babylonian, Persian and Indian, the Shiahs finally welded two unheard-of ideas which traditionists to this day abhor. Following the ancient Babylonian theory of Inner Light and the more recent Christian Gnosticism, they held that their leaders, the Imams, had incarnated in them the Divine Light which descended through successive generations of prophets from the time of Adam.

Among the Shiahs, therefore, the Imam is at once pope and emperor, gifted with sinlessness and infallibility. But more seriously, Mohammed is regularly credited with divine or near-divine prerogatives, which has deeply influenced the whole of Islamic thought. A European scholar (Abraham Kuyper) examined some two thousand prayer formulas in use by Moslems throughout the world, and discovered that in most of them Mohammed had usurped the place of Allah or God, being addressed three to five times in a single invocation.

The Shiahs differ greatly among themselves, ranging from the moderate Zaidis, who in the tenth century founded the state (now the country) of Yemen, to the extremist Ismailis, sometimes called the "Assassins," found in India and elsewhere. Shiahs favor temporary marriage, and because of their compromises with Christianity have found acceptance among certain Western peoples as esoteric cults, like the Bahais, who originated in Persia and have a sizeable following in the United States.

Besides Mutazilite nationalism and Shiah gnosticism, periodic strains of Moslem puritanism seek to reinstate the spirit of former days, and bring the people back to Allah and His prophet. Among the most recent and currently effective are the Wahhabis founded in the eighteenth century by Mohammed Wahhab (1691–1787) who castigated his contemporaries for their luxury and for their worship of Mohammed and neglect of God. Originally fanatical in preaching and propaganda, they created enemies on all sides, notably among the Turks. For a time they held Mecca and Medina, where they removed from the mosques all that they held was the accretion of later superstition. Although much restricted, the Wahhabis have lately risen with new strength as protagonists of the "Arab idea" in Islam. Their efforts to purify religion and restore its pristine monotheism now constitute one of the outstanding features of modern Islam. Even politically they have regained an Arabian empire under the leadership of Abd al-Aziz, founder of the new kingdom of Saudi Arabia.

RELATIONS WITH CHRISTIANITY

From the first beginnings of Islamic expansion, Christianity in the East found itself weak to resist the Mohammedan tide. There was a proliferation of Christian sects, universal dissatisfaction with Byzantium and sympathy with the innovators among the Arab Christians and schismatics chafing under the Greek emperors.

After the first period of conquest, we find numerous anecdotes describing the peace if not cordiality existing between Moslems and their Christian subjects. The father of St. John Damascene (674–749) was the chief representative (*Logothere*) of the Christians to the Caliph. But there were also acts of violence and humiliating conditions laid on the Christians— the payment of tribute and grave restrictions on freedom. Many Christians apostatized, often following the example of prelates whose position was secure if they catered to the religious prejudice of the civil rulers.

The West labored under the strangest notions about Islam, which some merely dismissed as another Eastern heresy and others looked upon as the vowed enemy of Christianity. Things became worse when the Moors invaded Spain (711) and occupied the coasts of Italy and France, and especially when the Turks made pilgrimages to the Holy Land impossible or extremely risky. Under papal exhortation and the preaching of men like Peter the Hermit and Bernard of Clairvaux, a series of Crusades was launched that lasted from 1096 to 1270, but finally Palestine was lost to the Saracens.

After numerous trials the kings of Spain succeeded in driving the Moors out of the Iberian peninsula (1492). Sicily was delivered by Norman princes in the twelfth century, but Moslem pirates continued to ravage the Mediterranean area for centuries, thus giving rise to the several religious orders destined for the redemption of Christian captives, like the Trinitarians (1198) and Mercedarians (1220). The founding of military orders, e.g., the Templars and Hospitallers (Knights of St. John), belongs to the same era.

In Central Europe, Islam was not fully checked until late in the seventeenth century, under the Polish leader Sobieski (1683), more than a century after the Popes waged a tireless Mediterranean campaign that ended in the victory of Lepanto (1570) under Pope Pius V.

The apostolate to the Moslems by the Eastern Christians was sporadic and only minimally effective. Pioneers in the West to undertake a methodical study of the Moorish religion included the abbot of Cluny, Peter the Venerable, and the Franciscan Ramon Lull. Franciscans and Dominicans began organizing schools to prepare missionaries to the Moslems, and the Council of Vienne (1312) ordered the creation of schools of Arabic in the larger universities. St. Thomas Aquinas wrote the *Contra Gentiles* to answer Moslem arguments on the grounds of natural reason, and his treatise on Averroes challenged the latter's claim that what is true in philosophy may be false in theology, and vice versa. Prospects of converting the Moors was a leading motive in the mind of Ignatius of Loyola when he organized the Society of Jesus.

In the last century, Cardinal Lavigerie established the White Fathers expressly to work among the Mohammedans. Parallel enterprises have been going on for years in North Africa, Syria, India, and the Near East, but after hard experience the missiological method has changed, or rather became stabilized to a long range evangelization of charity, patience and study, preparing the Moslem people for the Gospel and disposing them to accept what, by their standards, is only a prelude to the religion of Mohammed.

The more seriously Mohammedans take the Koran and live up to its precepts, the stronger becomes their unqualified belief in one personal God which they share with the Christian world; and correspondingly, the further they depart from the tradition or *sunna* of their ancestors, the more easily they compromise with polytheism or, in modern times, with Marxism.

On the other hand, the same Koran teaches them "take not the Jews or Christians for friends. They are but one another's friends. If any of you takes them for his friends he is surely one of them. Allah does not guide evildoers."[30] Uncompromisingly the Moslem is told "the Religion before God is Islam. If anyone desires a religion other than Islam, never will it be accepted of him. And in the hereafter he will be in the ranks of those who have lost all spiritual good."[31] With Oriental realism, the *sunna* tells him, "He who has denied a verse of the Koran, it is allowed to behead him."[32]

The one hopeful solution is a changing climate in Moslem circles towards the followers of "the son of Mary." Conscious of the threat of Red domination, spokesmen for their people are telling Christians, "It is a prime duty of our two monotheistic faiths to establish real and abiding friendship, not only among their own adherents, but also between themselves and the followers of the other faith as well. We should collaborate as believers in the one God in defending the world against the menaces of atheism and materialism."[33]

In the same spirit of tolerance, commentators on the Koran are reinterpreting its harsh passages in a way that leaves room for Christian influence if not for Christianization. "The Muslim does not claim," they explain, "to have a religion peculiar to himself. Islam is not a sect or an ethnic religion. In its view all Religion is one, for the Truth is one. It was the religion preached by all the earlier prophets. It was the truth taught by all the inspirited Books. In essence it amounts to a consciousness of the Will and Plan of God and a joyful submission to that Will and Plan."[34] If these sentiments appear strange against the background of more than a thousand years of Koranic intransigence, they suggest that not only new Moslem nations are coming into existence but also a new Islam.

THE NEW ISLAM

Since Mohammedanism from its origins has always been closely tied in with the State, its spirit and religious outlook at any given point in history can be accurately judged by the political structure of the countries that are dominantly Islamic.

Modern Islam in its church-state dimension is being shaped

by the heavy impact of Western thought and institutions, whose influence is commonly dated from the beginning of the nineteenth century, after the invasion of Egypt by Napolean in 1798. Moslem religious leaders for long resisted this West-ernization. Their historical traditions had little interest outside the Islamic world, and their educational traditions were mostly confined to the Koranic sciences and supporting disciplines. Civil and political leaders, on the other hand, were more than sympathetic with European technology and such phases of Western thought and culture as promised a competitive equal-ity with the nations of Europe.

As a result two conflicting tendencies are visible in the recent development of Mohammedan countries: a passive re-sistance to the influx of Western ideas and institutions, along with a reactionary Islamic renascence; and a ready ambition to adopt everything feasible from European sources, provided the adaptation can be grafted on the existing culture. While it would be an oversimplification to say that the first tendency has been directed largely by religious fervor and the second by hard-headed realism, these have been the principal motivat-ing forces behind a tension that it may take generations to resolve.

SECULAR-STATE EXPERIMENT. Turkey is the best example of Moslem experimentation in which the secular impulse has overridden the religious to create a novel situation, quite un-like anything else in the Islamic world. Since the early nine-teenth century, Turkey had reacted with political sensitivity to the ferment of Western ideas, most of which came from France and, specifically, from the ideals of the French Revo-lution.

At the close of the First World War, Turkey was on the verge of destruction when its destinies were taken in hand by a single individual who changed the course of its history. Mustafa Kemal Ataturk, first president of the Turkish Repub-lic, was born in 1882 at Salonika, at that time part of the Ottoman Empire. In 1915, Mustafa Kemal commanded the Turkish Army at Gallipoli. Four years later, following the defeat of the Central Powers (including Turkey), he organized the armies of liberation in Anatolia, and commanded the campaign which resulted in the achievement of Turkish independence.

In 1920, Ataturk took the lead in the establishment of the First Grand National Assembly, in Ankara, which in 1924 abolished the Sultanate and was the forerunner of the present Republic. To do this he had the Sultan's son, and heir-apparent to the caliphate, 'Abd-al-Majid, banished from the country, on the principle that a supreme religious leader recognized as such by the entire Moslem world, even against his will could become a focal point for reactionary ambitions. Indignation over this move was great, particularly among the Indian Mohammedans who had set their hopes for protection against British imperialism on the newly resurgent Turkish Republic. Moreover, all efforts to re-establish the caliphate in other countries necessarily miscarried, because conditions for it were nowhere so promising as in Turkey.

But Ataturk was not to be checked; he crushed a series of revolts and finally stopped active resistance by having the rebels deported to eastern Thracia. He continued the secularization of the government with far-reaching laws. The ministry for pious endowments (*Evkaf*) was dissolved in 1924 and joined with the ministry of education; in the following year all the dervish orders were forbidden, and all monasteries dissolved. In the early thirties even the number of mosques was severely limited, of which only one was to be allowed within a circumference of every five hundred meters; the number of preachers to be paid by the government was reduced to three hundred, and they were obligated to provide practical instruction on things like agriculture, in addition to preaching on religious topics.

Some of the most famous mosques were turned into museums or railroad depots, and the religious law (*Shari'ah*) was replaced by a purely civil code, even as regards domestic relations. One result was the end of polygamy, and another that family names, hitherto unknown in Turkey, were introduced by a law of July 2, 1934. Turkish women were now given equal legal rights with men, and soon obtained the active and passive right of election. Such details as substituting the hat for the fez (that previously supplanted the turban) and other items of European custom were symbolic of the radical changes made.

The new Turkish Constitution professedly found its inspiration in the ideals of Western democracy. Its basic principle became sovereignty of the people, and the republican form of government was declared inviolable. All citizens were held to be equal before the law, and special privileges were abolished. Inviolability of person and freedom of conscience, thought, speech, press, assembly, association, travel, labor and contract were formally stated to be "the natural rights of citizens." This meant that "the life, property, honor, and home of each and all are inviolable," and correlatively that, "no one may be molested on account of his religion, sect, ritual or philosophy." To insure these and similar provisions, primary education was made obligatory and given gratuitously in the government schools.

All phases of life were affected by the new regime, to a degree that the Turkish Revolution has been considered the most complete in the twentieth century, not only because its effects were so widespread but because the ideas on which it was based were, from the Moslem viewpoint, so revolutionary. Spokesmen for the nation repeatedly declared that their Constitution guaranteed all liberties, yet on the theory of a completely secularized society, which had no responsibilities to Koranic principles.

The intention was not only to adapt the people externally to Western customs, but to impregnate them with the spirit of Europe. To achieve this goal the Arabic forms of writing had to be discarded. A new law abolished first the Arabic kind of numerals and then also the script. Schools were built everywhere in the country for people of all ages to learn the new script, which was naturalized in a surprisingly short time. Soon after, the long-established custom of teaching Arabic and Persian, which had been considered necessary for understanding Turkish literature, was eliminated from the lycees. Use of Arabic type for printing Turkish books was prohibited, with the result that innumerable productions of Istanbul printing presses were exported to Egypt, Persia and India.

With the suppression of so many aspects of Turkish culture, however, the new government had the foresight to preserve, as far as possible, the genuine religious values of the people. Formerly the Koran could be read only in Arabic, which limited its accessibility; a Turkish translation appeared for the first time in 1931, and published with a Turkish commentary. Within months, excerpts from this translation were publicly recited in the mosques. Religious freedom even made possible some conversions to Christianity, which according to old Islamic law would have been punished by death.

The guiding genius behind this revolution was Mustafa Kemal, on whom the National Assembly bestowed the title *Ataturk,* i.e., Father of the Turks, as "the expression of the gratitude and veneration of the nation for the greatest son." A born statesman and ardent nationalist, he was not troubled with theological or cultural sensitivities. From the Moslem point of view, within Turkey and outside, the changes he effected were widely criticized.

What made his critics so hostile was the reduction of Islam from the status of a religiously sanctioned system to the position of a private and inferior religious opinion. It was unthinkable to them that this could be reconciled with the innate theocratic character of Mohammedanism. Students of Islamic history observed that the problem of Islam and of Turkey's Islamic past was not being solved, but forcibly eliminated. It could not but reappear.

Their predictions were verified to the extent that a "palace revolution" in 1960 ended the late regime, ostensibly in opposition to restrictive laws and civil decrees but really in answer to a deep-felt need for closer identification between the ancient religious culture of the people, who are almost one-hundred per cent Moslem, and the political structure of the country. It is assured that the Second Turkish Republic will be more sympathetic with these aspirations.

CONSTITUTIONAL ISLAMIC NATION. At the other end of the spectrum is another Moslem country which came into existence in recent years, but whose origins were quite the opposite from those in Turkey. Pakistan, now a republic, was founded in 1947, when Great Britain withdrew from the Indo-Pakistan subcontinent. Its name, coined by Moslem graduates of Cambridge University, is interpreted as "Land of the Pure," in which P stands for the Punjab and A for the Afghan regions, K for Kashmir, I for Islam, S for Sind, and "tan" for the last syllable of Baluchistan. In Urdu, the Hindustani language as spoken by Moslems, *pak* means spiritual purity and *stan* means the land. Thus in the very title of their country the founders of Pakistan implied devotion to religious ideals.

The Islamic beginnings of Pakistan are traceable to the first Moslem invasion from Arabia in 712 A.D., which conquered most of the Indus valley, although the main incursions came from the north and started in the eleventh century. Under successive domination by the Moguls, the East India Company, and the English, the country grew in size and prosperity, but mostly in its fidelity to the teachings of the Prophet. When India began urging her independence, Indian Moslems cooperated with the Hindus in the movement. But as autonomy drew nearer, the Mohammedans felt that independence would only mean changing British masters for Hindu ones. They were convinced that the two cultures, a monotheistic Islam and polytheistic Hinduism, could never coalesce; that only a separate country would enable the Moslems to develop their own cultural and religious heritage and only a separate nation could assure them freedom from religious persecution.

While an All Indian Moslem League was founded as early as 1906, the first serious efforts to establish a distinct nation came much later, due in large measure to the ideas of one man, Mohammed Iqbal (1873–1938), the poet-philosopher who is venerated as the Father of the country. His writings played a decisive role in crystallizing the twin spirit of Islamic India: that the true basis of nationhood is far less the animal ties of blood than a harmony of religious ideals, and that Islam should form a federation of nations linked by the same internal beliefs.

Iqbal's devotion to Islam was almost a passion. His prose and poetical compositions breathe a love of the Koran and dedication to its teachings that no other Moslem leader in modern times has shown. For the people of Pakistan he is the philosophical light and almost absolute standard on the cardinal issue of Islam's relation to the modern world. And for all Moslems he has given a re-interpretation of Islam and a program for realizing a true synthesis of Mohammedanism and Western culture. His manual on *The Reconstruction of Religious Thought in Islam* is a profound study of the problems which the followers of Mohammed must be willing to face and solve if they are to remain faithful to his memory.

Otherwise than his contemporaries, Iqbal approached the Islamic predicament as a philosopher who was deeply attached to his people's religion; and he handled the issue not from any preconceived notions but on the strength of years of experience at Western universities and of contact with the best (and the worst) of Western civilization. He could therefore speak with authority about the inherent values of Islam and the deficiencies of other cultural traditions.

His main contribution to shaping the Mohammedan mind was to convince the people to open their souls to the message of their own faith, and their own past as a community; and at the same time to close their eyes to the teachings of others, since the Western world had little to teach them which Islam did not know. He asked himself, "What, shall I tell you then, is a Moslem's life?" and answered his own question.

> Ecstasy's summit joined with profoundest thought!
> Even its setting flames like a rising sun;
> Single its hue, yet manifold age by age.
> Neither with these times sharing their scorn of virtue,
> Nor with times past their bondage to myth and magic,
> Firm in eternal verity's bedrock standing.[35]

He exploited what he considered the profoundest difference between the Moslem and European thought. "Through all the Western *politeia,* religion withers to the roots; for the white man, ties of blood and race are all he knows of brotherhood." Even a Brahmin, converted to Christianity, "ascends no higher in life's scale," by Western norms, "because the creed of the Messiah has numbered him with its recruits."[36] Preoccupation with material things, Iqbal taught, had blinded the West to the only true bond of unity, which is a common religious faith.

When the people of Pakistan framed their first Constitution, they incorporated these principles into its laws, from the first article of the Preamble to the most detailed provisions. "Pakistan," it was decreed, "shall be a Federal Republic to be known as the Islamic Republic of Pakistan."[37] And on the international plane, "The State shall endeavor to strengthen the bonds of unity among Muslim countries."[38] Both aspects of the Islamic faith were amply provided for.

> Steps shall be taken to enable Muslims of Pakistan, individually and collectively, to order their lives in accordance with the Holy Quran and Sunnah.
> The state shall endeavor, as respects the Muslims of Pakistan: to provide facilities whereby they may be enabled to understand the meaning of life according to the Holy Quran and Sunnah; to make the teaching of the Holy Quran compulsory; to promote unity and the observance of Islamic moral standards; and to secure the proper organization of *zakat* (almsgiving), *wakfs* (sacred foundations) and mosques.[39]

Implementing this general intent, the State was further concerned to protect the interests of Islam by forbidding "the consumption of alcoholic liquor, otherwise than for medicinal and, in case of non-Muslims, religious purposes," and at the same time recognized that in certain cases polygamy is necessary.[40]

Along with such explicit legislation in the spirit of Iqbal, the Constitution provided for the welfare of those outside the Mohammedan fold, recognizing that "all citizens are equal before the law and are entitled to equal protection of law," and supporting this general provision with a variety of specific guarantees.

> Subject to law, public order and morality: every citizen has the right to profess, practice and propagate any religion; and every religious denomination and every sect thereof has the right to establish, maintain, and manage its religious institutions.
> No person shall be compelled to pay any special tax the proceeds of which are to be spent on the propagation or maintenance of any religion other than his own.[41]

The freer and more relaxed aspect of Pakistan was also visible in the generous effort to safeguard the religious convictions of children who attend the private and (Moslem directed) public schools. Thus "no person attending any educational institution shall be required to receive religious instruction or take part in any religious ceremony, or attend religious worship if such institution, ceremony or worship relates to a religion other than his own."[42] Similar privileges were conceded to every religious community or denomination to establish and conduct schools of its own and, most significantly, "in respect of any religious institution, there shall be no discrimination against any community in the granting of exception or concession in relation to taxation," which theoretically placed Hindus and Christians on a par with Moslems in the critical area of tax exemption.[43]

Pakistan, therefore, was founded on a vastly different political theory than Turkey. In fact its foundations were less political than spiritual, with so many articles of the Constitution dealing with the subject of religion that the prominent impression was religious. True to the inspiration of Iqbal the rights of Mohammedans, who constitute almost nine-tenths of the population, were amply protected; and according to the same ideals were even promoted by juridical sanction. Yet, realistically, the minority Hindus and Christians were not ignored, either on paper or in actual practice, which compares favorably with the Arabic-speaking Moslem countries, and the discrimination against non-Islamic religions in some of the newly founded nations of Africa.

There is a tendency also to stress the ideology which Islam has in common with Western and not with Asian culture, which contrasts strongly with the studied effort to emphasize the Oriental in other rising nations of the East. But the number of conflicting forces in Pakistan had the same general effect as in Turkey, except from other quarters. Where Turkey was professedly a secular state seeking a compromise with the Moslem traditions of its people, Pakistan was founded as a Moslem nation trying to work its way in modern society. The fear of revolution in the late fifties led to a change of political structure and a revision of the Constitution, with corresponding reforms in law and education that illustrate the unsolved problem of Islam: how to retain its ancient heritage while adapting itself to modern needs.

Symbolic of the adaptation, the second Constitution of Pakistan began by simply declaring that "the State of Pakistan shall be a Republic under the name of the Republic of Pakistan."[44] Yet the Preamble provided for Mohammedan ideals by stating that "the principles of democracy, freedom, equality, tolerance and social justice, as enunciated by Islam, should be fully observed in Pakistan," and "the Muslims of Pakistan should be enabled, individually and collectively, to order their lives in accordance with the teachings and requirements of Islam."[45]

A new concept in modern Islamic jurisprudence was the formation in Pakistan of an Advisory Board of Islamic Ideology. As the name implies, its function would be advisory and not mandatory, mainly "to make recommendations to the Central Government and the Provincial Governments as to means of enabling and encouraging the Muslims of Pakistan to order their lives in all respects with the principles and concepts of Islam."[46]

ORTHODOXY AND ADJUSTMENT. More than any other religious culture, Islam is at the crossroads of its history. The situations in Turkey and Pakistan are only symptomatic of a deeper tension within the body of Mohammedanism, between orthodoxy and rationalism. All the available evidence suggests that orthodoxy is not only still in possession but promises to make a resurgence that may have lasting effects on the future of Asia and Africa, and corresponding influence on the major religions of the world.

An all-Moslem Colloquium, held at Lahore (Pakistan), clearly emphasizes this dominant trend. Delegates from every Mohammedan country were present, including representatives from Soviet Russia and Communist China. The subjects they treated show the wide range of new situations by which Islam is confronted: Islamic culture and its meaning, the Islamic concept of the State, the challenge of modern ideas and social values; the scope of legislation and the social structure of

Islam, Mohammedan attitude towards other faiths and potential contribution to international peace, Islam's influence on Western history and civilization.

The guiding theme at Lahore was remarkably orthodox. Occasional outbursts against opinions considered doctrinally dangerous heightened the fact that the prevailing spirit is how to adjust positions and principles, believed undebatable and unassailable, to a rapidly changing non-Moslem world. A rare note was struck with the regret that "such a beautiful expression of human tragedy" as the Crucifixion "is not reflected in the Holy Koran," implying that Islam offered no answer to the problem of pain and no substitute for the inspiration of the Cross.

Yet the most severe test of Islamic faith comes not from its contact with the traditional West, whether Christian or secular, but from its relations with a rampant Marxism. Upwards of fifty million Moslems are directly under Communist control, and subject to all the pressures that a hostile government exercises against a socioreligious system which, by Marxist standards, is a feudal tool for reactionaries. And more serious still, the Marxist appeal to humanitarian motives is a temptation to dedicated Moslems who are highly critical of the laissez faire individualism that has characterized so much of Western social policy in the past two centuries.

Moslems have the principles of resistance to Marxism built into their religion, even when they see, as did Iqbal, the shortcomings of a society whose sins deserve the divine judgment. In a powerful verse-essay, *Lenin before God,* Iqbal pictures the revolutionary standing before Allah and asking: Of what mortal race art Thou the God? Is it of those creatures formed of dust beneath these heavens?

> Europe's pale cheeks are Asia's pantheon, and Europe's pantheon her glittering metals. A blaze of art and science lights the West with darkness that no Fountain of Life dispels; in high-reared grace, in glory and in grandeur, the towering Bank out-tops the cathedral roof; what they call commerce is a game of dice: for one profit, for millions swooping death. There science, philosophy, scholarship, government, preach man's equality and drink men's blood; naked debauch; and

want, and unemployment. Denied celestial grace a nation goes no further than electricity or steam.

Omnipotent, righteous, Thou. But bitter the hours, bitter the laborer's chained hours in Thy world. When shall this galley of gold's dominion founder? Thy world, Thy day of wrath, Lord, stands and waits.[47]

Put into the mouth of Lenin, these thoughts are not the passing fancy of a social visionary. They express the mind of numerous Moslems who know their own faith, know the West, and await the "day of wrath" which their Prophet foretold would befall those who fail to share their wealth "for love of God, with their kinsfolk, and the orphans, and the needy, and the wayfarer, and with those who ask."[48] There is some fatalism in this attitude, but also a great deal of truth.

15

EASTERN ORTHODOXY

Eastern Orthodox writers justly complain that for over a thousand years Christianity has been identified with Europe. In the eyes of Asiatic and African people, Christendom is a Western religion and its culture equated with the civilization of Western Europe. Yet almost one-fourth of all contemporary Christians do not belong to the West but call themselves Eastern and their religious position Orthodoxy.

Geographically the Eastern Oriental Churches form a vast triangle, whose base is twelve thousand miles long, reaching across the Russo-Siberian plain from Petzamo in the West on the Arctic Ocean, to Alaska in the East where the Indians were evangelized by Russian missionaries in the last century. The western side of the triangle cuts through Finland, Estonia and Latvia, goes south towards Galicia and the Carpathian mountains, divides Yugoslavia in half, touches Albania on the Adriatic Sea and reaches the southern apex of the triangle in Egypt. On its eastern side, it passes across Palestine and reaches all the way to Japan and Korea. The great majority of Eastern Christians now live within this area, with substantial numbers in other countries, including the United States, as descendants of immigrants from the original Orthodox triangle.

It seems that historically the term "Orthodox" was coined to distinguish Christians who believed in the Council of Chalcedon (451), which defined Christ's divinity against the Monophysites. Originally the word was used to describe the Eastern Churches, in communion with Constantinople, who were orthodox or "right-believing," as against the heterodox, "wrong-believing," separated bodies like the Nestorians and Jacobites. Recently, however, the latter and also the Copts in Egypt have taken to adding "Orthodox" to their names.

In modern parlance, the Orthodox are those Christians who separated from Rome in the eleventh century through the great Eastern Schism, and whose distinctive liturgical feature is the Byzantine rite and doctrinal basis the acceptance of the first seven ecumenical councils, up to the second Council of Nicea in 787.

ORIGINS OF THE SCHISM

There are two views on the origin of the Eastern Schism, the Western and the Oriental, and their very divergence is symbolic of the difference in religious posture between Orthodoxy and Catholicism. According to the Latin version, it was not heresy but political issues that led the Greek Church to separate from Rome. The patriarchs of Constantinople had gradually acquired a dominant influence in the Byzantine Empire, by comparison with the patriarchate of Jerusalem, which was never of great importance, and of Alexandria and Antioch whose prestige had been all but lost because of heretical innovations. Moreover, they had fallen under the control of Islam in the seventh century.

Constantinople, therefore, became the official Church, and its dominance slowly developed into a disregard of Rome. Several schisms racked the capital between the fourth and seventh centuries, either because of administrative differences or as the result of the Eastern emperors' patronizing doctrinal error. This was aggravated by the invasion of the barbarians in the West, the independent growth of each church under the nominal tutelage of Constantinople, and especially by the establishment of the Holy Roman Empire of the West at the opening of the ninth century.

Then came the unfortunate conflict between Photius (810–895), Patriarch of Constantinople, and Pope (St.) Nicholas I. The latter decreed to excommunicate Photius, while admitting he was "a man of great virtue and world-wide knowledge," unless he gave up his see to St. Ignatius, the rightful occupant. Ignatius had been driven out by the emperor Michael III for refusing communion to Bardas Caesar, the emperor's uncle, who was living in notorious incest with his daughter-in-law, Eudokia.

Instead of yielding to the pope, Photius proceeded to condemn Nicholas on five charges, all but one of which arose from legitimate differences between Greek and Latin discipline. He urged these Latin "heresies": fasting on Saturdays in Lent, beginning Lent on Ash Wednesday instead of Monday, disapproval of a married clergy, objection to confirmation administered by a priest, and insertion of the *Filioque* (and from the Son) in the Creed. The last objection has made theological history and marked the beginning of Eastern accusations of heresy against the See of Rome. When Michael III died in 867, Photius fell from power and later retired to a monastery at Armeniaki where he died.

With mutual confidence between Rome and Constantinople thus shaken, the formal breach less than two hundred years later took place almost without opposition. Michael Caerularius, patriarch of Constantinople, suddenly attacked Pope (St.) Leo IX on charges of doctrinal innovation, regarding clerical celibacy, fast on Saturdays as well as Fridays, the use of unleavened bread in the Eucharist, and the *Filioque* in the Nicene Creed.

Personally ambitious, Caerularius defied pope and emperor, and struck Leo IX's name from the diptychs, or commemoration in the Liturgy. When negotiations broke down, the legates sent from Rome solemnly excommunicated Caerularius in the Church of St. Sophia on July 16, 1054. As the Liturgy was about to begin, the Roman Cardinals Humbert and Frederick and Archbishop Peter of Amalfi passed through the congregation, entered the sanctuary and laid Pope Leo's document of excommunication on the altar. "May God see to it and pass judgment," they pronounced, and departed.

The Greek version is quite different. Orthodox writers admit the foregoing facts but say they are not enough to explain the separation. No doubt the immediate cause for the first cleavage, under Photius, was due to his appointment to the See of Constantinople. But the real origins of the schism lay in the great political conflict that occurred at the beginning of the century, when in the year 800 Charlemagne restored the

Western Roman Empire. In the eyes of the Greeks the pope was guilty of a grave insult to the East when he agreed to crown a barbarian like Charlemagne emperor of the West. Perforce the Byzantine ruler had to bow to the inevitable and recognize his imperial rival in Rome, but the Greeks strongly resented the pope's action. Two competitive political powers came into being, and their respective close associations with the ecclesiastical authorities drew the patriarchs of Rome and Constantinople into the vortex.

Photius precipitated the earlier crisis by calling the West heretical; the Latins retorted by producing a similar list of Eastern heresies. In a short while, the original charges grew into a formidable indictment that covered more than fifty topics. Differences in custom and teaching which had been treated as legitimate expressions of religious diversity suddenly became outrages and ground for mutual incrimination.

Even the dramatic excommunication of Caerularius was not definitive. No one at that time had any idea that this was the beginning of a schism which would last for many centuries. It took two hundred years for the tension to become hardened into formal separation, due to the coming of the Crusaders.

If the Crusades are stripped of their romantic elements, they are revealed as mass exploitations of the Eastern Christians under the guise of a Holy War. The worst evil was that Crusaders used military aggression to advance Christianity, and believed the sword can more effectively serve the Gospel than preaching the word of God. They countenanced the idea that robbery, murder and rapine are permitted, if the victim has erroneous beliefs.

At the outset of the Crusades, the East was alarmed. It had lived in peaceful co-existence with the Moslems, and under their rule, for half a millennium. It was surprised, even irritated, at the sudden burst of zeal against the infidel generated by the Christian West. These fears developed into hostility when Eastern Christians came under the rule of the Crusaders. Heedless of the warnings and exhortations of Rome, they pillaged and oppressed, trying to convert the Orthodox to Latinism, confiscating church buildings, imprisoning the clergy, and treating them as though they professed a wholly foreign religion.

The sack of Constantinople, say the Orthodox historians, dealt the final blow to brotherly relations between these two branches of the Christian Communion. It was an occasion of plunder seldom equalled for horror in world history. The riches of its churches were unsurpassed in the whole world. Soldiers and Latin clergy vied with each other in their attempts to seize some part of these riches for themselves; even the precious Holy Altar of St. Sophia was polluted, broken in pieces and sold.

This day, April 3, 1204, marks the end of the fellowship between Eastern and Western Christians, which means that the split was brought about, not by quarrelsome theologians or ambitious prelates, but by the greed and lust of those who had embarked upon a war of aggression and conquest.

The two explanations have this in common: they both admit the historical events that finally caused the break were not basically dogmatic, and the severance of Constantinople from Rome was not due to irreconcilable positions in theology but to external factors in which personalities and emotions played the major role.

HISTORICAL DEVELOPMENT

Eastern Orthodox history from the beginning of the thirteenth century is the story of trial and conflict with the civil powers that have no parallel in Western Christianity.

Russia was the first to suffer oppression at the hands of the Mongolian tribesmen, called Tartars because of their ferocity, "the detestable race of Satan, rushing forth like demons loosed from Tartarus."[1] The Mongols under their great leader, Genghis Khan, swept across China, Bokhara, Georgia and Persia. They captured the principal cities of Central Asia and after three devastating campaigns (1237–1241) conquered Russia and for the next two and a half centuries kept her in submission, at first abject, then relaxed, but always sufficient to keep the Russian people from exercising religious liberty beyond the measure determined by the political rulers.

Nevertheless the Mongols showed marked respect for certain Orthodox prelates, notably those of Kiev, whom they exempted from taxation. Alternately Russians and Greeks were appointed by the government to the key ecclesiastical posts and one churchman, Theognost (1325–1352), decided to fix his residence at Moscow, which by then had become a leading national center. Due to the courageous support given by the abbot Sergius of Radonezh (1314–1392), the Russians defeated the Tartars at the battle of Kulikovo Pole, September 8, 1380. The resulting relaxation of control by the Mongols inaugurated the first period of Russia's spiritual renewal. Religious houses were founded all over the country, learning was revived and ikon painting reached its golden age. Over fifty monasteries were founded by the disciples of Sergius during his lifetime.

Ivan III, surnamed the Great (1462–1505), succeeded in so strongly welding the nation under his rule that the final liberation of the country from the Mongols was achieved without bloodshed. The obvious balance of power so favored Moscow that the Tartars were unwilling to oppose the Russians. Periodic attacks from Mongolian nomads continued until the absorption of the Crimea in 1783, but from 1479 (when Moscow's rival, Novgorod, was subdued) Russia became independent of the Mongols.

Yet almost simultaneously two new subjugations to the State took sudden effect, one in Russia under the Tsars, as Ivan III and his successors came to be called, and the other in Asia Minor under the Moslems.

The Russian Church's domination by the Tsars was occasioned by a split in the ranks of the churchmen, one party called "the Possessors" and the other "Non-Possessors." Those who were nicknamed Possessors emphasized unity in preaching and worship, beauty and dignity in ritual service and favored possession of material property by the monasteries and convents. Non-Possessors, on the other hand, were more concerned with freedom in religious practice and taught that God is most pleased with a simple, contrite heart, even in the absence of an elaborate Liturgy. They were the scholars and mystics, who upheld evangelical poverty and maintained that monks should support themselves by the labor of their hands.

As long as the two parties were equally divided and influential, religion prospered. But early in the sixteenth century a crisis arose which tipped the scales in favor of the Possessors. Tsar Basil III had no children by his first wife and wanted to marry another woman. He was opposed by the Metropolitan, Varlaam (1511–1521), a Non-Possessor, but supported by the Possessing prelates whose leader, Daniel, was put into Varlaam's place as Metropolitan and Basil had his second marriage blessed by the Church. The offspring of this union was Ivan the Terrible (1533–1584), the most despotic ruler in Russia until the Communist Revolution in the twentieth century.

This marked the turning point in Russia's religious history. For years the Possessors had upheld the political autocracy and allowed the State to take a leading role in the government of the Church. They preached the doctrine that the Tsars should be loved and obeyed as fathers, no matter how harsh or oppressive their rule. Now, with Basil's support, they avenged themselves on the Non-Possessors, whose leaders were imprisoned and their monasteries closed. At a time when the country most needed the saving influence of men who could withstand political tyrants, the leadership of Church and State fell into the hands of a single party. With periodic exceptions, this continued into modern times.

In the southern portion of Orthodoxy, Constantinople fell to the Moslems after the city had been largely depopulated by civil war and the ravages of plague. With only 10,000 men, the emperor Constantine IX (1449–1453) defended his capital against a powerful army of more than 150,000 Mohammedans. A renegade, Urban, aided the Turks to break through the wall and on May 29, 1453, the Eucharist was celebrated for the last time in the *Hagia Sophia*. The Islamic soldiers poured into the city, pillaging its treasures and destroying its people, including the emperor and patriarch. According to legend, the Eucharistic liturgy at St. Sophia's was not completed when Constantinople fell, and the Eastern Christians still believe the temple will one day be restored to

Christian worship, when the divine service interrupted by the Moslems will again be sung in the Cathedral of Holy Wisdom.

It is impossible to read the story of the Orthodox Church under Turkish rule without admiration and pity. True to Mohammed's teaching about Christians being "People of the Book," the Turks tolerated the Orthodox while enslaving them according to the most advanced Oriental standards of despotism.

Allowed to survive and practice their religion, the Eastern Christians suffered under a thousand disabilities. They were obliged to pay tribute, wear a distinctive garb, and conform to a list of humiliating regulations. In practicing their religion, external profession had to be curtailed to the minimum set by the ruling monarch or ruling magistrate. For long periods they were forbidden to use crosses on their churches or ring bells on feast days.

Worse still, the Moslem policy appears to have been one of slow annihilation. New churches were not to be built, the systematic training of the clergy was severely restricted, higher education made impossible, and the schooling of children reduced to a few rudimentary facts. Bribery and treachery wreaked havoc with the clergy; the Sultan had to be provided with Christian slaves.

Every five years, Christian boys between eight and fifteen were inspected by the Moslem overlords. Those who were strongest and most intelligent were chosen, taken from their parents, converted to Islam and impressed into the Sultan's service. Most of them were drafted into a special army corps, the Janissaries, and used for centuries as the main instrument of oppression at home and of conquest abroad.

For administrative purposes, the Orthodox Church under the Moslems was made into a *Rum Millet* (Roman nation) with the patriarch of Constantinople at the head and all other church officials under him. He was completely subject to the Sultan, yet given civil jurisdiction over his own people within the Turkish Empire. Before the Moslem ruler, he was responsible for the conduct of the Orthodox who could approach the government only through him.

As might be expected, the result was a mixture of political

and religious power that tended to secularize the Church or, if the patriarch resisted, to oppress the Christian believers. A climax was reached in the eighteenth century when the churches of Rumania, Bulgaria and Serbia came under the Turkish sway, and with it the patriarchate of Constantinople was extended from Asia Minor into the heart of Europe.

Historians of the Orthodox Church graphically describe the price their leaders had to pay for maintaining some semblance of religious authority over the people.

The patriarch received his *berat,* or confirmation of spiritual and secular authority, from an infidel source. He could be removed and, often more than once, reinstated at the Sultan's will, with consequent loss of dignity and the temptation to cater to the Moslem prince for the sake of recognition and prestige. There were notable exceptions, where some patriarchs suffered prison and death rather than compromise on religion. But the over all picture is depressing. Out of one hundred fifty-nine patriarchs in Constantinople from the fifteenth to the twentieth centuries, the Moslems on one hundred and five occasions drove the prelates from their see. There were twenty-seven abdications, often involuntary; six patriarchs suffered violent deaths, and only twenty-one died natural deaths while in office. In one short span, from 1625 to 1700, Constantinople had fifty patriarchs, or an average of a year and a half for each.

Since nominees for patriarch were promoted by a party, those who financed his promotion later expected to be reimbursed, at the expense of the suffragan sees subject to the Metropolitan. They in turn taxed the clergy, who obtained the necessary funds from the people. And behind this whole mechanism stood the power of Islam, which dominated Orthodoxy in Asia Minor until the opening of the twentieth century.

The current oppression of Orthodoxy in Soviet Russia and allied countries is unparalleled in religious history. After half a century of tension, conflict and compromise, the future is still uncertain, but the broad lines of contact between the Russian Church and the Soviet State fall into four distinct periods: from the October Revolution in 1917 to the revolt within the Church in 1922, from the revolt to the outbreak of the second World War in 1939, during the war years, and after the war to the present day.

In the first phase, following the Communist seizure of power, Orthodox churchmen reacted strongly against the wave of persecution waged against the Church by Lenin and Uritskii. Exactly a year after the Revolution got under way, the Moscow Patriarch, Tikhon, issued a ringing message to the Council of People's Commissars, in which he summarized twelve months of Soviet rule: a country running with blood in which "no one feels himself in safety; all live in fear of search, plunder, dispossession, arrest, shooting." He charged the government with inhuman armies against defenseless citizens, of ruthless execution of bishops, priests, monks and nuns "not guilty of anything, but simply on the wholesale accusation of some sort of vague, indefinite 'counter-revolution.'"

"Where," he asked, "was freedom of preaching in church? Already many bold preachers have paid with the blood of martyrdom." He closed with a powerful indictment.

> It is not our work to judge the earthly power; all power permitted by God would draw upon itself our blessing, if it truly showed itself to be "God's servant," for the good of those under it.
>
> Now, then, to you, who use power for persecuting your neighbors and for wiping out the innocent, we extend our word of admonition. Celebrate the anniversary of your taking power by releasing the imprisoned, by stopping bloodshed, violence, havoc, restriction of the faith. Turn not to destruction, but to organizing order and legality, give to the people their wished-for and deserved respite from fratricidal strife. Otherwise all righteous blood shed by you will cry out against you, and with the sword will you perish who have taken up the sword.[2]

Tikhon paid for his criticism by being placed under house arrest, although the Soviets took no other action against him. He further issued a solemn decree excommunicating those who attacked Christians and profaned church buildings, but he soon discovered that such a weapon was useless. The new masters of Russia assaulted not the Church, but God, and the threat of divine punishment only aroused worse anti-religious fervor.

In August 1922, Tikhon was arrested and kept in prison until June of the next year, at which time he published a retraction, declaring his loyalty to the Soviet government and his regret for opposing the confiscation of the sacred vessels. Till his death in 1925, Tikhon was acceptable to the Church and State, although some Christians were shocked by his act of repentance.

A more intransigent position was shown in the manifesto composed by a group of Russian churchmen who were exiled to the concentration camps on Solovetski Island. With calm dignity they explained that they had no political grievance against the Soviet State, that their only concern was over the teaching of materialism by the Communist Party which controlled the government.

> The Church recognizes the existence of the spiritual principle; Communism denies it. The Church believes in the living God, Creator of the world, Guide of its life; Communism does not admit His existence. The Church believes in the steadfast principles of morality, justice and law; Communism looks upon them as the conditional results of class struggle, and values moral questions only from the standpoint of their usefulness. The Church instills the feeling that humility elevates man's soul; Communism abases man through pride.[3]

Meantime a major revolt within the Orthodox Church shook its government to the foundation and split the leaders into opposing factions: Tikhon and the monastic, celibate prelates and clergy on one side, and the "white" married clergy, on the other. The monastic bishops were charged by their confreres with reactionary measures against the State, with ultra-conservative positions in worship and polity and, above all, with intransigence regarding Communism. The Living Church movement, as the progressives styled themselves, met in congress to depose Tikhon, decree that married priests might become bishops and widowed priests might remarry, and issue an appeal to the people, saying that capitalism was the highest form of godlessness.

The reform clergy soon split into dissenting parties, but the effect of their State-encouraged opposition to the bishops (all monastics) was to inflame the masses against their ecclesiastical leaders and weaken the Church's stand against Communism.

In spite of internal weakness, however, the conservative element rallied around their new leader, the Metropolitan Sergius, who was first imprisoned by the Soviets, then made his peace with the government and released. He was allowed to register the Orthodox Church in 1927, for the first time in five years, on the theory that since physical extermination was impossible legal control by the State was better policy. Soon after, on April 8, 1929, a revised law on religion was published by Stalin. Every form of religious propaganda became a civil offense. In addition, Article 17 of the Constitution forbade every kind of philanthropic and educational activity under Church authority.

"Religious unions (parishes)," the law read, "are forbidden: to establish mutual aid funds, cooperative and productive unions, and in general to use the property at their disposal for any other purpose than the satisfying of religious needs; to give material aid to their members, to organize either special meetings for children, youth or women, for prayer and other purposes, or general meetings, groups, circles, departments, biblical or literary, handwork for labor, religious study and the like, and also to organize excursions and children's play-grounds; to open libraries, reading rooms, to organize sanatoria and medical aid. Only such books as are necessary for the performance of services are permitted in the Church building and houses of prayer."[4] These prohibitions were reinstated in Article 124 of the 1936 Constitution and still remain effectively unchanged.

This new legislation marked a radical change in the Church's status. It was now faced with a crusade of anti-religion, while allowed under government supervision to conduct religious services for the people. An unequal competition opened between the inarticulate Church and the Soviet program of indoctrination, which centered on the public schools.

The war years, 1939–1945, proved a boon to the Orthodox

Church. With the outbreak of hostilities the antireligious campaign was softened to a low key; churchmen published statements of support of the government against the Nazi aggressor; and even the State promoted friendlier relations with ecclesiastical authorities. A climax was reached in 1943, when the Patriarchate of Moscow was re-established, after a lapse of two hundred years. Tsar Peter the Great had abolished the patriarchate in 1721 on the grounds that many Russians thought the patriarch was equal or superior to the emperor. A "holy governing synod," modeled on the German Lutheran synods, replaced the patriarchate. Re-establishing this office was a master-stroke of strategy to win the support of the Church for Soviet political needs.

At the Sobor (congress) which followed Sergius's death, the metropolitan Alexii was chosen patriarch in 1944. Next February at his investure, the Sobor issued a warm message of approval of the government, praying God "to increase the strength, health and years of life of our beloved Leader of the Soviet State, Joseph Vissarionovich Stalin."[5] After the defeat of Germany, Alexii published a statement to the effect that, "the most important thing the Russian Orthodox Church did in wartime was to demonstrate to the whole world its complete unity with its government."[6]

Since the war, the condition of the Orthodox Church in Russia has been precarious, in spite of ostensible growth. Honors and benefits have been conferred on dutiful churchmen by the Soviet government, and a *modus vivendi* marked out that gives the appearance of progress. But all the evidence points to a radical decline in religion among the people, due mostly to the steady pressure of Marxist teaching in the schools and control of available media of communication.

A recent survey made by the government showed there is still a widespread religious survival among the peasantry, partly explained by the concentration of women on the farms and of atheist propaganda in the cities. "Precise data on the sex ratio among the Orthodox do not exist. However, on the basis of various facts available to researchers in this field, it may be stated that about 75 to 80 per cent of all the faithful are women."[7]

This poses a new problem for the Church, to save itself and survive the Communist State by strengthening the religion of its women and, as far as possible, using their services in the interests of the faith. Aware of this fact, the government is more than ever stressing the need of teaching atheism in the homes. "The most effective form of antireligious propaganda is systematic individual work with the faithful within their homes, particularly with the mothers. Since religion is most widespread among women, attention must be directed chiefly to antireligious work among them. Women must be drawn into public affairs as active participants. This is the most important condition for liberating them from the narcotic of religion," and through them the next generation.[8]

SOURCES OF FAITH

It is not easy to specify the doctrinal principles of Eastern Orthodoxy. The very name, Orthodox, designates both "correct doctrine" and "correct worship." In Slavonic, Orthodoxy is rendered by the work *Pravoslavie,* which means "true glory," so that when a Russian, Serb, or Bulgarian calls himself Orthodox he proclaims his belonging to a community which praises and glorifies God in the right way.

Consequently for the Orthodox the Church's purpose is mainly to worship God, and to teach its members how to glorify Him in the right spirit. This de-emphasis of doctrine affects the importance given to different types of doctrinal positions, whether they belong to dogma, theologumena, or theological opinion. In the absence of an infallible defining authority, there is considerable overlapping of dogmatic teaching among churchmen, and numerous areas of uncertainty not found in Roman Catholicism. Dogmas are universally binding among the Orthodox, as emanating directly from divine revelation; theologumena are traditionally held doctrines hallowed by the authority of ancient and respected Church teachers; theological opinions are the vast body of disputed theories and explanations that scholars have devised over the centuries.

Until the seventeenth century, the Orthodox accepted the

same books of the Old and New Testaments as are found in the Catholic canon. Then Cyril Lukaris (1572–1638), patriarch of Constantinople, followed the Protestant pattern and denied the inspired character of the so-called deutero-canonical books of the Old Testament, namely, Tobias, Judith, Wisdom, Ecclesiasticus, Baruch, and the two books of Maccabees. This innovation was at first resisted, but closer relations with Calvinism confirmed many, if not most, Orthodox theologians in reducing the Old Testament canon to its Protestant form.

While the concept of biblical inspiration differs among the authors, a common notion is to consider it "an immediate movement and instruction of the sacred writers by the Holy Spirit. As a result, they are not only preserved from error but positively receive a revelation of God's truth, though without violence to their natural faculties. The biographers therefore become organs for transmitting divine revelation, while retaining all their native powers and activities."[9] So exalted is this type of inspiration that the sacred authors are said to have received and communicated divine truths even as the man Christ understood and expressed revelation by means of the Word which assumed His human nature.

Tradition as distinct from Scripture is a valid source of Christian doctrine in Orthodoxy. In general "sacred tradition is that form of preserving and propagating revelation whereby the faithful and worshipers of God, by word and example transmit one to the other, the predecessors to those who follow them, the doctrine of faith, law of God, the sacraments and sacred rites."[10] The significant feature of this concept is the essential part played by the faithful in forming and conserving tradition.

However, in spreading doctrinal tradition among all the faithful, the Orthodox recognize certain monuments of special import which differ in dogmatic value according to their greater or less respect among the people.

Highest in dignity are the Creeds: the Nicene, the Athanasian and the Symbol of St. Gregory Thaumaturgus (213–270). In the Nicene they do not include the *Filioque*, which declares the procession of the Holy Spirit from the Son. The

Athanasian Creed, known as the *Quicumque* (Whosoever), from its opening words, differs from other summaries of faith in embodying anathemas against those who deny the Trinity, Incarnation and other doctrinal essentials. Though dating from the time of St. Ambrose, it was not recognized as a standard of faith in the Eastern Church until the seventeenth century, when it began to appear in the Greek *Horologium* (liturgical manual) and in Russian service books. Surprisingly the Apostles' Creed lacks "ecumenical authority" among the Eastern Orthodox.[11]

Gregory Thaumaturgus' Creed is entirely Trinitarian, and has no reference to Christology. It owes more to tradition than to the Bible, and practically typifies the character of Eastern religious thought.

> One God, Father of the living Word, of subsistent wisdom, eternal power and likeness. Perfect source of the perfect One, Father of the only-begotten Son. One Lord, one alone from the only One, God of God, likeness and image of the Deity, active Word, wisdom comprehending the structure of the universe, and effective virtue of every creature. True Son of true God, Invisible of invisible, Immortal of immortal, Eternal of eternal.

> And one Holy Spirit, having substance from God, and who appeared to men through the Son. Image of the Son, perfect of the perfect, life which is the cause of the living, holy wellspring, sanctity which dispenses sanctity, in whom God the Father is manifested, who is above all and in all things, and God the Son who is through all things.

> Perfect Trinity, undivided and unseparated in glory and eternity and reign. Nothing created nor subservient nor introduced in the Trinity, as though it were absent before and had later come in. In like manner, the Father was never without the Son nor the Son without the Spirit; but always the same unalterable and unchangeable Trinity.[12]

Second in authority to the Creeds are the first seven general councils: two of Nicea, 325, 787; three of Constantinople, 381, 553, 681; Ephesus, 431; and Chalcedon, 451. The eighth council, of Constantinople in 869–870, deposed Photius as patriarch and by Orthodox standards marked the beginning of Western Christianity apart from the Eastern Church. All the future general Councils recognized by Rome, from First Lateran in 1123 to Second Vatican in 1962, have been held in the West, and are not accepted by the Orthodox.

The first seven councils dealt almost exclusively with the Trinity, the divinity of Christ, the divine maternity of the Blessed Virgin and the veneration of sacred images. As a result, doctrinal principles in Orthodoxy show little of the dogmatic development found in the West, through the clarifications and definitions of such major conclaves as the Council of Trent (1545–1563) or First Vatican (1869).

The Fathers of the Church most respected and followed by the Orthodox are Athanasius, the three Cappadocians (Basil, Gregory Nazianzen and Nyssa), Pseudo-Dionysius, Maximus the Confessor, Leo and Gregory the Great. It is of more than passing interest that two Roman Pontiffs are among the highest patristic authorities in the Eastern Church.

Below the Fathers but still within the concept of tradition are the symbolic books, described as "professions of faith of particular churches in recent times, especially those composed against Catholics and Protestants," or "professions of faith by certain enlightened persons in the churches, succinctly and clearly written to teach the faithful all or some of the doctrines contained in the Creeds."[13]

Among the more famous symbolic authorities are the *Confessions* of Gennadius (died 471), of Peter Mogila (1597–1646) and of Dositheus (1640–1707), and the *Catechism* of Philaret (1553–1646); Gennadius, however, is not acknowledged by many theologians. Mogila was a Wallachian theologian whose comprehensive survey of the Greek Orthodox Church was formally approved by the foremost patriarchs in 1643, re-approved by the Synod of Jerusalem in 1672, and is now a primary witness of Eastern Orthodoxy. Dositheus, as Patriarch of Jerusalem, wrote strenuously against Calvin and Bellarmine, and was a prime mover in combating Western influences in Orthodox theology.

Theodore Romanov Philaret, the Patriarch of Moscow, founded the Romanov dynasty. Under his cousin, Theodore I, the last Tsar of the Runik family, he fought against the Swedes and was later banished to a monastery. After his son Michael was elected Tsar, he became patriarch (1619) and until his death remained virtual ruler of Russia. A zealous reformer, he established a seminary in each diocese, promoted the study of theology and composed his famous *Catechism*.

Other writings of lesser authority are sometimes called symbolic, but their value varies and practically depends on the following they have in contemporary circles. Thus a man like Vladimir Solovieff (1853–1900) is highly regarded by the Orthodox, but his later entrance into the Catholic Church naturally colors the acceptability of his doctrines.

DOCTRINAL VARIATIONS

Consistent with the undefined nature of dogmatic sources, there is considerable fluidity among Orthodox teachers on many points of doctrine that have become defined dogmas in Roman Catholicism.

According to Eastern thought, nothing which has no direct bearing on divine worship should be made a matter of absolute belief. Confessions of faith for the Orthodox are mainly a part of doxology or liturgy. At most, dogmas safeguard the beatific vision of God and the Incarnation, and are enshrined in the Creeds and dogmatic pronouncements of the first seven councils. Catholicism has a doctrinal system which includes the nature of man, the constitution of the Church, the primacy, sin, grace and the ways of salvation. All these are "problems" for Eastern Christians, in the sphere governed by Theologumena. Even such basic issues as the concept of the supernatural and the real presence in the Eucharist are open to discussion and controversy in Orthodox theology.

Nevertheless, beyond the Trinitarian and Christological teaching of the early councils are many areas of substantial agreement among the Orthodox. These form their "deposit of faith," about which, however, opinions may vary.

SUPERNATURAL LIFE. Until very recent times, the influence of Protestant theology on Orthodoxy was notable but sporadic. Since the nineteenth century, the effect has been more profound and shows itself especially in the median position between Catholicism and Protestantism that Eastern churchmen have adopted on the subject of man's elevation to the supernatural order.

Current writings indicate that many Orthodox theologians do not admit a strict elevation of man to a supernatural destiny. They variously describe this elevation as suprasensible, transcendent, what is above the common mode of action of the forces of nature, or above the natural capacity of man. While apparently subtle, their concept allows for an exigency or demand for the beatific vision, which goes beyond mere tendency or desire.

The issue became crucial for the Orthodox through their frequent relations with the continental Reformation and since the sixteenth century has given rise to opposing parties within the Eastern churches. About 1400 A.D. translations of Latin works, including St. Thomas, made Catholic writings available to the Orthodox and divided them into Latinizers and Anti-Latins, Palamites and Anti-Palamites (generally Latinizers). With the advent of the Reformation, the lines were further sharpened. Cyril Lukaris, Greek patriarch, was ardently pro-Calvinist; his *Confessio* is a thoroughly Reformed interpretation of the Greek Orthodox faith and allows for no supernatural elevation in the Catholic sense.

Twentieth-century ideas are in a state of flux, with perhaps the majority favoring the Catholic position, without clearly distinguishing between grace as absolutely gratuitous and in no sense due to any creature, and grace as an exalted sublimation of human nature.

PROCESSION OF THE SON. Historically the principal divergence from Catholicism is on the procession of the Third Person of the Trinity. Symbolized in the term, *Filioque,* it has been the main object of Orthodox theological writing for centuries. Two attitudes are discernible: that the procession of the Holy Spirit from the Father alone is a dogma, and therefore the Latin *Filioque* is heresy; or that the procession from the Father is a dogma which the Roman Church admits, so that procession from the Son is only a theological opinion which may be professed by the Orthodox.

Historically the problem goes back to the insertion of the

words *Filioque* in the Nicene Creed, begun in Spain in the sixth century and later adopted by the whole West as the official expression of the revealed truth that the Holy Spirit proceeds at once from the Father and the Son, as from one principle. Photius and after him the Orthodox objected to what they called either a heretical tampering with the Creed, or an unjustified exercise of papal authority approving the insertion without an ecumenical council.

Since the turn of the century, Orthodox sentiment has been in the direction of considering the *Filioque* more irenically. In 1907 the Moscow Synodal Commission published a statement declaring that the *Filioque* had not been the cause of separation of the Churches; that the theory of Photius on the procession of the Spirit from the Father alone was a theological opinion and not a dogma; that the true meaning of the Greek Fathers who said the Holy Spirit proceeds *from* the Father *through* the Son corresponds to the Latin formula.

The Synod suggested that the two formulas concur essentially: the co-ordinating version (*Filioque*) and the subordinating (*per Filium*), since they both attest that Father and Son are the one Principle of the Holy Spirit. They also complement each other. While the former stresses the unicity and indivisibility of the Principle, the latter emphasizes that the Father is Prime Principle, while the Son as "God from God" is a Derived Principle, since with His essence He also receives from the Father the power of spirating the Holy Spirit.

More recently a leading theologian, Sergius Bulgakov, gave a critical judgment on the whole question. "The controversy about the Holy Spirit has been conducted in an atmosphere lacking in love and actuated by the spirit of schism; it has been therefore a pointless dispute."[14] Current writers ask themselves: if the controversy was so futile, why has it persisted for so long? They answer that the issue is not doctrinal but moral. A grave breach of mutual trust was committed by changing the Nicene Creed; all other factors are minor or irrelevant.

CONCEPT OF THE CHURCH. Orthodox ecclesiologists believe their concept of the Church is a balanced mean between the Reformation idea of an essentially invisible society and the

Catholic definition of the Church as a visible, hierarchical institution. Within the Orthodox system, however, two quite different notions prevail: the traditional and conservative, which is perfectly consistent with Orthodox professions of faith; and the liberal concept especially prevalent among the Slavophils.

Representative of the conservative theorists is Philaretus (Gumilevsky), who describes the Church of Christ as "the assembly of believers in Christ, instituted by the Lord and united by the divine word, sacraments and the hierarchy under the influence of the Holy Spirit, to lead people to eternal salvation."[15] This earthly society is united with the heavenly, the angels and saints, in one and the same Church of Christ. A heavy stress on the unitive character of the dual society is a feature of Orthodox ecclesiology. It is unlike the Protestant notion by its recognition of a hierarchy, and similar to the Catholic in conceiving the Church as visible in bodily structure and invisible as regards its soul.

Within the conservative camp, however, are different schools of thought, one in the direction of Rome and the other of the Reformation. Macarius Bulgakov defines the Church in terms reminiscent of Bellarmine, except for including the word "Orthodox" and excluding the Roman Pontiff. "The Church," he says, "is the orthodox society of the believers and the baptized in Jesus Christ, founded immediately by Him and through the holy apostles, and animated by Him; which is directed visibly through spiritual pastors, and by means of a teaching authority, the administration of sacred rites and a ruling body; and at the same time is led invisibly to eternal life through the most efficacious grace of the Holy Spirit."[16] Theophylact Gorskii, on the other hand, gives an almost Luthern definition, calling the Church "the assembly of true believers and saints, rightly called together by the preaching of the divine word to attain eternal life through the great goodness of God. Only those really belong to the Church who possess the true faith, by which they are united with Christ the Head. Hence they are called members of the Body of Christ, so that the wicked, the unbelieving and hypocrites are certainly excluded from membership."[17] This differs only in detail from the classic Protestant Church of the believers and the predestined.

Slavophil ecclesiology antedates Alexius Khomjakov (1804–1860), but his theory on the Church has deeply affected Orthodox thought and found expression in the unity movements now current in the Eastern Churches. He began by conceiving the Church in its broadest possible extension, including the Mystical Body of Christ in its triple form of militant, suffering and triumphant. Then he explained that only the Eastern Orthodox Church is the true Church. Western Churches, namely Catholicism and Protestantism, do not differ essentially as sects outside the true fold of Christ. The Catholic Church fell into rationalism in the ninth century, when it introduced the *Filioque*, Protestants when they embraced private interpretation of the Scriptures. In Khomjakov's vocabulary, the Church is "a living principle," or "the Church is the universal life of love and unity, along with organic and living solidarity."[18]

Not the least value of this expansive notion of the Church has been the function it served those who sought a rapprochement with contemporary Marxism. It also gave men like Nicholas Berdyaev (1874–1948) the principles required for adapting religion to the demands of the modern mind. This "spiritual Christianity," it is felt, has no need of doctrinal definitions, bourgeois morality, and set worship.

In the absence of an ultimate juridical authority to pass judgment on the relative value of these concepts, it is difficult to know which ideas are prevalent. Certainly those most closely approximating the standard manuals of doctrine are also nearest to Catholicism, in which the Church is not so spiritualized as to include almost anyone who calls himself a Christian even though he disbelieves what the first seven councils made mandatory on all the faithful.

Although the Eastern Orthodox generally admit that the Church is a visible institution, they say that Christ alone is the head, since a visible head would be irreconcilable with the doctrine of the Mystical Body. One body can have only one head, not two, as found in Catholicism. Christ, they teach, so reserves to Himself the whole life and government of the

Church that no vicar can take His place. Ministers in the Church can assist in the activity of the Head, but they cannot share in it; otherwise Christ's function would suffer encroachment and the Church which is divine would become subject to a human person.

No mortal man, they argue, can be head of the Church. He cannot exert influence over the scattered peoples of the earth; his action would supplant that of Christ and introduce into an indefectible society the fallibility and weakness of a human being. Most importantly, if the Church were to have a human head, it would cease to be celestial and become as one of the many secular kingdoms of earth.

The dominant principle in Orthodoxy is that Church authority is diffused among its members, and not as in the West, isolated in a definite source. This was strikingly illustrated in an exchange of letters between Pius IX and the Patriarchs of the East. In 1848 a reply of the Orthodox prelates, signed by thirty-one bishops and three patriarchs, informed Rome that "the Pope is greatly mistaken in supposing that we consider the ecclesiastical hierarchy to be the guardian of dogma. The case is quite different. The unvarying constancy and the unerring truth of Christian dogma does not depend upon any of the hierarchical orders; it is guarded by the totality of the people of God, which is the body of Christ."[19]

This answer reflects the common attitude of Orthodox towards the primacy and infallibility of the Roman See. "Does any one in the Church," they ask, "possess of himself infallibility in his judgment of dogma? No, he does not; every member of the Church is liable to error, or rather to the introduction of his own personal limitations in his dogmatic studies." According to this view, neither the hierarchy nor the councils are organs of doctrinal inerrancy. "Only the Church in its identity with itself can testify to the truth. It is the Church which agrees or not, with the council. There are not, and there cannot be, external forms established beforehand for the testimony of the Church about itself."[20]

Such corporate authority, however, is compatible with a hierarchical structure. Bishops and clergy have clearly defined functions in the ministry and norms of orthodoxy to maintain in their teaching. Councils on a local or provincial basis may be called, but when dealing with matters of conscience their decisions must have the approval of the whole community to take juridical effect, and even then there is no claim to infallibility.

SACRAMENTAL SYSTEM. Orthodox churchmen recognize seven sacraments, and stress the fact so solemnly they charge anyone who diminishes the number with trifling with Christian revelation. As one writer expressed it, "There are as many sacred mysteries or sacraments among the Greeks as among the Latins, namely, seven. And no one in either Church has ever called this into question."[21] The exceptional Orthodox who departs from this norm is considered outside the stream of Eastern tradition.

Nevertheless occasional doubts arise. Thus a prominent theologian in Europe, Jerome Tarasij, suggested that other rites should be added to the sacramental system, for example, entrance into monastic life, solemn blessing of water and funeral ceremonies; but matrimony could well be dropped because there was nothing spiritual about it.[22] Tarasij has since been supported by at least one metropolitan, Antonij Chrapovickij, whose diocesan catechism allowed considerable freedom on the subject. His comment that the Church has never defined the number of the sacraments is correct from the Orthodox viewpoint, although few would doubt that the number is seven.

Eastern commentators repeatedly say that the sacraments are not mere symbols or pure signs of grace, received independently of the rite and only occasioned by its administration. They use terms like "effect grace," or "give grace," and describe the sacraments as instruments, organs or means of divine sanctification.

Yet again there are sporadic dissenting voices. The same Tarasij explicitly teaches that the causality of the sacraments does not depend on special external rites but on union with the whole Church. In the same way, the "matter" and "form" of the sacraments, which in Latin terminology stand for the material rite and the ritual words, have never been clearly defined among the Orthodox and therefore variations appear among different churches. But in general there is a remarkable consistency between Eastern and Western beliefs and practices with regard to the sacraments.

The Orthodox always place baptism in the first place among the sacraments, and recognize its institution by Christ or, as some prefer, "by the words and actions of the Lord." Pure and natural water is required along with the Trinitarian formula and a triple immersion, using the words, "The servant of God (name) is baptized in the name of the Father, the Son and the Holy Spirit." Symbolically this signifies the death of the sinner, and his redemption and resurrection as a Christian.

The ordinary minister of baptism is a bishop or priest, but in case of necessity even a lay person (man or woman) may baptize. Some Orthodox canonists question the validity of a baptism performed by laymen, unless the latter are Orthodox and have the intention of conferring the true sacrament. Very like Catholic doctrine, the effects of baptism are said to be remission of sin, imprinting of a character, entering the fold of Christ, and receiving a title to heavenly glory. Consequently, with rare exception the necessity of baptism for salvation is taken for granted, and therefore children are normally baptized in infancy.

Confirmation, or holy chrismation, follows immediately after baptism. Although the priest confers the sacrament, the holy oil or chrism must have been blessed by a gathering of bishops of a self-governing church presided over by their senior. While anointing the various parts of the body, actually the whole body, the priest recites the formula, "The seal of the gift of the Holy Spirit." However, the Orthodox do not believe that an indelible character is imprinted; and only two sins can efface it, heresy and schism. As a consequence, confirmation is the regular way that converts to Orthodoxy (or fallen-aways) are received into the Church.

Orthodox theologians stress that chrismation is not a renewal of baptismal vows, but a kind of lay ordination, by which the laymen obtain special graces to participate in the life of the Christian community and receive the other sacraments. One important consequence of confirming infants is that from childhood they are considered full-fledged members of the Church, with all the rights and privileges of adults, including the reception of Holy Communion.

Confession of sins is an ancient practice among the Orthodox, which they base on three considerations: that people are normally responsible for their actions and can have their conscience trained, that their responsibility is a corporate affair that requires corporate means to cultivate and may not be left to each individual indiscriminately, and that sincere reconciliation with men secures divine forgiveness with a consequent removal of guilt.

A familiar custom is to have the penitent first visit his relatives and close friends before going to the priest. He asks their pardon, with or without specifying how he may have offended them. They answer, "God forgives you." Behind the practice is the centuries-old tradition of confessing one's sins publicly, which has now been largely abandoned, although early in the present century a certain John of Cronstadt revived in Russia the practice of public confessions.

Instead of kneeling before the priest, the penitent stands facing East, as a symbol that the confessor is not absolving in his own name but as a witness of the Christian community. At least this is the custom among many Orthodox churchmen. After the penitent tells his sins, he may be asked a few questions and then hears a brief exhortation.

> O Lord God of the salvation of Your servants, merciful, gracious and longsuffering. You offer repentance for evil and will not the death of a sinner but rather that he should be converted and live. Forgive now, O Lord, this Your servant (by name). Grant him the assurance of repentance, pardon, and remission of his sins, and absolve him from all his offences, voluntary and involuntary. Reconcile and unite him to Your holy Church through Jesus Christ our Lord, with whom be power and glory ascribed to You, now and for ever, even unto ages of ages. Amen.[23]

After this prayer follows the absolution, of which there are two main forms, one common to Russia and the other to the Greek Orthodox Churches. The Russian formula appears to have been influenced by Catholic divines in the seventeenth century. It is expressly indicative, i.e., the priest declares he is forgiving the sins in the name of God. "May our Lord and God Jesus Christ, through the grace and compassion of His exceeding love, forgive you, my son (here follows the Christian name), all your transgressions, and I, an unworthy priest, by the power that is given to me by Him, forgive and absolve you from all your sins in the name of the Father, and of the Son and of the Holy Spirit, Amen."[24]

The Greek version is more deprecative, i.e., the priest declares that God forgives the penitent. "May God, who pardoned David through the prophet Nathan when he confessed his sins; who received Peter bewailing the denial, the harlot weeping at His feet, and who took back the publican and prodigal; may the same God, through me a sinner, pardon you everything in this world, and cause you to stand uncondemned before His awful tribunal."[25]

After absolution the penitent is seldom required to say or perform a penance prescribed by the confessor. Its function is said to be only a subjective one, to strengthen the will of the penitent against future lapses or act as a salutary remedy for bad habits. Many Orthodox theologians do not consider satisfaction for sins necessary for the remission of punishment incurred, on the theory that Christ perfectly satisfied for our sins, so that the absolution of the priest delivers us from all penalty both eternal and temporal.

The frequency of confession differs. Four times a year is a common practice, although in the Russian Church no one may receive the Eucharist unless he has first confessed his sins. Other Eastern Churches have no set rules and may even prescribe confession only when grave sins have been committed. The same with faculties to hear confessions: some bishops restrict the privilege to a select group of priests, others allow all priests under their jurisdiction to absolve anyone who comes to them.

Holy Orders are almost, but not quite the same as in the Catholic Church. The Orthodox distinguish (as do Catholics) between major and minor orders, but they do not consider any of the minor, as well as the subdiaconate, sacraments;

only the episcopate, priesthood and diaconate are called sacraments, the rest are merely sacramentals. Sometimes even the subdiaconate is regarded sufficient to make the law of continence binding; so that subdeacons, as well as deacons and priests, are occasionally forbidden to marry or to contract a second marriage if their first wife dies.

In the ceremony of ordination, the actual conferral of orders is quite simple, although the surrounding liturgy is very elaborate. Essentially the sacrament is conferred by the imposition of hands (in the Byzantine ceremonial only the right hand) by the bishop on the ordinand; this is the same for all three major orders. The form of ordination is also practically the same for bishop, priest and deacon, except for a single phrase. "The grace of God, that always strengthens the weak and fills things that are empty, advances the most devout subdeacon N.N. to be deacon. Let us therefore pray for him that the grace of the Holy Spirit may come upon him."[26]

There follows a long prayer with biblical allusions to the deacon St. Stephen, while the bishop continues to hold his hand on the subject's head. The deacon is then vested in the sanctuary and given a horarion or stole decorated with crosses and placed over the shoulders. In the ordination of priests the same formula is used, except for the words, "the most devout deacon N.N. to be priest," and for bishops, "appoints the most devout elect N.N. to be Metropolitan of the most holy Metropolis N." A priest receives the vestments and sacred vessels, the bishop is given a miter and insignia of his office.

In the Russian Church a theory prevails that ordained clerics lose their sacerdotal character when they ask for reduction to the lay state or the same is imposed on them for a grave crime. The result is that reordinations to the priesthood and reconsecrations to the episcopate are not rare in the history of the Russian Orthodox Church.

The sacrament of matrimony is called the Crowning in the Eastern Churches. Its purpose is to bestow the Church's blessing upon husband and wife, and assist them to remain faithful to each other and their respective duties until death. Husband and wife wear crowns during the ceremony, and in some places for a week afterwards. Marriage vows are pronounced

during the Eucharistic Liturgy, with appropriate readings from
the Gospel of St. John about the marriage feast at Cana and
from St. Paul's classic epistle to the Ephesians, that "a husband is head of the wife, just as Christ is head of the Church."

Although in the marriage formula words are used to suggest a permanent union, and this is still considered the ideal,
divorce with the right to remarry is commonly recognized
among the Eastern Orthodox. A few dogmatists still hold that
only adultery gives the privilege of a perfect divorce, but
canonists and the normal practice extend this condition to a
broad variety of causes. A divorce law promulgated in Russia
after the Communist Revolution typifies the general attitude
of the Church, which juridically reserves to itself the right to
dissolve the marriage bond.

Among other grounds for dissolving marriage, besides antecedent physical impotence, are abandonment of the Orthodox
faith by either party, adultery whether of one or both parties,
voluntary mutilation which makes marital relations impossible,
grave disease like syphilis, prolonged absence of one partner
for two or three years, physical violence or injury to the
spouse or children or threat of death, incurable mental illness,
malicious neglect of duty proved before an ecclesiastical
tribunal. In practice the two most common grounds urged
before the Church are prolonged absence and malicious neglect, with the dissolution taking automatic effect after a
specified time and previous adjudication by Church authorities.

Provisions are made for marriage ceremonies following a
divorce. They are much different from the Crowning at a first
nuptials, and contain a clearly penitential note to emphasize
that those who enter on a second union have failed to preserve
the purity of their first intention. A salutary prayer is read
over the couple by the priest. "O Lord Jesus Christ, cleanse
the iniquities of Your servants because, being unable to bear
the heat and burden of the day and the hot desires of the
flesh, they are now entering into the bond of their second
marriage, as You did render lawful by Your chosen vessel
the Apostle Paul, saying for the sake of us humble sinners, 'It
is better to marry in the Lord than to burn.' "[27]

The penitential ritual is used both for divorcees remarrying, and for those who were widowed. However no permission is given to deacons and priests to marry more than once, and they are required to espouse a virgin. If they contract a second marriage, they must give up the active work of the priestly ministry and may continue to function in some subordinate position.

There is an Orthodox equivalent of the Catholic sacrament of extreme (or "final") unction called "Holy Unction," to distinguish it from the idea of a final anointing in grave sickness or at the time of death. Holy unction has a broader significance, since it is administered in cases of bodily and mental illness, even when there is no danger of death, and may be received by anyone seeking spiritual renewal and purification.

Generally the priest is invited to the sick person's home and administers the unction there, but recently the practice has arisen of offering the benefit of the *Euchelaion* to everyone who presents himself at the church during certain seasons, as in Lent, or who visits some place of pilgrimage. In a few localities anointing becomes a special preparation for Holy Communion.

There are seven lessons or readings which deal with the healing ministry of Christ, each followed by an anointing, whose original form was, "Holy Father, Physician of bodies and souls, You sent Your only-begotten Son our Lord Jesus Christ to cure every ill and to deliver us from death. Heal also this Your servant N.N. of the sickness which afflicts his body and enliven him through the grace of Your Christ."[28] This formula has since undergone many additions and changes, including invocations of the Blessed Virgin and Saints Cosmas and Damian. Seven priests are recommended to perform the unction, although one is sufficient in case of necessity. A brush is used to anoint the various parts of the body: the forehead, chin, cheeks, hands, nostrils and chest. However the practice is not uniform among the churches. Each priest performs the same ritual with an amalgam of olive oil which, at least in Russia, is mixed with wine, in memory of the Good Samaritan.

SAINTS AND FAITHFUL DEPARTED. Among the saints, the
Orthodox reserve a special place for the Blessed Virgin.
"Warm veneration of the *Theotokos* (Mother of God),"
writes one of their theologians, "is the soul of Orthodox piety."[29] Priests and people invoke her name constantly in liturgical and private prayers; they love her not only as the
Mother of Christ but as the spiritual mother of all men. Her
ikons are worshiped everywhere, and the majority of Orthodox prayers and hymns are addressed to Mary under a variety
of titles and with a profusion of feast days that has no counterpart in the rest of the Christian world.

In their theological reflection on this Marian piety, Eastern
writers are quite technical, distinguishing between the kind of
worship offered to God and to His Mother. "We worship our
Lady, the Virgin-Mother of God, with hyperdulia, but not as
God; as the Mother of God, but not with latria. God forbid,
that would be blasphemy. For God only do we worship with
latria and make our intercession with Him for sins committed
after baptism, and by her we hope for remission from
Him."[30]

Underlying the devotion to Mary is a profound veneration
for the saints, who are considered bound to the faithful on
earth by ties of grace and through a common bond in Christ.
This was brought out forcefully at the Evanston Assembly of
the World Council of Churches, at which the Orthodox delegates took issue with the prevalent opinion that the Church
is only a community of wayfarers en route to their destiny.

> It is misleading to describe the Church simply as "the pil-
> grim people of God" and forget that the Church Triumphant
> and Church Militant are but one Body. It is precisely in this
> unity that the Christian Hope is grounded. The Church is the
> great Communion of Saints. We upon earth live and strive
> in communion with the glorious "cloud of witnesses" revealed
> through the ages and are strengthened by the intercessions of
> the *Theotokos* and the Saints with whom we join in adoration
> of Christ our Redeemer.[31]

The Russian Catechism explains how the faithful who belong to the Church Militant on earth, in offering their prayers
to God, call at the same time to their aid the saints who be-

long to the Church in heaven. Since the saints stand on the highest steps of the approach to God, "by their prayers and intercessions they purify, strengthen, and offer before God the prayers of the faithful living upon earth, and by the will of God work graciously and beneficently upon them, either by invisible virtue, or by distinct apparitions and in divers other ways."[32]

Recognizing that their devotion to Mary and the saints is a major obstacle to the acceptance of Orthodoxy by the Protestants, Eastern churchmen have gone to great lengths in clarifying what to them is an essential part of Christianity. "The Orthodox Church asks nothing of the saints except the acting as ambassadors towards God for us and the supplicating for all things needful—not even of the Holy *Theotokos* herself. Inasmuch as of her own power she can do nothing except act as an ambassador, we ask nothing of her except that, and to plead with her Son and her God for us."[33]

It comes somewhat as a surprise that the Immaculate Conception should not be admitted. Actually the Orthodox had always venerated Mary's absolute sinlessness, but since the definition by Pius IX spokesmen for the Eastern Churches have denied the doctrine, at any rate in Catholic terms. Anthimos VIII of Constantinople officially declared against it in 1895. The more common Orthodox opinion is that Mary was freed from original sin at the Annunciation.

The subject of an intermediary state between earth and heaven has been controverted among the Orthodox for centuries. They offer the Holy Sacrifice for the faithful departed and pray for the dead, but their theologians insist they do not accept the Catholic doctrine of purgatory. A measured statement about the condition of the dead occurs in the highly respected Confession of Kritopoulos.

> The Church teaches that their punishment is not material, nor in their members, nor by fire nor any other material thing, but by the pain and sorrow of conscience which come to them from the remembrance of those things which in the world they did in violation of reason and against sanctity. Therefore we pray for the departed by name for each. As often as the Lord's Supper is celebrated, no matter on what day, they are remem-

bered in common. For all who have compiled the prayers of that Sacrament, Basil the Great, Gregory the Theologian and John Chrysostom, make mention of them who are fallen asleep. It is not for us to fix the time of their purification.[34]

Other writers further speculate on the lot of the souls in purgation, but their main difference from the accepted Catholic position is a denial of the name, "purgatory," and the existence of a purgatorial fire. The latter is common teaching in Catholic theology, but at the reunion Councils of Lyons (1274) and Florence (1438–1445), out of consideration for the separated Greeks the official declarations speak only of purifying punishments (*poenae purgatoriae*), not of purifying fire.

CHURCH AUTHORITY AND MONASTICISM

The most characteristic feature of the Eastern Churches is their constitutional organization as a visible society. Many Orthodox agree that the Church is essentially hierarchical; they admit that bishops are the successors of the Apostles and visible heads of particular churches; and they invest the universal Church (including the faithful) with supreme transitory authority during an ecumenical council. But in the absence of a permanent, divinely instituted visible head, endowed with immediate jurisdiction over each diocese, they have developed a system of government known as autocephalism.

SELF-GOVERNMENT. Literally autocephalous means "self-headed" and was used in the early Church to describe bishops who were under no superior authority in their metropolitan area. Eventually the term came to describe the whole juridical structure of Eastern Orthodoxy, which may be compared to the United Nations in contrast to a monarchy such as the Catholic Church. In theory there may be as many autocephalous churches as there are dioceses or bishops, because the Orthodox recognizes no ultimate primate, and individual bishops by equal right succeed the first Apostles. But in practice there are as many autocephalous churches as distinct political units or racial bodies speaking the same language, even though not united politically.

The interior government of each autocephaly is synodal or collegial, since a monarchical form of jurisdiction is excluded not only from the universal Church but also from each autocephaly. Instead the supreme authority is vested in a college or synod. The principle holds good even in autocephali presided over by a patriarch or exarch (lower metropolitan primate), where the real governing power is a synod of bishops together with the primate. Without the synod, the latter can do little or nothing of his own accord.

Yet even the synod is only partially authoritative, because the supreme jurisdiction governing each autocephaly is twofold: the Church and State. In the territory where the synod is located, the civil government has extensive power, comparable to the rights of ecclesiastical superiors in the Catholic Church.

In defense of the synodal system, Orthodox writers appeal to Sacred Scripture, which shows that the Apostles settled controversies and treated questions of moment by means of synods. Collegial government, they add, is also more in conformity with fraternal charity. The dogmatic foundation for this system is found in the text of the Byzantine Nicene Creed. In the Slavonic version of the Creed, the word *Katholike* is translated *subornaiia,* which etymologically means synodal or conciliar. Orthodox theologians say that the ancient translators by this version wished to show that the true Church of Christ is recognized by its collegial character.

At the convention of all Patriarchal Churches held in Moscow in 1927, the assembly declared that the term *sobornost* must be understood of the conciliar form of the Church. It means "conciliarity," and stands for the joint possession by all the members of the Church of all its gifts and properties. Thus the prerogatives of ultimate authority and infallibility belong to the whole ecclesiastical community. *Sobornost,* from the Russian *sobor,* "assembly," has no exact English equivalent, but generally denotes the quality needed for charitable collaboration, with stress on the cooperation of the people. It is a feature of their Church, say the Russians, in contrast with the emphasis on authority in Roman Catholicism and the individualism of the Protestant communions.

Theoretically national autocephalism precludes anything like a real primacy of jurisdiction on the part of any prelate. Even the Ecumenical Patriarch of Constantinople has only a primacy of honor and precedence, but not of ultimate authority. In practice, however, the autocephalous churches do acknowledge a kind of primacy of jurisdiction, whether to their local prelate or the metropolitan or the patriarch. Yet the acknowledgment fluctuates and differs with the regions and the degree of autonomy from State control.

Mutual relations between the autocephali vary. On principle they enjoy equal rights, like politically independent nations. They call each other sister churches, and are urged to practice fraternal love and ecclesiastical unity, which they manifest in several ways. When a new prelate is elected, he informs each autocephaly of his appointment. The prelates of each autocephaly inscribe each other's names in the diptych and make a commemoration during the Sacred Liturgy. Those admitted into communion by one autocephaly should be accepted by the others; those excommunicated by one are to be ostracized by all. Doctrinal or disciplinary decisions should be communicated to all the Orthodox churches; and in the same spirit correspondence on problems and methods of procedure is encouraged, and when a council is convoked, each autocephalous body is to be represented.

A midway theory of government, between autocephalous and monarchical, was strongly advocated in Orthodox circles until modern times, and has recently found favor among Eastern theologians. The idea is basically an ecclesiastical oligarchy, founded on the notion that the Apostles were of equal authority but they gave supreme jurisdiction not to one of their number but to a number of prelates equal in power. Two forms have been advocated, the pentarchy and tetrarchy, each within the limits of authentic Orthodox ecclesiology.

According to the pentarchical theory, supreme authority in the Church would be ascribed to five mutually independent Patriarchs, equal in authority and simultaneously governing the universal Church, namely Rome, Constantinople, Alexandria, Antioch and Jerusalem. Just as the body is ruled by five senses, so God is said to have willed His Church to be directed by five Patriarchs, among whom is included the Roman Pontiff.

Theologians who exclude the pope from the universal Church on account of schism and heresy logically adopted the tetrarchical theory, which consigns the supreme jurisdiction of the Church to the four Oriental Patriarchs, minus the pope, whose primacy of honor passed from Rome to Constantinople with the change of empire at the time of Charlemagne.

MONASTIC LIFE. Monasticism is an essential feature of Eastern Orthodoxy. Yet its concept is quite different from the religious life in the West, where a great variety of rules and apostolic needs has produced a corresponding variety of communities dedicated to following the Christian counsels. Harnack once remarked that an Orthodox monastery is the most perfect relic of the fourth century left in the world. Its spirit and ideals are still those which St. Benedict found and developed in Europe, but which the Orthodox have inherited from St. Basil and retained practically unchanged.

With rare exception, Orthodox monks do not engage in teaching, preaching, or the ministry. That is the concern of the bishops and secular (white) clergy, as distinct from the black clergy in monasteries, who are only a small fraction of the total monastic population. Practically all of them follow the Rule of St. Basil; the monastery on Mt. Sinai and some others in Lebanon and on the Red Sea prefer the Rule of St. Anthony the Hermit.

Each monastery (*laura*) is independent of all the rest, with no ultimate superior like a provincial or general; although most lauras are under the jurisdiction of the local Metropolitan or even the Patriarch. However daughter monasteries (*kellia*) are subject to the abbot of their parent laura. The abbot (*Hegumenos*) is elected by his own monks, approved by the Metropolitan, enthroned in a special ceremony and governs for life in cenobitic monasteries.

Of the thousand or more Orthodox monasteries scattered

throughout Europe and Asia, the most famous is the monastic republic on the Holy Mountain, Athos, at the northernmost of the three peninsulas that jut from the Chalcis in Greece. There are twenty monasteries on the mountain, eleven following the cenobitic rule and nine the idiorrhythmic.[35] The word cenobite is derived from the Greek *koinos* (common) and *bios* (life); idiorrhythmic comes from *idios* (one's own) and *rhythmos* (fashion or mode).

The cenobitic rule insists on perfect obedience to the abbot, elected for life by monks who have been in religion at least six years. He is spiritual master of the community, but has the assistance of others in external administration. Monks receive property, clothing and food from the abbot; they eat their meals in common.

Idiorrhythmic monasteries first appeared in the fifteenth century and are directed by two annually changed trustees, elected from the ten or fifteen senior monks, whose decisions they enforce. A spiritual father (*pneumatikos*) has charge of the interior life of the monks. Individual members retain their property, eat meals in their own cells, which may be two or three rooms, and are left to their own judgment on matters of austerity. The cenobites consider the idiorrhythmic rule lax; but they are answered that personal initiative in the spiritual life is not stifled under the broader discipline. Actually the cenobitic are more austere and cater to a more hardy type of ascetic.

Before entering one of the monasteries on Athos, a man "from the world" visits several and chooses one, at which he presents his application. He must be at least eighteen, a member in good standing of the Orthodox Church and entering without coercion. After about three years of probation, he has the option of remaining a "beginner" without vows, or seeking advancement by taking the four vows of stability, obedience, poverty and chastity. In token of his new status, he receives a first name identical in initial with the rejected Christian name. The new name is that of a deceased saint, who serves as an inspiration; the surname is that of the monastery. Religious on this level are called "monks of the little habit."

Those who seek greater perfection may do so after years of experience, to become "monks of the great habit," with duties of more prayer, stricter fasting, and more severe discipline.

The monks on Mount Athos are generally called from bed at eleven at night for an hour's private prayer, and later in the small hours for Matins and the chanting of communal hymns. There are two meals a day, with household duties interrupted by regular community prayers. Supper and Compline are between six and seven. Monks are to occupy the stalls assigned to them, and are regularly checked by the abbot to note any absentees.

Two characteristic practices in Orthodox monasteries are keeping the liturgical vigils and fasts. There are more than fifty vigils a year, which call for continuous services throughout the evening, night and following morning. Fasting varies between the cenobitic and idiorrhythmic rule. One meal without oil is taken about noon in the *coenobia* on Mondays, Wednesdays and Fridays throughout the year; and two meals on other days. No meat is served, but fish is allowed. The idiorrhythmic rule requires abstinence from cheese, butter and meat on Wednesdays and Fridays, with a stricter diet during the season of Lent, which begins on Quinquagesima Sunday, and on certain fast days before the great feasts of the year.

The general principles of Orthodox monasticism apply equally to men and women, except that before the Russian revolution "unenclosed" nuns were practically unknown. But now they engage in active works of mercy among the sick and indigent. The same change has affected some monasteries of men, who were pressured by the government and public opinion to undertake teaching in schools, conducting agricultural colleges, preaching missions and otherwise becoming involved in secular affairs. However, the number of monks and nuns who have made the turn over is fractional, and one of the major tensions they experience is the conflict of ancient ideals with the increased demands, often under severe sanction from civil authorities, to abandon what the Fathers of Eastern monasticism call the "angelic life" of separation from the world and contemplation of God.

LITURGY AND WORSHIP

The liturgy and ritual of the Eastern Churches are the product of a long process of development reaching back to the
early centuries, and find their roots in the traditional doctrine
of the Eucharist. Although their writers avoid the term "transubstantiation," they commonly believe in a very real presence
of Christ in the Eucharist. In fact their ecumenical efforts with
the Protestants often reach an impasse in the unequivocal insistence on a complete change taking place at the consecration
of the elements at Mass.

> We believe that the substance (*ousian*) of bread and wine
> remain no longer, but the very Body and Blood of the Lord,
> under the form and figures of bread and wine, that is under
> the accidents (*sumbebêkosin*). Also that under every part or
> smallest bit of the bread and wine there is not a part of the
> Lord's Body, but the entire whole Lord Christ according to
> His substance: that is with the soul and divinity as He is
> perfect God and perfect Man.
>
> So that though there be many Eucharists celebrated in the
> world at one and the same hour, there are not many Christs,
> or many bodies of Christ, but one and the same Christ is
> present in all and every Church of the faithful, and there is
> one Body and Blood. Not that the Body of the Lord which is
> in heaven descends upon the altar; but because that Bread
> which is laid on the altar, and there offered in every Church,
> is by consecration changed and transubstantiated and made
> one and the same with that which is in heaven.[36]

When modern Orthodox theologians balk at the word
"transubstantiation," their objections may be generally reduced to an unwillingness to accept the Latinized version decreed by the Council of Trent. They prefer the Greek
metousiôsis or "transelementation," but the concept behind
the term is practically the same.

THE EPIKLESIS. A more serious problem concerns the moment at which the Eucharistic change takes place. With the
doubtful exception of the Nestorian Christians, all the Eastern

liturgies contain the words of institution in the Holy Sacrifice, "This is my Body," and "This is the chalice of my Blood." But they consider these words either nonessential or inadequate, on the score that another prayer, the Epiklesis or invocation of the Holy Spirit, is necessary. In the Orthodox liturgy, the Epiklesis is that ritual prayer in which God the Father is asked to send down the Holy Spirit and to effect the Eucharistic conversion, changing the sacred gifts by His divine power.

In the Liturgy of St. John Chrysostom, after the words of institution, the priest recites the prayer, "We offer You this reasonable and unblood sacrifice, and we pray You, beg You, and implore You to send down Your Holy Spirit on us and on these present gifts; and to make this bread the precious Body of Your Christ, and what is in this chalice the precious Blood of Your Christ, changing them by Your Holy Spirit."[37] Similar prayers are found in the other Eastern liturgies.

Three schools of thought exist among the Orthodox on the Epiklesis. One group attributes the consecration to the words of institution and the Epiklesis taken together; another says the Epiklesis fructifies what is only seminally expressed in the previous formula; and a third holds that the entire consecratory power is in the Epiklesis. In the last theory, the words of institution are taken as a mere historical narrative. The trend in recent years has been away from the intransigence previously shown on the subject towards an acceptance of the Catholic doctrine which identifies the form of consecration with Christ's words instituting the Sacrament.

STRUCTURE OF THE LITURGY. Orthodox writers summarize the differences between Western and Eastern celebrations of the Eucharistic Liturgy by saying that the Eucharist for an Orthodox Christian is not so much a sudden intervention of the divine from above, as a gradual revelation of the divine presence which is always here but remains hidden because of the sinfulness of men. A mystical union of the soul with God, through the operation of the Holy Spirit, also typifies the Eastern approach to the Liturgy.

Special emphasis is placed on the Eucharistic Sacrifice as a re-enactment of the whole life span of Christ, in which priest, deacon and the laity have essential roles to play. The service itself is divided into three parts, corresponding to three phases in the life of the Savior. In the *Prothesis* or preparation, the infancy and hidden life of Christ are commemorated; the *Synaxis* or assembly, which in Catholic terms is the Mass of the Catechumens, reminds the faithful of the teaching and healing ministry of the Redeemer; while the third part, the *Anaphora* or offering of the gifts, properly speaking the Liturgy of the Faithful, recalls the final events of the Gospel narrative: the Last Supper, the Cross, Resurrection, Ascension and descent of the Holy Spirit.

Among other functions during the Prothesis, the round loaf of leavened bread is cut into particles, placed on the diskos and repeatedly incensed; litanies are recited for various causes like peace, the Church, bishop, civil rulers, and fruits of the earth; and a series of antiphons is sung by the choir and ministers.

In the Mass of the Catechumens, the Trisagion is sung daily, invoking "Holy God, holy strong One, holy immortal One, have mercy on us," three times, followed by the *Gloria Patri* and then again, "Holy Immortal One, have mercy on us," and finally the whole invocation, "Holy God." While the choir sings, the priest is reciting other prayers; a reader sings the Epistle, and the deacon the Gospel, after incensation. When the deacon announces, "All catechumens go out; not one catechumen shall stay," the Synaxis is over.

Although the Anaphora is strictly speaking the Canon of the Mass, the Mass of the Faithful begins with the invitation to the faithful to "pray to the Lord in peace," along with other prayers and the famous *Cherubikon* when the choir sings, "Let us, who mystically represent the Cherubim, and who sing to the life-giving Trinity the thrice-holy hymn, put away all earthly cares so as to receive the King of all things escorted by the army of angels." At the word, "King," the Great Entrance takes place, which is the dramatic moment of the Orthodox Liturgy. The royal doors are opened and after prayers and incensation a solemn procession goes through the church, carrying the elements to be consecrated.

The sequence of prayers from the Creed to Communion is not unlike that familiar to Catholics of the Latin rite, but the external ceremonies are quite different. Choir and priest alternate more frequently, the doors separating celebrant from people are closed and shut several times, special litanies are said, a little hot water is added to the consecrated chalice, and the consecration takes place behind the *Ikonostasis* or screen which divides the sanctuary from the nave. It is pierced by three doors, the central or Royal Door admitting to the altar, and those on the right and left corresponding to the sacristy and place of preparation of the elements for Mass.

Holy Communion is received by priest, deacon and people under both species. However in administering to the sick or from the tabernacle, the consecrated Host is dipped into unconsecrated wine. Practice differs, but the Orthodox laity receive the Eucharist only rarely; one custom is four times a year on the major feasts. In the liturgy of St. John Chrysostom, the priest takes with a spoon part of the Host which is in the chalice, soaked in the consecrated wine, and gives it to the communicant, saying, "The servant of God, N.N., receives the holy and precious Body and Blood of Jesus Christ, Lord, God and Savior, for the forgiveness of his sins and for life everlasting."

The final part of the Liturgy includes a short litany with the singers, a prayer to the image of Christ, consuming the remnants of the consecrated elements, blessing and distribution to the people of the unconsecrated bread and concluding orations. At the end the doors are again shut to separate the celebrants from the congregation.

RITES AND OFFICES. Besides the Eucharistic Liturgy and the sacraments, Orthodox prayer books contain more than forty other rites and sacred blessings, covering every need and phase of human life. In all these ceremonies the stress is on the Church, which the people believe has power to sanctify and purify all life, both matter and spirit, and that whenever a benediction is received the blessing comes through the assembly from the Holy Spirit who animates the body of His faithful.

The Divine Office is held in high respect, although its full recitation and chant are limited to religious communities. Unlike the Roman Breviary, it is not combined into a single set of books but various parts must be drawn from different sources. Consisting essentially of the Psalms, it also contains numerous hymns, prayers, litanies and antiphons. Secular priests say as much as devotion and time allow, because the complete office (in at least one rite) is said to take eight hours to complete.

Prayers to the Virgin are featured in the office, addressing her, "Honored above the Cherubim, bearing the incarnate Word, Mother of God, we praise you. Hail, cause of our joy; hail, end of the curse of Adam; hail, throne of the King; hail, bearer of Him who bears all things. Spouse and Virgin, hail." An evening hymn that dates from at least the third century, the *Phos hilaron* (Kindly Light), was Newman's inspiration for the prayer he wrote shortly before his conversion. "Kindly Light of the Father's glory, blessed and holy Jesus Christ, now that we see the setting sun and light the evening lamps, again we worship God, the Father, Son and Holy Spirit. At all times it is right to praise You, Son of God and Life-giver, and so the whole world shall always tell Your glory."

Current services of the Orthodox Church follow a complex system of cycles, of which the first is the seven days of the week. Sunday is dedicated to the Resurrection, Monday to the angels, Tuesday to John the Baptist and the prophets, Wednesday and Friday in honor of Christ's Passion, Thursday is in honor of the apostles, St. Nicholas and all the saints, and Saturday commemorates all the faithful departed, especially the martyrs. Another cycle is based on the eight musical modes, each with its own set of hymns. A new mode is introduced on Saturday night and dominates the offices of the Church for the rest of the week. After eight weeks the cycle is repeated.

The annual cycle is the most comprehensive, with each day commemorating its own saints and some important event in biblical or Christian history. A special book, the *Typicon*, gives the rules and rubrics for conducting services and choosing prayers and hymns for each day. For two periods of the year the liturgical tempo changes. Lenten services are unusually long and penitential, calling for kneeling and prostration; whereas Easter is celebrated with signs of joy and festivity. The Royal Doors are not closed for seven days, and no one kneels during the six weeks following Easter Sunday. To care for all these liturgical needs, the Church provides a variety of books, in addition to the Missals and books of the Divine Office. Besides the *Typicon* at least seven are commonly used: the *Horologion* covers the unchangeable parts of the services and serves as a scaffolding for the rest of public worship, the *Octoekhos* incorporates the eight modes of musical chant, the *Menaia* (in twelve volumes) gives the hymns for daily commemoration, the *Triodion* and *Pentikostarion* serve the Lenten and Easter seasons, the *Litourgion* and *Euchologion* are used for conducting Easter worship. Manuals of prayers are also designed for the laity, and may include daily Bible lessons for private recitation.

Orthodox liturgical worship is designed to inspire by appealing to all the senses: the eyes by beholding the sacred painting of ikons, the ears by hearing the songs, the incense surrounds the worshiper with aromatic fumes, the palate is served by tasting both species of the Eucharist and the sacred bread (*antidôron*), the body joins in prayer by means of symbolic gestures. More than in any other branch of Christendom, Orthodox liturgy stresses the element of mystery and sense of community in public worship, based on the principle that religion is primarily a raising of the mind and will to God and that communal prayer is most pleasing to the Trinity, which itself is a social concept of the Divinity.

HETERODOX EASTERN CHURCHES

Although the Orthodox Christians represent by far the majority membership in the Eastern Churches not in communion with Rome, two other groups, the Monophysites and Nestorians, are also called Eastern and follow much of the Oriental ritual but their theology is heterodox by traditional Christian standards.

The Monophysites, from the Greek *monos* (one) and

phusis (nature), hold, in general, that Christ had only a divine nature, as opposed to the orthodox teaching that He was true God and perfect man.

The essentials of Monophysite doctrine go back to Apollinaris of Laodicea (c. 310–390), for whom the man Christ had no human spirit, which was replaced by the divine Logos. But the real foundations of Monophysitism were laid by Eutyches (c. 374–454), archimandrite of a monastery at Constantinople, who said he was only repeating the doctrine of St. Cyril of Alexandria. His opposition to Nestorianism led Eutyches to the other extreme of claiming that the manhood of Christ was transformed into or absorbed by the divine nature. On this theory the redemption of the world by the passion and death of Christ became theologically impossible.

While there is some question of how unorthodox Eutyches was personally, the doctrine attached to his name and developed by his followers was condemned by the Council of Chalcedon in 451. In the classic form of Eutychian Monophysitism, the two natures of Christ are considered mixed or blended to produce a composite who is not properly God nor really man, but one and the other simultaneously, much as a drop of water dissolves in wine or as the elements of hydrogen and oxygen combine to make water.

A dominant type of Monophysitism was started by Julian of Halicarnassus (died after 518), who so spiritualized the man Christ as to make Him incorruptible and immortal from the moment of incarnation. Dubbed the Phantasiasts, Julian's followers were like the earlier Docetists, for whom the humanity and sufferings of Christ were only apparent and not real.

The Julianists were opposed by Severus, patriarch of Antioch (c. 464–538), who rejected Eutychianism and ostensibly professed that Christ was both God and man. Yet he and his disciples were not orthodox because they accused the Council of Chalcedon of Nestorianism, refused to accept the Church's terminology to describe the Incarnation, and explained the union of the two natures of Christ by analogies and in language that openly favored Monophysitism.

The adversaries of Chalcedon were soon divided into opposing sects and later formed churches which catered to their respective beliefs. They finally consolidated into three principal bodies: the Copts and Abyssinians; the Syrian Jacobites, named after their leader, Jacob Baradaeus (*c.* 500–578), and the Armenians. All three bodies still exist and accept the Fathers of the Church prior to Chalcedon, but they differ among themselves, partly in doctrine and mainly in liturgical practice.

Coptic Christians number about a million and are concentrated in Egypt. Their liturgy is derived from that of St. Mark, and a characteristic custom is the five great fasts: of Nineve before Lent (14 days), Lent (55 days), Advent (28 days), before the Ascension (9 days), and before the Assumption of the Virgin (15 days). In 1948 the Monophysites of Abyssinia became independent of the Egyptian Copts, and today the Ethiopian Church counts the majority of that country's sixteen million population.

Syrian Jacobites number less than half a million, and follow the Antiochean liturgy of St. James. One of their customs is to make the sign of the cross with one finger, to express belief in the one nature of Christ. However the term "Jacobites" is also used to describe the Monophysite Christians in Egypt.

Unlike the Copts and Jacobites, the Armenians were not represented at Chalcedon, but around the year 500 for political reasons they repudiated the council and formed a church which has a current membership of three million. The Armenians never entered into full communion with religious bodies that are professedly Monophysite.

Present-day Monophysites are closer to the mitigated variety of Severus than the radical form of Eutychianism. Their churchmen consistently oppose the latter as heresy, and in their creedal formulas approximate the wording if not the full doctrine of traditional Christianity.

Nestorianism was a fifth century heresy which held there were two distinct persons in the incarnate Christ, one human and the other divine, as against the orthodox teaching that Christ was a divine person who assumed a human nature.

Its name was taken from Nestorius (died *c.* 451), a native of Germanicia in Syria. As a monk in Antioch he came under the influence of that school of exegesis, with its emphasis on the literal instead of the spiritual or merely typical sense of

Scripture. A powerful speaker, he became bishop of Constantinople in 428, but in the same year gave offense by his preaching against the expression then popular in the city, of *Theotokos* (Mother of God), as applied to Mary. When his chaplain, Anastasius, forbade the use of the term as savoring of heresy, Nestorius supported him, but soon came into conflict with St. Cyril of Alexandria and the Egyptian monks.

Both sides appealed in 430 to Pope Celestine I who sustained Cyril and threatened Nestorius with excommunication. When he refused to submit, an ecumenical council was summoned at Ephesus through the intervention of the emperor Theodosius II (431). Nestorius was promptly condemned and told to retract. Complications arose when John, the Patriarch of Antioch, led forty bishops to side with Nestorius. However, on arrival of the papal legates from Rome, 198 prelates upheld the first condemnation, deposed Nestorius, and repudiated the rebel council of John of Antioch. After two years of negotiation, a "creed of union" was adopted by the dissenters and in 435 Nestorius himself was forced into exile where he died not long afterwards.

The theology of Nestorianism can best be understood as a reaction to Apollinarianism, which separated the two natures in Christ to the point of denying His humanity. While properly insisting against Apollinarius that Christ had a perfect human nature, Nestorius could not conceive a complete existing nature that was not also a person, namely, an autonomous subject of existence and its own activity. Consequently, though he admitted that in Christ there was a divine person, he claimed there was also a human personality.

Postulating two separate persons in Christ, when Nestorius came to describe their union, he could not have them joined ontologically (in their being) or hypostatically (constituting one person), but only morally or psychologically. They would be united only by a perfect agreement of the two wills in Christ, and by a harmonious communication of their respective activities. This harmony of wills (*eudoxia*) and the communion of action to which it gives rise, are what forms the composite personality (*henosis*) of Christ.

In the Nestorian system, therefore, we cannot speak of a

true communication of idioms, i.e., that while the two natures of Christ are distinct, the attributes of one may be predicated of the other in view of their union in the one person of Christ. Accordingly it could not be said that God was born, that He was crucified or died; Mary is not the Mother of God, except in the broad sense of giving birth to a man whose human personality was conjoined to the Word of God.

Nestorianism did not disappear with the Council of Ephesus. Twenty years later the Council of Chalcedon (451), which condemned Eutyches for confounding the two natures in Christ, also took issue with Nestorius. In the next century, the II Council of Constantinople (553) again rejected the Nestorian theory while extolling the orthodoxy of Cyril of Alexandria.

Through the efforts of Ibas, Bishop of Ephesus from 435, and Barsumas, Bishop of Nisibis from 457, Nestorianism was developed into a rounded theology and transported to Persia and Asia Minor where a small but influential sect was founded. The Nestorian Church survives to the present day under the name of Assyrian Christians.

Among other divergences from the Eastern Orthodox, the Nestorian Church has dropped a number of the sacraments. Confirmation was at first identified with baptism and then omitted altogether; the sacrament of penance has gone out of use except in the rare case of reconciliation of an apostate; holy unction has also practically disappeared. An unusual fact about the Nestorian celebration of the Eucharist is that their original liturgical books had omitted the words of institution; and, in spite of efforts by certain missionaries of the Anglican Church to have books printed which include the words of Christ at the Last Supper, some Nestorian priests still omit the formula of consecration.

A studied comparison of the orthodox and heterodox Oriental bodies would further reveal the cleavage that separates these two segments of Christianity. It would also show how much the majority of Eastern Churches have in common with one whom they call the "Mother Church of the West."

16

PROTESTANTISM

There is a legitimate sense in which Protestantism refers to all Christian movements, other than the Roman Catholic Church, that share the heritage of Western Christianity. Even the Churches of Eastern Orthodoxy have been called "Protestant," because they place the seat of ecclesiastical authority outside the papacy and within the believing community.

But these are extensions of a term which has historical rootage. Protestantism as a type of the Christian religion stems from the Reformation, and especially from the work of Luther and Calvin. Four hundred years have changed many things in Protestantism, but they have not effaced the spirit and theological emphases first created by the Reformers in the sixteenth century. Indeed every effort at renewal within Protestant ranks has been based on the principles of the Reformation, whose importance in religious history can scarcely be exaggerated. It marked a turning point in Western civilization and developed a form of religion that is baffling in its complexity, and yet so influential there is no part of Christianity whose life has not been affected by the faith and polity of Protestantism.

HISTORICAL ORIGINS

The great Luther monument at Worms, unveiled in 1868, includes a number of statues of men who are popularly considered heralds of the Reformation. Luther's central figure is encircled by statues of Savonarola, Huss, Wyclif, Reuchlin and Peter Waldo. By implication these men were precursors of the principal doctrines of Luther and of Protestantism, whereas their contribution was definitely minor and often tenuous, with only the single thread of unity that all had some-how come into conflict with the papacy.

More recent historians admit the disparity of ways which led the Reformers away from Rome, and consider it super-fluous to find any forerunners of the original Luther whose genius alone, they feel, produced the Reformation and laid the foundations of Protestantism. However, one exception is admitted, namely, the influence of contemporary Nominalism, particularly in the form in which it was taught by William of Ockham (1300–1349). "I am a member of Ockham's school," Luther boasted. Time and again he referred to the debt he owed the fourteenth century philosopher for the ideas he used in his contest with Rome. Ockham's teaching was so much that of the schools through which Luther passed that the latter simply described him as "Magister meus."[1]

Ockham questioned the power of reason to prove the exist-ence of God, the immortality of the soul, and human freedom. He held that these truths can be known with certainty only through faith. A proposition may be true in philosophy and false in theology. The ultimate cause of the eternal law he placed in the divine will. Absolutely speaking, an unworthy person might be found worthy of heaven if God so willed it. According to his theory of acceptation, everything depends on the will of God; and no supernatural virtue is necessary in the justified. Repression of reason and opposition to ecclesiasti-cal authority were characteristic of Ockham. His political theories played an important part in the development of the conciliar movement, which placed a general council above the pope; and his radical separation of the Church from the world became tinder for the reforming zeal of Luther who looked with horror at the immorality of churchmen in high places and decided the only remedy was to sever relations with this "Babylon of iniquity."

Yet Ockham's influence on Luther must not be overstated. Too often the Reformation is conceived as only the end of a long line of lesser reforms, from the Lollards in England, through the Hussites and Waldenses on the continent, to the final conflagration. There were preludes, of course, of a prac-tical type, as with Wyclif, and more theoretical ones, as in

Ockham. But no precursors explain the changes which the Reformers introduced into Christian thought, or the revolutionary positions they adopted in theology.

The birthday of Protestantism is commonly dated October 31, 1517, when Martin Luther nailed his ninety-five theses to the church door of the castle at Wittenberg. Within ten years, every major difference from the parent Roman Catholicism had been stated by Luther, and whatever subsequent development took place only built on the foundations he laid with a clarity and vigor that prompted his friend Melanchthon to say that "Luther is a miracle among men. What he says and writes grips the heart and leaves a marvelous deep impression behind."

His basic principle was an appeal to conscience, personally enlightened by the Spirit, against what he called the accretions of the Roman Church. Standing before the Diet of Worms in 1521, and charged by the Empire with promoting heresy, Luther replied in a statement that has become famous. The imperial judges asked him for a plain reply to this accusation. In a word, was he prepared to recant or not?

> Your Imperial Majesty and Your Lordships demand a simple answer. Here it is, plain and unvarnished. Unless I am convicted of error by the testimony of Scripture or—since I put no trust in the unsupported authority of Pope or of councils, since it is plain that they have often erred and often contradicted themselves—by manifest reasoning I stand convicted by the Scriptures to which I have appealed, and my conscience is taken captive by God's word. I cannot and will not recant anything, for to act against our conscience is neither safe for us, nor open to us.
>
> On this I take my stand. I can do no other. God help me. Amen.[2]

During the next twenty-five years, until his death in 1546, Luther elaborated this theory of conscience to include the whole construct of the Reformation. The conscience, he taught, is bound up with the word of God in the Scriptures. Therefore, instead of popes and councils, Scripture alone (*sola Scriptura*) became the source of religious knowledge. By the time of the Formula of Concord (1577), this had been canonized into an article of faith, that "Holy Scripture alone is acknowledged as the only judge, norm, and rule, according to which, as by the only touchstone, all doctrines are to be examined and judged, as to whether they are godly or ungodly, true or false."[3] Language could not be clearer on the Scriptures as the fountainhead of all doctrine and the only standard of Christian belief.

However, Scriptures themselves need an interpreter. Since ecclesiastical authority was ruled out, the alternative was the indwelling Spirit of God. Both the antecedent question of which books of the Bible are inspired, and the problem of determining what a given passage means, are subject not to the whims of a human institution (like the Church) but to the ever-present divine light in the soul. If this idea was thematic in Luther, it was systematized by John Calvin in his *Institutes of the Christian Religion,* first published in 1536, to become the greatest single legacy of the Reformation and the *Summa Theologica* of Protestantism.

Accordingly, the principle that by the Spirit alone (*solo Spiritu*) do we understand the Scriptures was axiomatic. "The testimony of the Spirit is more excellent than all reason. For as God alone is a fit witness of Himself in His Word, so also the Word will not find acceptance in men's hearts before it is sealed by the inward testimony of the Spirit." So that "those whom the Holy Spirit has inwardly taught truly rest upon Scripture," and "the certainty it deserves with us, it attains by the testimony of the Spirit. For even if it wins reverence for itself by its own majesty, it seriously affects us only when it is sealed upon our hearts through the Spirit. Therefore, illumined by His power, we believe neither by our own nor by any one else's judgment that Scripture is from God," or that a given meaning attached to a biblical text is divinely true. "But above human judgment we affirm with utter certainty, just as if we were gazing upon the majesty of God Himself, that it has flowed to us from the very mouth of God."[4]

Among the verities that Luther and Calvin were convinced the Spirit had taught them by the ministry of the Word was the complete depravity of human nature since the fall, and consequently that whatever good we do or hope we have of heaven come only from grace (*sola gratia*) and not at all from the effort or good works of man.

Basic to the Reformation theology of grace was the principle that original justice was due to human nature by a strict right of essence. "Original justice," wrote Luther, "was part of man's nature."[5] As a result, when Adam fell and lost the righteousness he possessed, his nature became essentially corrupt and his faculties were intrinsically vitiated. Nothing in the literature of historic Protestantism is more emphatically asserted against the "scholastic innovators" who misinterpreted revelation and the teaching of St. Augustine.

"See what follows," urged Luther, "if you maintain that original righteousness was not a part of nature but a sort of superfluous or superadded gift. When you declare that righteousness was not a part of the essence of man, does it not also follow that sin, which took its place, is not part of the essence of man either?"[6] If this were so, "there was no purpose in sending Christ the Redeemer," whose unique function was to win the grace we need to supply for our complete helplessness and inability to do any good. If, then, we are saved all the credit belongs to God and none to us; grace alone accounts for man's salvation and not in any sense the works of man, whose corruption is capable of nothing but sin and whose freedom, in Luther's phrase is "only an empty phrase." To God alone the glory, therefore, and to His grace the thanks.

One final element belongs to the foundations of Reformation thought, the doctrine that by faith alone (*sola fide*) are we saved, namely, by an absolute trust in God's mercy that in spite of our sinfulness the merits of His Son will hide our sins and spare us from the hell fire that we justly deserve. In the words of the Augsburg Confession (1530), "Our works cannot reconcile us to God or merit remission of sins and grace and justification. This we obtain only by faith, when we believe that we are received into grace on account of Christ." And to make sure there is no mistaking this trust for the dogmatic faith of Catholics, who made acceptance of revealed truths the first requisite for salvation, "Men are warned that the word *faith* does not signify the knowledge of an event— the devils and impious men have that—but it signifies a faith which believes not in an event merely, but also in the effect of an event, namely this article, the remission of sins, i.e., that we have, through Christ, grace, righteousness, and remission of sins."[7]

Thus we have the full complement of principles on which the structure of classic Protestantism was built, likened to the pillars of a massive building: the interior conscience instead of external authority, the Scriptures rather than ecclesiastical tradition, the interior Spirit supplying for the pope and councils, divine grace making up for the innate deficiency of will, and confident trust relying on the promise of the Savior, "because consciences cannot be quieted by any good works, but by faith alone, when they believe assuredly that they have a God who is propitiated for the sake of Christ."[8]

In the four centuries since these concepts were propounded, they have undergone much development and seen applications that Luther and Calvin never suspected, but their original spirit has not been lost. This spirit has remained fairly constant, and still serves to unite what is externally the most fragmented form of Christianity in existence, whose very beginnings were marked by cleavage and division. For although it is true that Luther was the first of the Protestant Reformers, the churches of the Reformation really had four beginnings: under Luther, Calvin, Henry VIII and the Anabaptists, all within a generation of that Eve of All Saints in Wittenberg. Each prototype has since grown into a multitude of churches and denominations that, in spite of mergers and overlappings, still retain characteristic elements that are traceable to their respective ancestry, along with the common features that first marked the origins of Protestantism.

LUTHERAN AND EVANGELICAL CHURCHES

The religious crisis which Luther and his followers precipitated in Germany occasioned a series of conferences which became landmarks in the history of Protestantism. Summoned by Charles V to the Diet of Worms, Luther refused to submit and was condemned as an outlaw, but taken by the Elector of Saxony into protective custody. Eight years later, at the Diet

of Speyer (1529), the Lutheran princes refused to agree that
Catholic worship should be free everywhere and the new religion be allowed only in places where it already had some
followers. Their "protest" at Speyer became symbolic of the
whole movement and gave the name by which the Churches
of the Reformation have since become known. When the Diet
of Speyer proved inoperative, the Emperor called the Diet of
Augsburg (1530) to effect a reconciliation between the Catholics and Reformers. While this attempt failed, a compromise
was reached among the factions in the Protestant camp and
the agreement was stabilized in the Confession of Augsburg,
for which Melanchthon wrote an Apology after the creedal
statement was challenged by the Catholics. Both documents
are now doctrinal standards in Churches of the Lutheran
tradition.

Luther's productivity was phenomenal. There are four Weimar editions of his writings, amounting to eighty-three volumes. The current English translation will run to fifty-five volumes in octavo. His two catechisms, a larger and smaller,
were originally intended "for the improperly indoctrinated
Roman clergy who had joined the evangelicals and to the
teachers of the parochial schools." They have since been recognized as the most unique of his writings and the most influential, in marked contrast with the polemic tracts he was
forced to compose to meet the steady opposition toward leaders of the Reformation.

After Luther's death, the area of conflict widened between
his own evangelical disciples and the followers of Calvin and
Zwingli. Questions of sin and grace, justification and free will,
the ministry and the Lord's Supper, baptism and predestination divided the different groups, even among the Lutherans,
who were partially reconciled by the Formula of Concord,
which is the last of their fundamental confessions of faith.

By the middle of the seventeenth century, Lutheranism had
been established not only in Germany and Central Europe,
but in Denmark, where the Church was organized in 1536
with the king as ruling prelate, in Sweden, East Prussia, Ice-
land, Hungary, Silesia, Poland, and Transylvania. The first
Lutherans to make a permanent settlement in America came

from Holland to the Dutch New Netherlands (Manhattan) in 1623. Their estimated world membership is eighty million.

DOCTRINE AND WORSHIP. Justification by faith alone lies at the heart of Lutheranism, which strenuously opposes any kind of synergism (Greek *syn*, "with," and *ergon*, "work"), that in the act of conversion the human will can cooperate with the Holy Spirit and God's grace. Its emphasis is always on God's sole activity in the process of salvation.

According to the Augsburg Confession, man has some freedom of the will in matters which do not concern salvation. But in things spiritual, no freedom is left to the natural man, who "cannot work the inward motions, such as the fear of God, trust in God, chastity, patience and the like."[8] Everything in the moral order is the fruit of grace alone. Modern Lutheran manuals of theology are equally intransigent. "One of the consequences of the hereditary corruption is the loss of free will in spiritual matters." And "if by free will is meant the ability to will or desire what is spiritually good . . . we deny that since the Fall man has a free will."[9]

Unlike the Reformed Churches, however, Lutheran bodies abstain from examining too closely into the mystery of predestination which is painfully raised by the denial of freedom in contact with grace. They concentrate on the confidence we should have in God's mercy and the gratitude we owe Him for His promised redemption. In the Evangelical tradition, therefore, God has done everything for us; we have only to trust and give Him thanks. He has already forgiven us; we need only accept His benefit with appreciation. He has already come to us in the person of the Savior; so that nothing can separate us from this treasury of goodness.

Lutheran Churches retain in large measure the pre-Reformation idea of the Atonement as something objective, and not merely personal to each individual. One modification, however, is that they do not consider the sufferings of Christ a satisfaction for sin but a punishment which Christ underwent vicariously on our behalf. This concept of the Atonement is a prominent feature of Lutheran preaching and liturgical hymns.

No area of Lutheran theology more clearly distinguishes it from others, notably the Calvinist, than the doctrine of the Eucharist. Lutherans repudiate any idea of the presence of Christ in the Eucharist in a purely spiritual manner. They hold that He is present in a bodily way, and the communicants partake physically of His body and blood, along with the visible elements. "The body and blood of Christ are received with the bread and wine, not only spiritually by faith, but also orally, in a supernatural and celestial way, because of the sacramental union. He who eats this bread eats the body of Christ."[10] Unlike the Catholic belief, there is no transubstantiation but a kind of impanation (in-breadness) in which Christ's presence exists alongside the substance and accidents of bread and wine, the union between elements and Christ being called sacramental. In the Formula of Concord, the body and blood are said to be present "in, with and under" the bread and wine. Technically the doctrine is known as *consubstantiation.*

Behind this theory is the application of a principle of Christology, adapted from the teaching of Chalcedon, that the two natures in Christ are not commingled or confused, yet are inseparably united. The Reformed Churches maintained that after the Ascension Christ's human nature was on the right hand of the heavenly Father, and therefore only His divinity was really present in the Eucharist, together with a virtual (but not bodily) presence of His humanity. Lutherans objected that such separation is impossible, so that wherever Christ is present, He is there both as God and man, hence also in the Eucharist.

Upholding the ancient faith that Christ is true God and man, Lutherans made the miracle of the Incarnation central in their tradition and the focus of all their teaching. It was, particularly, concern to preserve such fundamental doctrines as the divinity of Christ that has led Lutheran Churches the world over to promote Christian day schools and, at great sacrifice, build an impressive system of religion-centered education. When civil pressures threatened the parochial schools, they were quick to defend their educational policy.

Whereas the Word of God, our rule of life, enjoins upon all Christian parents the duty of bringing up their children in the nurture and admonition of the Lord; therefore all Christians who educate their children in schools are in duty bound to entrust their children to such schools only as secure the education of children in the nurture and admonition of the Lord, while at the same time it is with us self-understood that we are willing to make good citizens of our children, to the utmost of our ability.[11]

In the development of Lutheran forms of worship, the basic structure was the Roman Catholic Mass, "purged of non-evangelical elements and adapted for the ordinary worshiper." Among the major changes, the most important was the removal of sacrificial prayers from the Canon of the Mass. Luther himself carried out this reform. His idea was to give expression to the doctrine of the Eucharistic Presence without the concept of sacrifice.

The normal sequence of the Canon is the Preface, Sanctus, Words of Institution, Lord's Prayer, Pax Domini, Agnus Dei, and distribution of Holy Communion. In giving the elements to the faithful, the minister says, "Take, eat; this is the true body (blood) of our Lord and Savior Jesus Christ, given into death for (shed for the remission of) your sins. May this strengthen and preserve you in the true faith unto life everlasting."

Another change was to make the sermon an essential part of the Eucharistic service. The word of God, in the sense of the word that is preached, remains to this day a prominent feature of Lutheranism. Orders of worship prescribe the sermon after the Nicene Creed and before the Offertory.

Another innovation that has since become part of most other Protestant churches was the singing of hymns by the congregation during the Communion service. As early as 1526 Luther composed his German Mass (*Deutsche Messe*), in which the *Credo* and *Agnus Dei* were replaced by German hymns so that the whole congregation could sing together. He also replaced the Latin Introit by a hymn in the vernacular and added a prescriptive hymn after the Epistle in place of the Gradual. Luther's love of music was proverbial, and faithful to his memory the churches have made religious songs almost coextensive with divine worship.

Among the authors in common use are Saints Ambrose, Bede, and Bernard of Clairvaux, the Dominican Savonarola, non-Lutheran Reformers like John Huss and the two Wesleys, and more recent writers like John Keble and William Cullen Bryant. Most of the composers are Protestant, but a few Catholics (Palestrina, Gounod and Tallis) are included in standard hymnals. Typical of the robust virility and authentic evangelical theology of the hymns is the well-known masterpiece of Luther, *Ein' feste Burg ist unser Gott.*

A mighty Fortress is our God, a trusty Shield and Weapon;
He helps us free from every need that hath us now overtaken.
   The old evil Foe now means deadly woe;
Deep guile and great might are his arms in fight; on earth is not
      his equal.
      With might of ours can naught be done, soon were our loss
      effected;
But for us fights the Valiant One, whom God Himself elected.
      Ask you, who is this? Jesus Christ it is, of Sabbath Lord,
And there's none other God; He holds the field forever.
      Though devils all the world should fill, all eager to devour us,
We tremble not, we fear no ill, they shall not overpower us.
      This world's prince may still scowl fierce as he will, he can
      harm us none,
He's judged; the deed is done; one little word can fell him.[12]

Customs differ greatly in different countries. In Germany, for instance, the liturgical heritage of Lutheranism has been much reduced; in the United States it is growing at a pace so rapid that concern has been expressed over the "ritualistic movement," comparable to the High and Low Church types in Anglicanism. Lutheran bodies closer to the Reformation spirit have altars, altar candles, vestments, and an order of worship which are remarkably Roman Catholic in external form.

RECENT DEVELOPMENTS. All the principal Lutheran Churches of Reformation times were established institutions following the norm of the Augsburg Treaty of 1555, *cujus regio, ejus religio,* which meant that civil rulers determined the religious affiliation of their subjects. To this day, Lutheranism is the state religion of Norway, Sweden, Denmark and Finland. In Germany the Lutheran Churches continued to be established bodies until the Weimar Constitution of 1919, when Church and State were declared separated throughout the country.

In Scandinavia, the national bodies are supported financially by the civil authorities and administered by a ministry of ecclesiastical affairs, which is a joint Ministry of Church and Education in Norway and Sweden. Except for assistant pastors, bishops and clergy are appointed by the Crown, and Parliament acts as the Church's highest legislative body, in spite of the fact that members of Parliament need not belong to the Lutheran Church.

The European trend has been in the direction of emancipating the Church from political control, and giving it independence in purely spiritual matters. Sweden has a national Church Assembly that can vote on ecclesiastical issues, present recommendations to Parliament, and exercise a kind of veto; but the legal competence of the assembly is naturally limited as long as the Church is officially established. In the United States the congregation is the basic unit of Lutheran church government, with no semblance of the close tie-in with civil powers as in Europe.

During the nineteenth century, two competing theological trends in Lutheranism struggled for mastery in Europe, with heavy overtones in America. In 1821, Friedrich Schleiermacher (1768–1834) published his *Christian Faith* which dates an epoch in the history of modern theology. While rationalists and supernaturalists carried on their fight in schools of divinity, Schleiermacher took the ground from under their contention by removing its main premise. The Christian faith, he claimed, does not consist in any kind of doctrinal propositions. It is a condition of devout feeling and, like all other internal experience, simply an object to be described.

Against the supernaturalists Schleiermacher maintained that Christianity is not something to be received on authority from without, but an inward state of our own self-consciousness.

Against the rationalists he said religion is not a product of rational thinking, but an emotion of the heart, a feeling which occurs independently of the mind.

The net result of this emphasis on subjective experience was to usher Low Church mentality into Lutheran circles, with an undervaluation of the sacraments and a new stress on revivalism. There was a correlative downgrading of church authority and the development of an ecclesiastical structure built along Free Church and Congregational lines.

In the opposite direction, Lutheran confessionalism reacted against the liberal tendencies of the Enlightenment and the "religion of feeling" to inaugurate what can only be called a Lutheran Renascence. Since the beginning of the present century, interest in Luther's theology and Reformation thought has become the dominant characteristic of the Evangelical Churches. German and Swedish scholars have been the mainstay of the movement, but supported by Danish and Flemish theologians.

One effect of this renascence has been the discovery in Reformation sources of doctrinal principles that lay hidden for centuries, principles that are being exploited in the current drive for Christian unity. The *Una Sancta* movement brings together priests, ministers, theologians and laymen to discuss the prospects of uniting Catholic and Evangelical Christianity. *Die Sammlung* (The Gathering) is a more advanced group of Lutheran pastors which sees in Roman Catholicism a balance that Lutherans desire to reach the fulness of their own Reformation ideals.

In a declaration of principles, *Die Sammlung* calls upon Catholics and Lutherans alike to re-examine their respective positions to find out whether a corporate reunion is possible, without compromise of doctrinal convictions. Under title of the League for Evangelical-Catholic Reunion, the leaders of the movement bear witness to the fact that Christ founded only one Church, which exists in the realm of the visible and is always present, and that according to Scripture and universal Christian belief visible unity is inherent in the nature of the true Church.

The League considers the present division of Christians

against the will of Christ. "It is a sin and scandal." Without seeking to blur or level off confessional differences that exist within the Evangelical Church, *Die Sammlung* believes that these contrasts can be overcome only if it should first enter into Catholic unity. Its duty is to strive for the gathering together and the formation of an Evangelical church community united with the Roman Catholic Church.

> Corporate reunion with the Catholic Church is commanded because the Catholic Church is the closest to Evangelical Christendom historically, geographically, and spiritually, in comparison with the Churches of the East. It is also commanded because the essential Catholic content of Revelation is already explicitly and visibly transmitted in Sacred Scripture as confirmed in great measure by Evangelical exegetes of modern times, and this content is preserved and defended by the Catholic Church. In it is also found subordination to the authoritative rule of the Apostles and of the Bishops, established by them. From this flows a duty insufficiently comprehended by the Reformation.
>
> Evangelical Christendom must learn that the Bishops, having at their head the possessor of the Petrine Office, make decisions with the authority of the Holy Ghost, which are binding in conscience for the individual Christian.[13]

If sentiments like these are comparatively rare, the spirit behind them is becoming more deeply felt in Lutheran writers and churchmen on both sides of the Atlantic. They are impelled, they say, by the will of God, by Evangelical responsibility for Catholic unity, and a concern to save the Church of Christ from the assaults of Communism.

An interesting sidelight of the *Sammlung* approach has been the restoration of community religious life in the Lutheran Churches. While still on a microscopic scale, the idea has taken hold in Germany and the States and shows signs of further development. The Sisters of St. Mary on the continent were founded in 1944 at Darmstadt. One of their main concerns is to pray for the unity of Christendom. Members wear a religious habit of austere gray, and they all pledge to live according to the three evangelical counsels of poverty, chastity and obedience. After a year's probation, the novitiate lasts from four to five years. The Sisters maintain a continuous vigil of prayer, holding services in a chapel, and engage in works of charity by caring for children, helping the sick, imprisoned and delinquent. They also do catechetical work.

In America a similar organization was started by a group of men who call themselves the Congregation of the Servants of Christ. The articles of incorporation set forth that "the rule, life and worship of the Congregation shall be in agreement with the Augsburg Confession."

CALVINIST AND REFORMED TRADITION

Reformed Protestantism stems from the teachings of John Calvin, synthesized in his massive *Institutes of the Christian Religion,* and for that reason often simply called Calvinism. Its doctrinal position has been stabilized in the Reformed Churches of Europe and America, and the Presbyterian bodies in France, England and the United States. Baptists have also been deeply influenced by Calvinism.

Similar to the symbolic writings of the Lutherans, there are Reformed confessional documents, but they have never played a major role in the Churches' life and policy. The main reason is that the Scriptures hold a towering position in Calvinism, with everything else, including "articles of faith," relegated to second place. Yet the importance of doctrinal standards should not be minimized; it is only that they are relatively less binding than their Evangelical counterparts.

In Switzerland the most important confessional statements are the two Helvetic Confessions of 1536 and 1566, and the *Consensus Tigurinus* of 1549. Where the Confessions are strongly Zwinglian, the *Consensus* is a compromise document drawn up by Calvin. A feature of all three is the doctrine of the Eucharist, which oscillates between the pure symbolism of Zwingli (1484–1531) and the Calvinist theory that Christ is present in Holy Communion "for all who truly believe."

In France the composition of Calvin, *Confessio Gallicana,* first drafted in 1559 at a general synod of St. Germain, is still the confessional document of the French Reformed Church. Predestination is lucidly expounded in a long article and the Eucharist is said to be received by the communicant *spirituellement*. Germany produced a parallel statement of faith in the Heidelberg Catechism of 1563, a practical and edifying work with a moderate Eucharistic and Christological doctrine. In order to avoid offending the Lutherans, there is no express mention of Predestination, but a strongly anti-Catholic tone pervades the document. The Heidelberg Catechism has become popular also in Switzerland, Hungary and Poland. In 1566 the Netherlands adopted their *Confession Belgica,* approved by a synod held at Antwerp, as the last continental document of this type compiled during the Reformation.

The Reformed faith was recognized as the national religion by the Scottish Parliament in 1560, and in the same year published the *Confessio Scoticana,* which is mildly Calvinist, with an almost Lutheran doctrine of the Eucharist and the doctrine on Predestination expressed in ambivalent terms.

However the most significant statement of Calvinist teaching is not a *Confessio* but a set of Canons formulated (1619) by the Synod of Dortrecht (Dort) in the Dutch Reformed Church. The document arose out of a heated controversy on the question of Predestination. Most ministers and theologians in Holland held the doctrine in its full severity. God had from eternity arbitrarily chosen some persons for heaven and predestined others to damnation, irrespective of their faith or good works and dependent solely on the inscrutable will of God.

A less absolute tendency was advocated by the Arminian party, named after Jacob Arminius (1560–1609), professor at Leyden. Under adverse pressure from the orthodox clergy, they submitted a Remonstrance to the government in which they stated five theses that favored Catholic teaching on grace and became the subject of a celebrated controversy. God's predestination, they stated, rests upon His foreknowledge that certain people will persevere to the end; Christ died for all men, although only believers share in His merits; divine grace is not irresistible and it is possible for a person once in grace to lose the friendship of God.

In view of its importance, the synod invited Reformed representatives from other countries, including delegates from England. In its one hundred and thirty-seventh session, the Arminians were declared heretics and a detailed statement of orthodox Calvinism was compiled. It said in substance that the election of the predestined depends solely on God, Christ died only for the predestined, grace cannot be resisted, and those who have received irresistible grace cannot subsequently fall away.

The Westminster Confession was formulated in 1646, to become the standard of doctrine for Presbyterian Churches in the British Isles and America. A critical passage in the American version was changed with regard to the papacy. From an originally polemic statement, the present text reads, "the claim of any man to be the vicar of Christ and the head of the Church is unscriptural, without warrant in fact, and is a usurpation dishonoring to the Lord Jesus Christ."[14]

DISTINCTIVE FEATURES. The guiding motif of Churches in the Reformed tradition is the affirmation of God's sovereign majesty. Every phase of doctrine, worship and church policy is affected by this stress. Where Lutheranism might be described as anthropological, because its central doctrine is man's salvation, Calvinism is theocentric in that its governing principle is the service and glory due to God from His creatures.

Confessional standards repeatedly speak of the Glory of God which is man's universal purpose in existence. Thus the Genevan Catechism begins with the statement that "God has created us, and put us into this world in order that He might be glorified by us," and the first response of the Shorter Westminster Catechism reads, "Man's chief end is to glorify God."

Consistent with this accent, the distance between God and man is brought out in the strongest terms. In the Westminster Catechism, it is said "the distance between God and the creature is so great that although reasonable creatures do owe obedience unto Him as their Creator, yet they could never have any fruition of Him, as their blessedness and reward, but by some voluntary condescension of God's part, which He hath been pleased to express by way of covenant."[15]

Predestination and Election are organically connected with this notion of sovereignty. Since man's salvation is due entirely to God and man contributes nothing, all the praise is due to the Creator, even when He condemns the damned to eternal sufferings.

Unexpectedly the Reformed doctrine on grace has not paralyzed human activity. If anything it stimulates action, though of a particular kind. Predestination serves the function of an ethical motive, on the assumption that those who reflect on this mystery are all chosen to heavenly glory. Armed with the conviction that they are predestined, believers can afford to rejoice at their happy lot and go about life's affairs with a nonchalance that might scandalize less hardy Christians.

The whole complex of Reformed mentality on this subject is illustrated in Karl Barth, the Swiss theologian, whose commentary on the Lord's Prayer is a witness to the abiding Calvinist tradition in modern times. In the fifth petition of the Our Father are two suppositions that seem irreconcilable with orthodox Calvinism. For when we ask God to forgive us our trespasses, we imply that in some sense our sins are not yet remitted and that our prayers will contribute to this remission. When we add, "as we forgive those who trespass against us," the implication is that our own practice of merciful charity somehow determines the degree of mercy that God will bestow on us.

But Barth will have none of either. We pray, "forgive us our trespasses," and with good reason, because our lives are continuously sinful. Can our prayer for mercy avail us to obtain pardon? Not at all. "Neither man's offense, nor man himself as a sinner can be exculpated. Man is unpardonable. He has no right whatsoever to ask for a remission of his debt."[16]

Perhaps, Barth suggests, we place some kind of condition when we pray that shows God's forgiveness is somehow determined by ourselves. "No, the phrase: as we forgive those who trespass against us, is only a necessary sign to make us understand the pardon of God." When He forgives us, we become conscious of His mercy and confident of salvation.

This confidence "necessarily opens wide our hearts, our feelings and our judgment with regard to our fellowmen." Some people mistakenly suppose the words, "as we forgive," are an appeal for the practice of charity. They are wrong. "This is not an exhortation, 'Come, be merciful,' but a simple statement of fact: 'When you receive forgiveness from God, you become capable of forgiveness to others.'"[17] In other words, prayer is essentially an expression of gratitude for graces received, not a petition to obtain them, and for the elect who are sure of their destiny this gratitude can well pour itself out in deeds of generosity.

Reformed teaching on the sacraments is distinctive. God is not bound by the sacramental instruments of grace, and, in any case, they are effectual only to the elect. They are "holy signs and seals of the covenant of grace," whose efficacy somehow depends "upon the work of the Spirit, and the word of institution, which contains, together with a precept authorizing the use thereof, a promise of benefit to worthy receivers."[18]

Baptism does not remit sin, but signifies becoming "ingrafted into Christ," and though it does not effect regeneration, yet infant baptism is retained. The Eucharistic doctrine has been the focus of controversy with Evangelical Protestantism since Reformation times and, like the Calvinist position on Predestination, has been much modified through tension. Present-day Reformed theology steers a middle course between the purely symbolic conception of Zwingli, who limited the sacrament to a commemorative meal and a confession of faith in Christ, and the Lutheran idea of a bodily presence and oral participation. Christ is in the Eucharist, they say, really but not bodily; and only the believers partake of Him. Familiar terms are "dynamic presence" and "virtual presence," whereby the communicant receives "the sacrificial virtue or effects of the death of Christ on the Cross."

Most characteristic of Reformed Protestantism is its unitary concept of the governing ministry. There is only one type of authority, the presbytery, but four kinds of office: pastors, teachers, elders and deacons. Presbyteries are usually organized on a geographical basis, but some exist to care for separate language groups or racial minorities. Although there are two grades of jurisdiction technically higher than the presbytery, the latter is the principal ruling body. Presbyteries consist of clerical and lay representatives within a given district, with power to receive and issue appeals or complaints, examine and license candidates for the ministry, resolve questions of doctrine and discipline, unite and divide congregations and, in general, care for whatever pertains to the spiritual welfare of the churches within the presbytery. It is more than coincidental that the only layman among the major Reformers in the sixteenth century, John Calvin, should have developed a form of polity that gives the laity equal share with the clergy in church government. This idea was soon borrowed by other religious bodies and is now practically universal in Protestantism.

FREE CHURCH MOVEMENT

The basic idea behind the Free Church Movement is nonconformity with established Protestant religions, which took different forms in different countries. On the continent the Anabaptists, Mennonites, and Brethren; in England the Separatists, including Quakers, Baptists and Congregationalists—professed the Free Church principle of dissociating from the doctrines, polity and discipline of the dominant Protestant body in their respective territory.

Continental Free Churchism began with the Anabaptists, the "rebaptizers" who refused to allow their children to be baptized and instituted the baptism of adult believers. They argued that the Reformers were unfaithful to their own tenet of *sola Scriptura* by allowing children to be baptized, since the Bible knows only the baptism of adults. Gradually the Protestant theory of private interpretation led to a cluster of other Anabaptist beliefs and practices which have remained in possession to modern times.

One of the earliest non-conformists was Thomas Munzer (1490–1525) and the Zwickau prophets who appeared at Wittenberg in 1521. Munzer favored the Peasants' Revolt (1525) and taught a doctrine of the Inner Light which reappeared later among the English Quakers. The Swiss Brethren reintroduced believer's baptism as a condition for church membership at Zurich in 1525, along with non-resistance and rejection of Christian participation in civil government. Soon these views spread throughout Switzerland and into Germany.

Communities that found asylum in Moravia, and led by Jacob Hutter (died 1536), founded settlements based on the idea of common property. After many wanderings and trials, the Hutterites became established in Central Europe or migrated to America. A group of Anabaptists in Munster attempted to form a Kingdom of the Saints, whose left-wing segment advocated polygamy. The idea was later revived among the American Mormons or Latter-Day Saints, under the reputed revelations of Joseph Smith (1805–1844). After the Munster episode, the Mennonites were reorganized in Holland and Friesland by Menno Simons (1496–1561), who first left the Catholic Church, joined the Anabaptists, and then founded his own denomination on the twin principle of independent church organization and no common doctrine.

The Anabaptists were vigorously denounced by Luther, Zwingli and Calvin, who encouraged their suppression by force of arms. Their influence on the English Separatists (Baptists, Congregationalists, and Quakers) places them in lineal relationship to the Free Church movement in Anglo-Saxon countries.

John Smyth (1570–1612), exiled Anglican minister, started the Baptists at Amsterdam in 1609, when he instituted the baptism of conscious believers as the basis of fellowship in a gathered church. Many Baptists were associated with the more radical spiritual and political movements in England in the seventeenth century. They were pioneers in pleas for freedom of conscience and religious liberty. John Bunyan (1628–1688), author of *The Pilgrim's Progress,* was an outstanding figure among them, not only because of his writings but because he advocated a Church community which should include Baptists and paedo-baptists (those who baptized infants).

Most of the Baptist population of the world (about ninety percent) is in the United States, divided into more than twenty bodies and following a modified Calvinism, tinged with Lutheran and Zwinglian elements. Since the stress is on baptism of believers, the attitude towards this sacrament is characteristic of Baptist theology as a whole. Baptism does not bring about the remission of sins or provide salvation. It is a symbol and "only a symbol of the blessed truths upon which remission of sins, salvation, and eternal life depend." There is nothing that comes after faith that is essential to salvation. With rare exception, baptism by immersion is considered essential.

In spite of their variety and individualism, most Baptists have remained strongly attached to the truths of evangelical Christianity. The popular evangelist, Billy Graham, became a Southern Baptist early in youth. Their worship is mainly in the Reformed tradition, and their church organization an American type of independency. Majority rule prevails in Baptist polity, "in accordance with the law of Christ." So that, "the will of the majority having been expressed, it becomes the minority to submit."[19]

Congregationalism is that form of church structure which rests on the independence and autonomy of each local church. It professes to represent the principle of democracy in Church government, said to have been the original type of organization founded by Christ and recognizing only Him as its head. Since all the members of the Church are Christians, they are all equally priests unto God. He is in their midst, wherever two or three are gathered in His name; their thoughts and actions are led by His spirit and, with no authoritarian laws to bind them, they are nevertheless united in Christ with the Church Universal.

The beginnings of Congregationalism are commonly dated from the founding, in 1581, of a church in Norwich, England, by Robert Browne, a Separatist Anglican minister. Browne was demoted from the ministry for teaching "seditious doctrines," notably that the basis of church membership was not submission to episcopal authority but acceptance of a covenant, to which a group of people gave their mutual consent. Pressure from the government forced Browne's followers to move to Holland, and then to America, where, as the Mayflower Pilgrims, they landed at Plymouth, Massachusetts, in 1620.

A few years later they were joined by a group of immigrant Puritans, with whom they signed a compact in 1629, and from whom they inherited a strong Calvinist creedalism that lasted almost two centuries. The Salem trials for witchcraft belong to the early period of New England Congregationalism. By 1730, however, the churches had become quite thoroughly secularized. This induced a reaction, called the Great Awakening, ushered in by Jonathan Edwards (1703–1758), pastor at Northampton, Massachusetts, who was consumed by the sovereignty of God, the fateful brevity of life and its eternal issues.

For more than two centuries, American Congregationalists were mainly concerned with higher education. Harvard was founded in 1636, Yale in 1701, to prepare students for the ministry. At present fifty-one colleges and universities in the United States have professedly Congregationalist affiliations. With expansion, however, came internal tension over doctrinal issues. Two conflicting tendencies threatened to dissolve Congregationalism. By the middle of the last century, about two thousand churches, originally Congregationalist, became Presbyterian; they were looking for a more authoritative and dogmatic church polity. And during the same period a smaller, but even more influential, group of liberals seceded to form the American Unitarian Association.

The current history of Congregationalism has been largely a story of mergers and unitive movements. In 1925, the Protestant Evangelical Church joined the Congregationalists. Six years later the Christian Churches merged to form the Congregational Christian denomination, and in 1957, the Evangelical and Reformed entered into organic union to produce the United Church of Christ, leaving only a segment of less than a hundred thousand Congregationalists still dedicated to the full import of their doctrine of local church autonomy.

Congregationalism has given a major impulse to the ecumenical movement. The constitutional basis of the World Council of Churches as "fellowship of churches" whose function is to "offer counsel and provide opportunity of united action" among its constituents, is a paraphrase of Congregational principles expanded to global proportions.

Quakers are the most distinctive form of Free Church ideology extant in English-speaking countries. More accurately known as the Society of Friends, the Quakers were organized as a separate Christian group in England in 1668, when George Fox (1624–1691) drew up his *Rule for the Management of Meetings*. They soon engaged in missionary work and in 1682 William Penn founded Pennsylvania on a Quaker basis.

The religious tenets of the Friends center around the idea of the Inner Light, first professed by George Fox and since become their focal doctrine. No Quaker has improved on the description of this Light given by Fox, and all Quakers subscribe to his definition.

> The Lord hath opened to me by His invisible power how that every man was enlightened by the divine Light of Christ; and I saw it shine through all; and that they that believed in it came out of condemnation and came to the Light of Life, and became the children of it; but they that hated it, and did not believe in it, were condemned by it, though they made a profession of Christ. This I saw in the pure openings of the Light, without the help of any man, neither did I then know where to find it in the Scriptures, though afterwards, searching in the Scriptures, I found it. For I saw in that light and Spirit which was before the Scripture was given forth, and which led the holy men of God to give them forth, that all must come to that Spirit—if they would know God or Christ or the Scriptures aright—which they that gave them forth were led and taught by.[20]

According to the theory of the Light, its possession consists mainly in the sense of the Divine, and the direct working of God in the soul, by which a man is freed from sin, joined to Christ, and enabled to perform good works. From the paramount importance given to the Inner Light derives the Quaker rejection of the sacraments, the ministry, and all set forms of worship. Their meetings are ideally held in bare rooms and begin in silence, in "holy expectation before the Lord" until some member of the congregation feels inspired to speak.

Church organization is democratic, ranging from Preparative Meetings which consist of single congregations, to Yearly

Meetings that comprise a whole country (as in England) or the Five Years' Meeting that forms one of several Quaker denominations in the United States.

The Quaker refusal to give military service and take oaths involved them in frequent conflict with civil authorities, more in Great Britain than America, and since the early nineteenth century the Friends have pioneered in promoting legislation in favor of conscientious objectors to war. Their devotion to social and educational work, as well as their high standards of personal integrity, have won popular support to their side and helped in the advancement of such humane movements as the elimination of slavery.

ANGLICAN HERITAGE

When the Tudor sovereigns in the sixteenth century decided to measure their strength against the Papacy, they found many elements in Great Britain to encourage their efforts. Criticism of ecclesiastical wealth, sporadic risings of antipapalism, remnants of the spirit of Lollardy which John Wyclif (1329–1384) initiated, merchants casting hungry glances at monastic property, religious dissatisfaction encouraged by the Renascence revolt against Scholasticism—all these were in the air when Henry VIII tried unsuccessfully to secure a divorce from his wife, Catherine of Aragon.

The historical origins of Anglicanism covered a period of thirty-six years, from 1527, when Henry VIII first proposed his divorce to ecclesiastical authorities, to 1563, when his daughter, Queen Elizabeth, promulgated the Thirty-nine Articles of the English Church. Between these dates the religious character of England completely changed.

Under pressure from Henry, the higher clergy disavowed the pope's spiritual jurisdiction in a famous "Abjuration of Papal Supremacy." At the Convocation of Canterbury in 1534, in reply to the question, "Whether the Roman Pontiff has any greater jurisdiction bestowed on him by God in the Holy Scriptures in this realm of England, than any other foreign (*externus*) bishop," they voted: Noes 34, Doubtful 1, Ayes 4. In the same year, the Convocation of York "unanimously and concordantly, with no dissentient," affirmed the same.[21]

During the minority of Henry's son, Edward VI, the Book of Common Prayer was published in two editions (1549 and 1552), first along Lutheran and then Calvinist lines. A new Ordinal was issued (1550–1552) following a Lutheran pattern, in which every mention of a priesthood offering sacrifice was carefully omitted from the ordination ritual. However the complete rupture with Catholicism did not come until 1563, when the Elizabethan Parliament made the Articles of Religion obligatory on all citizens under heavy penalties.

The main credit for establishing the English Church should be given to Queen Elizabeth (1533–1603) who inherited a religious problem at her accession and tried to solve it according to political expediency. When she became queen in 1558, the country as a whole was still predominantly Catholic, though with strong Calvinist undercurrents. Elizabeth disliked Catholics because they denied her legitimacy and spiritual supremacy, and the Calvinists because they abolished the episcopacy which she considered essential for the welfare of kings. Penal legislation was consistently directed against both elements. Among other laws, two Acts of 1593 were sweeping condemnations "of seditious sectaries and disloyal persons" who obstinately refused to attend Anglican church services, to be "committed to prison" and there to remain until they conform "according to Her Majesty's laws and statutes."[22]

After a century of controversy against Catholics and Puritans, the English Church settled down from 1689 to a period of quiet. The Methodist departure in the eighteenth century and the Oxford movement in the nineteenth marked the critical stages in a new Anglicanism, whose main features are still rooted in the Reformation but whose present status in the English-speaking world is in the nature of a compromise between historical Protestantism and the Catholic Church.

Episcopalianism, as the English Church is known in America, was brought to the colonies in 1607 by a group of English settlers who founded what is now Jamestown, Virginia. The Episcopalians officially left the parent Church at the time of the American Revolution, and proceeded to revise their juridical structure in a way compatible with a non-established denomination. They adopted the name Protestant Episcopal Church, which has been the subject of much discussion but emphasizes the unique character of American Episcopalianism: a democratic church united in spirit with the Anglican Communion throughout the world and committed to a policy of cooperation with other Protestant bodies, irrespective of their doctrinal traditions.

DOCTRINE AND WORSHIP. Although the Thirty-nine Articles are still included in manuals of instruction, they are not considered representative of what many Anglicans believe. Commentaries on the Articles range from extreme Reformed positions to an almost Roman Catholic interpretation, depending on the author and the tradition within which he is writing.

More typical of present-day Anglicanism are the broad principles enunciated at the General Convention of the Protestant Episcopal Church held at Chicago in 1886. In a revised form the Articles were approved two years later by the Lambeth Conference, the periodic assembly of Anglican bishops held at Lambeth Palace under the presidency of the Archbishop of Canterbury. The Lambeth Quadrilateral states the Anglican viewpoint on the essentials of religion. Its text has remained unchanged and serves as basis for reunion overtures with other Christian bodies.

> We believe that all who have been duly baptized with water in the name of the Father, and of the Son, and of the Holy Ghost, are members of the Holy Catholic Church;
>
> That in all things of human ordering or human choice relating to modes of worship and discipline, or to traditional customs, this Church is ready, in the spirit of love and humility, to forego all preferences of her own;
>
> That this Church does not seek to absorb other communions, but rather, cooperating with them on the basis of a common faith and order, to discountenance schism, to heal the wounds of the body of Christ, and to promote the charity which is the chief of Christian graces and the visible manifestation of Christ to the world.[23]

However, conscious that union among Christians is possible

"only by the principles of unity exemplified by the undivided Catholic Church during the first ages of its existence," the Quadrilateral isolates the four essentials of "this sacred deposit," which at once describes the substance of Anglicanism and the foundation for solidarity among the separated Churches.

> The Holy Scriptures of the Old and New Testaments, as the revealed Word of God.
>
> The Nicene Creed, as the sufficient statement of the Christian faith.
>
> The two sacraments, Baptism and the Supper of the Lord, ministered with unfailing use of Christ's words of institution, and of the elements ordained by Him.
>
> The Historic Episcopate, locally adapted in the methods of its administration to the varying needs of the nations and peoples called of God into the unity of His Church.[24]

Equally representative of the wide range of Anglican belief is the Book of Common Prayer, which historians believe has been the single most cohesive force in the English Church. The formula that the law of prayer is the law of belief expresses a fundamental norm of the Anglican Communion in modern times. Its liturgical life sets the standard for the Church's doctrine, and the past few generations have seen a number of far-reaching changes of emphasis. Today the liturgy is the keystone of harmony within the Churches derived from the English Reformation.

There are two main forms of the Book of Common Prayer, the revision made in England (1928) and the editions used in various countries, like the United States, where the Churches are juridically independent of Canterbury. The English revision was made over the protests of Parliament that refused to approve the moderately Anglo-Catholic version which the bishops submitted for government approval; it was therefore published without formal authority from the Crown. Different Prayer Books are substantially the same. All have set orders for Morning and Evening Prayer, for the administration of the Lord's Supper, baptism, and such "ordinances" as matrimony, visiting the sick and "making, ordaining and consecrating bishops, priests and deacons." Numerous Collects, Epistles and Gospels are offered for prayer on Sundays and Feast Days; they are drawn largely from the Roman Missal or other Catholic formularies. The complete Psalter is part of the Prayer Book, along with a Catechism, forms of prayer to be used in families, and the Articles of Religion.

Typical of the changes going on in Anglicanism, when the American Prayer Book was revised in 1928, most of the alterations affected the ultra-Protestant edition of 1552 and were a partial return to the more Catholic one of 1549. In the Offertory, Cranmer was by-passed in the direction of giving the Eucharist a definitely sacrificial tone. Answering to the demand for post-biblical saints to the liturgy, a new Proper was included, corresponding to the *Proprium Sanctorum* of the Roman Missal. Requiem Masses for the Dead were made legal, and prayers for the faithful departed were formally sanctioned. Since 1928, the Church at every Eucharistic liturgy has been remembering the souls of deceased persons, and beseeching God to grant them continual growth in His love. In the same way, extreme unction was at least partially restored as a sacrament of healing.

After three centuries of suppression in the Established Church, religious life was brought back in the middle nineteenth century, and today there are over one hundred Anglican religious communities of men and women in all parts of the world. While growing in size and influence, the communities are still in a fluid state. The most serious problem is ambiguity on the concept of religious life within Anglicanism. At the Lambeth Conference in 1958, the assembly declared how greatly it valued "the special form of vocation evident in Religious Orders and Communities" and hoped that "this form of vocation may find its expression in a wide range of ecclesiastical tradition." Yet the basic issue remained unsolved. The fourteenth of the Articles of Religion states that "voluntary works besides, over and above God's commandments, which they call works of supererogation, cannot be taught without arrogance and impiety." Newman had difficulty with this article when setting up his community at Littlemore. The tension has yet to be resolved.

Some years ago, the Archbishop of Canterbury, Geoffrey

Fisher, appointed a commission to study and report on the differences between Catholic and Protestant traditions within the Anglican Church, their causes and possible solution. Among other significant judgments which the commission reached was its estimate of the Papacy.

> It is one of the most remarkable facts in Christian history that the Papacy of the sixteenth century first cleansed itself of its vile and most notorious Renascence scandals, and then itself directed and impelled the cleansing of the Renascence Church.
>
> The easy way in which the Reformers, almost from the first, simply wrote off the Papacy even as a possibility, illustrates clearly the extent to which they ignored from the outset both the New Testament doctrine of the Universal Church as an inherent part of the Gospel, and the inherence of the Divine-human society in the here-and-now of history.
>
> If such an institution as the Universal Church is to exist, as more than a sentiment and an ideal, then some such central institution would seem to be more than just a convenience. It is at least a pragmatic necessity, as is shown by the obvious temptation of the modern ecumenical movement to try to provide a substitute for it.[25]

Sentiments like these are not uncommon in Anglican circles. They accentuate the middle-ground which the English Church and its derivatives occupy, between the individualism of the Protestant tradition and the visible unity of Catholicism under the Roman Pontiff.

METHODISM

The founder of Methodism, John Wesley (1703–1791), was an ordained priest of the Church of England who until the day of his death insisted he did not want to sever connection with the Church in which he was reared. Yet even before he died, the principles he elaborated and the stress in church policy he advocated led him to organize a distinct denomination, whose current membership in the world compares favorably with Anglicanism and, in the United States, is about three times the size of the Protestant Episcopal Church.

It is not easy to describe Methodism in doctrinal terms because Wesley himself stressed the minimal importance of belief, in the sense of confessional doctrine, and described his followers in a passage that has since become classic.

> The distinguishing marks of a Methodist are not his opinions of any sort. His assenting to this or that scheme of religion, his embracing any particular set of notions, his espousing the judgment of one man or of another are all quite wide of the point. Whosoever, therefore, imagines that a Methodist is a man of such or such an opinion is grossly ignorant of the whole affair; he mistakes the truth totally.
>
> We believe indeed that "all scripture is given by inspiration of God"; and herein we are distinguished from Jews, Turks, and infidels. We believe the written word of God to be the only rule both of faith and practice; and herein we are fundamentally distinguished from those of the Roman Church. We believe Christ to be the eternal, the supreme God; and herein we are distinguished from the Socinians and Arians. But as to all opinions which do not strike at the root of Christianity, we think and let think.[26]

Among the "opinions which do not strike at the root of Christianity," and on which his followers were free to dissent, were the character of the priesthood and the episcopate, the nature of Christ's presence in the Eucharist, and the role of the sacraments in the life of the Church.

But if Methodism allows considerable range in matters of doctrine, there is one element of its faith which not only distinguishes Methodists from their Anglican forebears but from orthodox Protestantism in general. This is their teaching on sanctification, which so closely resembles the Catholic doctrine on grace that some have called Wesley a "papist in disguise."

In his sermons and writings, Wesley constantly opposed the Calvinist theory of predestination. Even when he affirmed that God is the source of all human good, and that grace does not depend on any power or merit in man, he labored to show the untenability of any view that restricted salvation to the few who are elected by the unsearchable decrees of an arbitrary God. "The grace of God," he wrote, "whence cometh our salvation, is free in all, and free for all."[27]

When he revised the Thirty-nine Articles of the Anglican creed and sent them to America as a doctrinal basis for the new Methodist Episcopal Church, he eliminated the most extremely Calvinistic passages of Article nine, deleted the qualifying adverb *necessarily* from Article twelve, which says that good works "spring out necessarily of a true and lively faith," and entirely dropped Article seventeen, with its unqualified statement of predestinarianism.

Wesley's concern was mainly with the salvation of all men. He was convinced that Christ came to seek and save that which was lost, and the Church is commissioned to preach the Gospel of redemption. But if predestinarianism is true, Christ's advent was in vain and the whole task of evangelism a sham, because there is no need (or possibility) of saving the unsavable. Multitudes are beyond the love of God and nothing can be done to help them. He considered this a repudiation of the central truth of Christianity.

Methodism has since developed a well-integrated system of sanctification that rests on the prior belief that salvation is more than justification in the sense of removal (or hiding) of sin. It is a vital process that God intends to have grow with the passage of time and develop through man's cooperation. "Sanctification," according to the *Methodist Discipline*, "is that renewal of our fallen nature by the Holy Ghost, received through faith in Jesus Christ, whose blood of atonement cleanseth from all sin; whereby we are not only delivered from the guilt of sin, but are washed from its pollution, saved from its power, and are enabled, through grace, to love with all our hearts and to walk in His holy commandments blameless."[28]

Parallel with the Methodist teaching on sanctification is an emphasis on the Witness of the Spirit, who bears testimony to those who are reborn to God after a life of sin. By this witness is understood an inward impression on the soul, whereby the Spirit of God is believed immediately and directly to testify that a person is a child of God, that his sins are blotted out and that he is on the road to salvation.

This doctrine has inspired much of Methodist hymnology, composed by John Wesley's brother, Charles, in which the joyous experience of personal salvation is the dominant theme.

> No longer am I now afraid;
> Thy promise must take place.
> Perfect Thy strength in weakness made,
> Sufficient is Thy grace.
> Confident now of faith's increase,
> I all its fruits shall prove:
> Substantial joy, and settled peace,
> And everlasting love.
> Lord, I believe and rest secure
> In confidence divine
> Thy promise stands for ever sure,
> And all Thou art is mine.[29]

Correlative with a stress on religion as personal experience has been the Methodist conviction that Christianity is essentially social. "Solitary religion," declared Wesley, "is not to be found" in the Gospel. "'Holy solitaries' is a phrase no more consistent with the Gospel than holy adulterers. The Gospel of Christ knows no religion but social; no holiness, but social holiness."[30] This has deeply influenced Methodist thought and action, and stimulated what has since become a new religious dimension in the Western world. Wesley's followers were introduced into a fellowship in which moral, economic, and racial issues became an integral part of living the faith; Methodists became pioneers of the "Social Gospel" which has characterized so much of American (and Anglo-Saxon) Protestantism in modern times.

A typical area of Methodist social evangelism is the temperance movement. In the spirit of John Wesley, who forbade anyone even to touch "that liquid fire," Methodists have been leaders in opposing the sale and consumption of alcoholic beverages. "Our Church," they state, "reasserts its long-established conviction that intoxicating liquor cannot be legalized without sin." And "to be true to itself the Church must be militant in opposition to the liquor traffic," as evidenced in the Methodist promotion of what became the American Volstead Act. "Adequate relief can come only through total abstinence for the individual, and effective prohibition for the state."[31] Ministers are forbidden to indulge, and may be penalized for proved breach of their abstinence pledge.

Methodism has affected the religious thinking of many denominations outside its own immediate family. The Holiness movement stems from Wesley's doctrine on sanctification from which certain Methodist churches felt the general stream of his followers had departed. The result was a score of religious bodies, like the Nazarenes, Churches of God and Holiness Churches, which are juridically distinct but united in professing a number of basic tenets of Protestant perfectionism.

Besides justification, they hold, there is a "second blessing" in which a person feels himself closely united with God. This is an emotional experience produced in the heart by the direct action of the Holy Spirit. Although instantaneous, the "second blessing" may require years of preparation. As a group, Holiness bodies claim that the teachings and practices of the larger denominations have departed from the true faith and compromised with modernism. The favorite method of preaching is popular revivals, which used to be the regular mode of Methodist evangelism in colonial America. Most of the churches profess, without always stressing, the imminent second coming of Christ which is to inaugurate a millennium of earthly peace and happiness before the last day.

The extreme left wing of the Holiness movement developed into the Pentecostal Churches. They are similar to the Holiness churches in admitting the fundamentalist principles of Christ's divinity, inerrancy of the Bible, the Virgin Birth and Resurrection, Christ's atonement and the early second coming. There is also an emphasis on sanctification as a separate work of grace which follows justification, but with an added feature that characterizes the Pentecostals and accounts for their distinctive name. When the Holy Spirit comes to perfect a soul, His advent is not merely invisible; it manifests itself by an external outpouring of spiritual gifts, not unlike those bestowed on the Apostles at the first Pentecost, especially glossolalia or "speaking in foreign tongues, even as the Holy Spirit prompted them to speak."[32]

ECUMENICAL MOVEMENT

A new spirit has entered the body of American and world Protestantism. For the first time since the Reformation leaders in every denomination are deeply concerned about their cleavage in doctrine, worship and practice, and are seriously trying to heal what they brand the "sin of disunity."

Protestant writers have taken the term "ecumenical," long used to describe the general councils of the Catholic Church, and invested it with a new connotation. They speak of the ecumenical movement as the search for a world-wide unity "from the Church as men have conceived it, to the Church as God wants it to be."

Reunion efforts began on the international level, under stimulus of the need for coordinating the Protestant foreign missions. How could pagans be asked to believe that Christianity is true unless the missionaries themselves witnessed to the truth by professing the same message of the Gospel? The idea was first broached at Edinburgh, Scotland, in 1910, and by 1921 the International Missionary Council was formed at London to become the chief organ of liaison for Protestant evangelism.

According to its constitution, the "sole purpose of the International Missionary Council is to further the effective proclamation to all men of the Gospel of Jesus Christ as Lord and Savior." Its function is not to command but to advise, by furnishing information, studying policy and strategy, "as an agency through which all the forces of world-wide missions can think and act together."

Though historically first, federating Protestant missions was only a logical outcome of reunion labors at home, one in the field of doctrine and worship, called *Faith and Order,* and another to deal with social and economic problems, under the title *Life and Work.* At the charter meeting of *Faith and Order* in Lausanne, Switzerland (1927), the leading spirit was Bishop Brent, an Episcopalian, who frankly told the delegates from seventy denominations that "in our hearts most of us are devotees of the cult of the incomplete—sectarianism. The Christ in one Church often categorically denies the Christ in a neigh-

boring Church. It would be ludicrous were it not tragic."
Two years before representatives from thirty-three countries
met at Stockholm for the opening congress of *Life and Work*
to face the problems of social morality that are insoluble for a
divided Christianity.

By 1948 the two movements had sufficiently matured to fuse
at Amsterdam into the World Council of Churches, which has
since met regularly in formal assemblies. As expressed by the
Secretary General, who asked himself what is the purpose of
the Council, "Our name gives us the clue to the answer. We
are a Council of Churches, not the Council of the one undivided Church. Our name indicates our weakness and our
shame before God. Our plurality is a deep anomaly. Our
Council represents therefore an emergency solution—a stage
on the road."[33]

As a stage on the road, the World Council has done more
in the short years of its existence to make Protestants unity-
conscious than any other movement in the past four centuries.
Even adding the forty years of preparation, its achievements
are monumental. Presently combining about two hundred
Protestant and Orthodox Churches in fifty nations, its membership covers most of the Christians who date from the
Reformation.

The Council opened its third assembly at New Delhi by integrating with the International Missionary Council, which
represents non-Catholic missionary groups in forty countries.
By this historic action the three basic strands of the ecumenical
movement were united: doctrine and worship through *Faith
and Order,* social service in *Life and Work,* and evangelism
under the International Missionary Council.

From its headquarters in Geneva the World Council has
given Protestantism a new sense of solidarity. In spite of their
divisions, they feel that God has not left them without some
tokens of unity.

> In our separateness we have attested the operation of the
> one Christ across all boundaries that divide us. We have
> heard the voice of the one Good Shepherd in the testimony of
> communions other than our own. We have experienced the
> power of the Name of Christ in their prayers. We have ac-

knowledged the love of Christ to which they have borne witness in word and deed. In the fellowship of the ecumenical
movement we have come together in a way which forbids us,
in spite of all stresses, to break away from one another. Thus
we have been led to see that the reality of Christ is more
comprehensive than the limitations of our confessional traditions, and have confessed in faith our oneness in Christ.[34]

At the same time the Churches recognize how widely they
are separated, not only in accidentals but in essentials of the
Christian faith. They confess that their divisions are contrary
to the will of Christ, and they pray God "to shorten the days
of our separation and to guide us by His Spirit into fulness of
unity."

But the obstacles that stand in the way are humanly speaking insurmountable. In a study of the non-theological and cultural factors in church divisions prepared for the World
Council, no less than thirty areas of conflicting interest were
analyzed: national antagonisms, distrust of the unfamiliar, historic isolation, political pressures, institutional pride, race, indifference, property ownership, doctored history, love of status
quo, personal ambition—all were exposed to view and scru-
tinized.

Yet the doctrinal issues are admittedly deeper, and involve
differences of understanding on almost every major element
of the Christian faith. The very concepts of the Church and
of the unity the Churches seek are in dispute. "If we were
agreed on the nature of the Church's oneness," observed the
chairman of the *Faith and Order* Commission, "our struggle
between each other would be over."[35]

Two principal opinions prevail in the ecumenical movement
on what should be done about this cleavage. There is first the
theoretical position which represents the traditional Reformation concept of man, the fall and the Church of Christ. According to this opinion, the disunity among the churches is
certainly sinful, but unavoidable, in view of man's depraved
nature. Thus, "we may think of the Church as we are able
to think of the individual believer, who may be said at one
and the same time to be both a justified man and a sinner
(*simul justus et peccator*)."[36] The Evangelical theory of man's

justification is also the speculative basis for the Church's simultaneous unity and disunity. In the same way that individual believers are and ever remain sinners, although justified by God, in Christ who alone is *just;* so the Churches are divided among themselves, while they are somehow united because of Jesus Christ their Founder, who is *one.*

Disunity, therefore, is no less inevitable in the Churches than sin in the individual Christian. They cannot help being divided, no more than he can help committing sin. After all, the members of the Church are human beings, suffering from the common effect of Adam's fall which destroyed man's intrinsic power to do any spiritual good. If any unity is to be found in the Church, it can only be something extrinsic, a kind of appropriation, where the unity of Jesus Christ is imputed to the Society which He founded.

Is there any hope of unifying the dismembered bodies of Christendom on these principles? Not from man's side. The only hope is that through prayer and patient waiting for the Spirit, God may see fit to unify the Churches in a way similar to the way He justifies sinners: by permeating them with His grace to the extent of removing the subjective conflicts that separate the denominations, and enabling them to live with one another in amicable charity.

A far different attitude towards Christian disunity does not prejudge the case on principle but, while assuming the need of prayer and divine help, insists on the corresponding need of human cooperation. The former theory was cited by the Secretary General of the World Council of Churches, who realized that on this point rests the whole success or failure of the ecumenical movement. There are many, he said, who think that the present relationship of the Churches in the World Council is the limit of all that can be hoped for. "The danger of this is that the World Council can thus become a narcotic instead of a stimulant. We must react against this temptation of accepting the present established disorder of our ecclesiastical world simply because it has been made to look less shocking" as it has been provided with an ecumenical façade.[37]

The sanguine element in the World Council looks to find the way that leads beyond co-existence or even cooperation, "to a true unity which will make it clear to the whole world that as there can only be one Body of Christ, so there is only one Body which is the Church of His people."[38]

In the past years, however, new and unexpected elements have appeared on the ecumenical scene. The admission of Russians and other non-Protestant bodies has greatly increased the strength of Orthodoxy in the World Council of Churches. No doubt the ecumenical movement was never intended to be exclusively Protestant. But until recently a large majority of the Council of Churches has been Protestant, and probably a majority has preferred it this way. It is now evident that Christian reunion must be built on a wider base than could ever be provided by the Churches stemming from the Reformation. The entrance of several Pentecostal Churches reinforces the point, and illustrates what certain promoters of a limited ecumenism had disavowed: that the hopes of a united Christianity cannot be realized without the combined effort of the whole Christian world.

More importantly, Protestant ecumenism has revealed a kindred desire for unity in the Roman Catholic Church. Interest in Rome hovered over the first beginnings of the World Council. In 1919 when the founders were canvassing for member churches, they called on Benedict XV and invited his assistance, which he courteously declined. In 1937 at the opening service of the Edinburgh conference on Faith and Order, the Archbishop of York declared that "we deeply lament the absence from this collaboration of the great Church of Rome —the Church which more than any other has known how to speak to the nations so that the nations hear."[38] In 1948 at the first assembly in Amsterdam, one of the principal topics was on "The Roman Catholic Church and the Ecumenical Movement." At New Delhi, in 1961, there were official observers from the Vatican, whose presence was not only welcome but showed what no amount of argument could prove, that the pope and Catholics generally are deeply impressed with the unitive spirit of Protestantism and ready to do all in their power to advance the cause of true Christian unity.

It was more than symbolic, as the head of the Council of Churches declared, that the two world assemblies of New

Delhi and Second Vatican should have met within less than a year of each other. He felt "it would undoubtedly mean much for Christendom and for the world, if it became clear in the decisions of both, that these councils do not meet against each other and that each does not seek its own advantage, but seeks only to serve the Lord Jesus Christ."[39] The deliberations at New Delhi and the decrees of Second Vatican give every promise that the hopes of reuniting a separated Christianity are brighter now than they have ever been since the Reformation.

SPIRIT OF PROTESTANTISM

If it is difficult to analyze the essence of any religious faith, it is doubly hard with Protestantism, which is more a movement than a system and consequently not subject to easy classification. Yet visible as a theme in Protestant faith and practice is a respect for the person of Christ that may baffle other Christians whose theology is more consistent and who therefore tend to overlook the attachment to the Savior bequeathed by the Reformation to its followers.

The focus on Christ appears in all the great Protestant writings since the sixteenth century and, before Luther and Calvin, reaches into the *devotio moderna* of the late Middle Ages and the Brethren of the Common Life. Under the topic of prayer, Calvin pointedly stated the place that Christ should occupy in the life of a believing Christian. Alone and of himself, a man lacks everything necessary for salvation. If he is to be saved, this can only be from resources furnished him by God in the person of Jesus Christ.

> In Christ, the Lord offers all happiness in place of our misery, all wealth in place of our neediness. In him He opens to us the heavenly treasures that our whole faith may contemplate His beloved Son, our whole expectation depend upon him, and our whole hope cleave to and rest in him. This is that secret and hidden philosophy which cannot be wrested from syllogisms. But they whose eyes God has opened surely learn it by heart, that in his light they may see light.[40]

So uniquely was Christ interpreted as the object of devotion that the first commandment of the decalogue, "Thou shalt have no other gods besides me," was taken to exclude every other mediation of grace; and all claims to the contrary were summarily dismissed as idolatry.

On this principle the Mass was removed from liturgical worship as a human invention which derogates from the one sacrifice of the Savior on Calvary; priestly ministration of the sacraments, veneration of the saints and the Blessed Virgin, the use of sacramentals and relics, in a word, the very notion of the Church itself as a divine creation through which the grace of Christ flows to a fallen human race, were reinterpreted in the light of what some have called the two words that best synthesize the Protestant spirit, *Kurios Christos*, "Christ is the Lord," meaning that He alone is directly the agent of man's salvation, with no one and nothing else besides.

The Lordship of Jesus Christ in the economy of redemption has been imbedded in the principal confessions of Protestantism under various aspects depending on the denominational emphasis. Among Lutherans the stress is on the merciful Savior in whom sinners may implicitly trust that their sins are not imputed because of the merits of Christ; in the Reformed tradition it is Christ the Lord of creation and sovereign master of human destiny; for the Anglicans He is the object of liturgical worship and for Methodists the motive for works of zeal and social welfare; and in the Free Churches only Christ's authority is recognized in ecclesiastical polity, to the exclusion of synods, bishops, and even of mandatory creeds.

Subscription to this principle was dramatically illustrated when the Evangelical Church in Germany came into conflict with the totalitarian pretensions of National Socialism. Faltering for a while under the impact of the new tyranny, church leaders soon rallied to make a solemn affirmation that Jesus Christ is the one Word of God whom men have to trust and obey, all other claims to allegiance to the contrary notwithstanding. Under title of the Barmen Declaration, they stated their position as Christians and Protestants.

"I am the way, the truth, and the life. No man cometh unto the Father but by me" (John 16:6).

Jesus Christ, as He is attested to us in Holy Scripture, is

the one Word of God, whom we have to hear and whom we have to trust and obey in life and in death.

We condemn the false doctrine that the Church can and must recognize as God's revelation other events and powers, forms and truths, apart from and alongside this one Word of God.[41]

Commenting on the Barmen statement, Karl Barth saw in it more than a protest against the Nazi overlords. It was a stand against all the heterodox movements within Protestantism "which for more than two hundred years had slowly prepared the devastation of the Church. The protest was without doubt directed against Schleiermacher and Ritschl. The protest was directed against the basic tendencies of the whole eighteenth and nineteenth centuries and therefore against the hallowed traditions of all other Churches as well."[42] At its best, then, Protestantism asserts against all who teach otherwise that Christ is the only way, truth and life, and that all other claimants are false.

Parallel with its Christocentrism among Protestants in the biblical tradition is the same principle from another perspective among Protestants who philosophize about their distinctive contribution to the Christian way of life. Again the first commandment is invoked, this time not to exclude other mediators than Christ but other objects of loyalty than God. Paul Tillich has developed the idea in what he calls "the Protestant principle." It is the insistence that no partial allegiance may take the place of an ultimate object of loyalty. Nothing that is man-made, or less than God, may be respected and honored as though it were divine.

What makes Protestantism Protestant is the fact that it transcends its own religious and confessional character, that it cannot be identified wholly with any of its particular historical forms.

Protestantism has a principle that stands beyond all its realizations. It is the critical and dynamic source of all Protestant realizations, but it is not identical with any of them. It cannot be confined by a definition. It is not exhausted by any historical religion; it is not identical with the structure of the Reformation or of early Christianity or even with a religious

form at all. It transcends them as it transcends any cultural
form. On the other hand, it can appear in all of them; it is a
living, moving, restless power in them; and this is what it is
supposed to be in a special way in historical Protestantism.

The Protestant principle, in name derived from the protest
of the "protestants" against decisions of the Catholic majority,
contains the divine and human protest against any absolute
claim made for a relative reality, even if this claim is made
by a Protestant church. The Protestant principle is the judge
of every religious and cultural reality, including the religion
and culture which calls itself "Protestant."[43]

Tillich further explains that the Protestant principle is "the
guardian against all the attempts of the finite and conditioned
to usurp the place of the unconditional in thinking and acting.
It is the prophetic judgment against religious pride, ecclesiastical arrogance, and secular self-sufficiency and their destructive
consequences."[44]

Others than Tillich have spelled out the persons and agencies in modern times against which authentic Protestantism
lodges its protest whenever something less than God assumes
divine prerogatives. Social and political entities, industrial
combines and philosophical systems, ecclesiastical bodies in
the Catholic and Protestant tradition are all guilty in varying
degrees of obscuring "the chasm between the human and the
divine, which the prophets of Israel had understood so well,"
to pretend there were persons "in control of God's redemptive
powers and purposes; and were in possession of the 'keys of
heaven.' "[45]

Consistent with this protest against divinization is the idea
that Protestantism itself should reflect on its own character
and always see it as a church of sinners. "The Reformation,"
it is stated, "was not completed in the sixteenth century; it is
never completed. We may for the sake of comfort try to trans-
form Protestantism into a closed system; but it breaks out
again. It has no 'infallible' voice to silence other voices in
decrees that are 'irreformable.' Protestantism cannot be
static."[46]

There is more to this claim than admission of human frailty
or ignorance, more even than a confession of human guilt. It

is the positive assertion that a Christian may turn his judgment upon the Church; that he must allow for reformation not merely *in* the Church but *of* the Church, to the extent of changing not only its policies but doctrines, and looking to the future for greater changes still. By this standard, the Church is indeed reformed but always in need of further reformation, *Ecclesia reformata sed semper reformanda*, not merely in externals but, if necessary, in the very constitution of its being. To question such necessity is to fall victim to the illusion that a human creation can, in any part of its nature, be above improvement or intrinsic change.

If the Church is always a human institution, the Protestant will treat the religious group to which he belongs accordingly. He will go beyond it for his commitment in a way that the Catholic or Eastern Orthodox would not do. They believe the Church possesses the Spirit of God and speaks to its members in His name; the Protestant considers the Spirit as somehow outside the Church, not unlike the theory of imputed justification of Christ's merits to a man who still remains a sinner. The institutional Church is not literally animated by the Spirit of God to be equated, as Catholics and Orthodox believe, with the Mystical Body of Christ. It rather waits for the Spirit and lives in *ad hoc* dependence on His mercy. It is not, as Reinhold Niebuhr correctly observed, an extension of the Incarnation in the Catholic sense of these terms.

Accordingly the whole history of the Church is the history of the reformation of the Church by the Spirit. Always the Christian must accept the fact that God is leading forward His Church and changing it, that the Church may never "settle down in a revelation which it treats as if it were its own property." Instead it is constantly on the watch to receive the new order which the Spirit brings. "The Church of Jesus Christ in history is at once the congregation of sinners and the new creation, for although it continues to live and work within the brokenness and estrangement of this world and to share in its divisions, the Church belongs to the new age and the new creation. As such the Church is summoned to perpetual renewal, to put off the old life, and by the renewal of its mind to be conformed to Christ, looking beyond its historical forms to the full unveiling of its new being in the coming Lord."[47]

Here, perhaps, we come nearest to the essence of Protestantism, which sees itself in a constant process of renewal, so that all its affiliations with visible ecclesiastical structures, its adoption of various liturgical forms, and even the acceptance of certain confessional creeds are tentative. Only the Spirit of God is adhered to absolutely, and everything else with reservation.

17

OLD CATHOLIC CHURCHES

The origins of the Old Catholic movement go back to Reformation times, and its theological principles derive from a Calvinist theory of grace. As a historical phenomenon the movement is sometimes described almost exclusively in terms of national aspirations which came into conflict with Rome. This is correct enough as a partial explanation, but fundamentally the issue was not a tension between groups of zealous Catholics in Belgium or the Low Countries striving to rise above their environment and inhibited by papal authority; it was mainly a clash of two opposing theologies of man's relations with God, the Catholic, which holds that human nature has been elevated to a higher than natural order, and the Jansenist, which claimed that such elevation never took place, so that when Adam fell he lost for himself and posterity not the gifts added to nature but something essential to nature itself.

Although full-blooded Jansenism began with Jansenius himself, its antecedents were much earlier. They are traceable to Michael Baius (1513–1589), contemporary of Luther and Calvin and chancellor at the University of Louvain. Shortly after his appointment to Louvain, he announced his twofold intention to free dogma from the foreign elements that Scholasticism had introduced and that constituted the sole obstacle to the conversion of Protestants; and then to study the Catholic doctrine on grace in its true sources, not the anathemas of the popes but in the Bible and the writings of the early Fathers, especially of St. Augustine.

According to Baius, when man came from the hand of God he possessed perfect righteousness, which theology has called sanctifying grace but which is really a native human possession because it was Adam's by right of nature. So far, Baius was teaching straight Calvinism. But then he added a clarification. Calvin implicitly denied that grace can be resisted, but he never fully explained what this meant. Taking Calvin's principles, Baius postulated two kinds of love that necessarily attract the will: a vicious love and the love of charity, on the prior assumption that our will has been ruined by concupiscence and therefore capable of nothing but evil in the spiritual life. Charity does not rule in sinners, so that all their words and actions are sinful; in the predestined charity reigns, and they will be saved, but only because of irresistible divine action, and not for any merit or cooperation with grace on their part.

Baius was condemned by the Holy See and submitted formally, although his later writings show that he never actually gave up his opinions. His influence might have stopped with his death, except for Jacques Janson, his successor at Louvain, who discovered and encouraged one of his students, Cornelius Jansenius (1585–1638), to carry on the work of the former chancellor.

Jansenius' master work, the *Augustinus,* was not published until two years after his death. It was a bold defense of Baianism that profoundly stirred the theological world within months of its first appearance. In 1653 five propositions summarizing Jansenism and culled from the *Augustinus* were condemned by Innocent X for heresy. Meanwhile the Jansenist cause became identified with opposition to papal authority and the Gallican theory that national churches are independent of Rome. As a result, Jansenists refused to accept the condemnation of their leader and protested that the five censured statements were certainly erroneous, but they had never been taught by Jansenius.

Three years later Alexander VII published a Constitution in which he solemnly defined that his predecessor's condemnation was valid in fact and by law. "We declare and define," the document read, "that the five propositions were taken from the book of the aforementioned Cornelius Jansenius, Bishop of Ypres, whose title is *Augustinus,* and that they were condemned in the sense intended by the same Cornelius."[1]

Still the tension continued, until nine years later when Alexander composed a formula of submission to his own and predecessor's Constitutions, to be taken under oath, as a condition for ordination to the priesthood and consecration to the episcopate.

In spite of repeated censures, Jansenism not only continued in existence but spread to other countries. Under pressure from Louis XIV, Jansenius' great disciple, Antoine Arnauld (1612–1694), took refuge in Holland, where his followers were supported by the sympathetic Calvinist government. When Spain lost control of the Netherlands, the Dutch Catholics had come under the administration of a vicar apostolic at Utrecht. Since 1688 this office was held by a Jansenist bishop, Peter Codde (1648–1710), who was deposed by Clement XI in 1702. During the resulting schism, Codde obeyed the papal injunction to the extent of not exercising his episcopal functions.

After Codde's death, the schismatic party found another Jansenist prelate, Dominique Varlet, who befriended their cause and in 1724 consecrated the former vicar general, Cornelius Steenhoven, bishop of the new movement. Three others were consecrated by Varlet, but only the last, Peter Meindaerts, consecrated his own successor. Fearing that an episcopate which depended on a single place might be lost, Meindaerts consecrated Jerome de Bock bishop of Haarlem in 1742, and John Byevelt for the see of Deventer in 1758. All parties to the action were excommunicated by the pope, but until the present day the Church of Utrecht has continued in existence on the grounds of its possession of episcopal dignity.

In the early nineteenth century, the Dutch government would not recognize the titles of the bishops as "of" Utrecht, Haarlem, and Deventer, but only "at" those cities. At the same time Leo XII sent a nuncio to bring about a concordat with the civil authorities and, if possible, reconcile the Old Catholic Churches with Rome. In 1827, the nuncio, Monsignor Capaccini, invited the Archbishop of Utrecht (John van Santen) to a conference, which turned out to be the last formal attempt at a reconciliation.

Van Santen asked why the pope should attach so much importance to signing the Constitution drafted by Alexander VII as an affirmation that Jansenius actually taught the doctrines attributed to him. The nuncio answered he could not believe the prelate would defend his own opinion against the wisdom of the Church. There is a record of van Santen's reply.

> I do not wish to set my judgment above that of others. I only ask, let the Five Propositions be shown me in Jansen's book, stated in the sense in which they were condemned—that is, not in the sense in which anything similar is found in St. Augustine, for the Pope never professed to condemn St. Augustine.
>
> Am I to understand that His Holiness asks that I should call God to witness that I do believe what I do not believe, what the Pope knows that I do not believe, what Almighty God knows that I do not believe? Is Catholic unity to be maintained by perjury?[2]

Since the negotiations broke down, the Old Catholics in Holland continued under the jurisdiction of the three original sees, of Utrecht, Haarlem and Deventer, with episcopal succession continuing in unbroken line into the twentieth century. Meantime another protest movement arose on the continent, after the definition of papal infallibility by the Vatican Council in 1870.

Although the bishops of the Catholic world subscribed to the definition, the acceptance was not universal among the lower clergy in certain areas of Germany, Switzerland and Austria-Hungary. The churches under their care seceded from Rome and joined hands with the Jansenist groups in Holland. Three names stand out among the German segment: John Döllinger, Joseph Reinkens and Franz Reusch.

John Döllinger (1799–1890) was a prominent church historian and theologian, and author of numerous books on the Eucharist, the Reformation and comparative religion. After his excommunication in 1871 he became a leader of the critics of the Vatican Council, but more concerned with reuniting the separated Christian Churches than with advancing the Old Catholic cause. More dedicated to the movement was Reinkens (1821–1896), also a church historian, who had himself consecrated first bishop of the German branch of the Old Catholic Church in 1873 with his see at Bonn. The principal organizer was the Scripture scholar Reusch (1825–1900), who took a leading part in setting up the Reunion Conferences that were later held at Bonn. But when the Old Catholics abolished clerical celibacy in 1878, Reusch objected and retired into lay communion.

All the continental Old Catholics received their episcopal succession from the Church of Utrecht. Two years after Reinkens' elevation, the first Swiss bishop, Eduard Herzog, was consecrated and given headquarters at Berne. Owing to the opposition of the government, bishops were not consecrated for the Austrian communities until much later. A bishop of Warnsdorf (Bohemia) was consecrated in 1924 and of Vienna in 1925. In 1939 the three bishoprics of Bonn, Warnsdorf and Vienna were united into one Church.

The most significant event among the Old Catholics in the past century was the series of international conferences held at Bonn in 1874 and 1875 under the presidency of John Döllinger. Their purpose was to foster reunion between the Churches which had retained the faith and order of historic Christianity. Their direction was in the hands of the newly formed branch of the Old Catholics, though Döllinger never formally joined them.

Two main interests occupied the conferences: to clarify the basic position of the Old Catholic Churches, and arrive at some agreement between the Old Catholics on the one hand and the Eastern Orthodox and Anglicans on the other. The fundamental statement of belief had to wait fifteen years, but the principles of reunion were broadly agreed upon in a series of declarations that have more than historic value because they paved the way for similar ventures in the ecumenical movement of the present century.

Outstanding among the fourteen articles of unanimous agreement with the Anglicans were the acceptance of the Protestant canon of the Old Testament, denial of real merit before God for good works performed, rejection of "works of supererogation" in the practice of the counsels, belief that five of the seven sacraments are the fruit of later theological speculation, acknowledgment of the unbroken apostolic succession in the English Church, denial of the Immaculate Conception and that the Eucharistic celebration is a "repetition or renewal" of the sacrifice of Calvary.

Concord with the Orthodox centered around the procession of the Holy Spirit in the Trinity, which included the admission that "the Holy Spirit does not issue out of the Son, because in the Godhead there is only one beginning." The Anglicans did not universally accept this compromise with the Orthodox. Among others, Edward Pusey of Oxford Movement fame was quite intransigent in his opposition to any tampering with the Western tradition on the *Filioque* in the Nicene Creed.

When the Declaration of Utrecht was drafted in 1889, the Old Catholics settled on eight principal doctrines which, they said, characterize their concept of Christianity. Most important were the rejection of the Roman primacy and the acceptance of the Council of Trent in its dogmatic decisions "only so far as they are in harmony with the teaching of the primitive Church."

As now constituted, the Old Catholic Churches include not only the Jansenist bodies of Holland and the groups that refused to accept the decrees of the first Vatican Council but a number of national churches in the Slavonic tradition that came into existence since the late 1800's. Minor groups were organized among the Czechs and Yugoslavs, but the largest contingent was formed among the Poles in the United States. Their bond of union with the Old Catholics was a common grievance against the Roman primacy.

The Polish National Church had two independent beginnings within two years. In 1895 the Chicago priest, Antoni Kozlowski, organized an independent parish and two years later was consecrated bishop by the Old Catholic prelate, Herzog, at Berne in Switzerland. Before his death in 1907, Kozlowski had established more than twenty parishes scattered from New Jersey to Manitoba.

In 1897 another Catholic priest, Francis Hodur, followed the same course at Scranton, Pennsylvania. He also went to Europe to have himself consecrated, receiving episcopal orders from the archbishop of Utrecht in 1907. During the interim, the two national groups had merged with Hodur at the head. Until his death in 1953, Francis Hodur developed the Polish National Church into a dominant partner of the Old Catholic family, with a communicant membership exceeding that of all the other affiliates combined.

Typical doctrinal positions of the Polish nationals are their concepts of original sin and the sacraments. "We do not teach," their Catechism states, "original sin as in the Roman Catholic Church—that it comes down to us from the origin of the human race, and that we inherit it through Adam." The Eucharist is said to contain "the mystical Body and Blood of Christ under the forms of bread and wine," and in the ritual the stress is on the Eucharist as spiritual food rather than sacrifice.

In 1946 the Polish National Church joined with the Church of England and the American Episcopalians, on the basis of the Bonn agreement which the Anglicans had made with the Old Catholics about fifteen years earlier. The foundation of their intercommunion rested on three cardinal points, that have since played a major role in deepening the bond between two ostensibly different religious bodies.

> Each Communion recognizes the catholicity and independence of the other, and maintains its own.
> Each Communion agrees to admit members of the other Communion to participation in the Sacraments.
> Intercommunion does not require from either Communion the acceptance of all doctrinal opinion, sacramental devotion, or liturgical practice characteristic of the other, but implies that each believes the other to hold all the essentials of the Christian Faith.[3]

The Anglican communions in England and America accepted the Poles as associate members. Each group then appointed a Joint Intercommunion Committee to meet from time to time for discussing mutual problems and needs. After their first meeting the delegates reported that "the two Churches are dealing with a situation which has never before existed. Their separation is not due to schism. They are in fact two National Churches which, maintaining the doctrine and fellowship that have come down to them from the Apostles, find themselves in the same territory through the accident of immigration combined with the barrier of language."[4] At the Lambeth Conference in 1948, this achievement of full intercommunion was noted "with satisfaction and approval." Besides clarifying the nature and spirit of the Old Catholic movement, this merger also sheds light on the ecclesiastical structure of the Churches which stem from the English Reformation.

QUOTED REFERENCES

The references follow the numerical sequence in the text, with complete bibliographical information and credit lines (where needed) to the respective publishers. In quoting from the sacred writings of the various religions, the text used was based on standard translations which were carefully collated, so that the version given may differ verbally, though not substantially, from the original text.

The two most extensive translations consulted were those in the *Harvard Oriental Series,* and the Oxford *Sacred Books of the East,* to both of whose publishers the author is deeply grateful for permission to quote and paraphrase.

A full complement of titles on the religions of the world would fill another sizeable volume. Yet if the works cited in the text are combined with the select bibliography which follows, a representative library on world religions is offered to the reader.

12. EARLY CHRISTIANITY

1. *Testament of Levi,* XVIII, 2–5, 8–9.
2. *John* IV, 25–26.
3. *Luke* IV, 18, 21.
4. *II Peter,* I, 16.
5. *I Corinthians,* XV, 3, 19.
6. *I John,* I, 1.
7. St. Ignatius of Antioch, *Epistle to the Trallians,* 9–10.
8. *II Epistle to the Philippians,* 7.
9. *John,* X, 30–39.
10. *John,* VI, 48–70.
11. *Matthew,* XIX, 3–12.
12. *Matthew,* X, 37.
13. *John,* XV, 5; XIV, 13.
14. *Mark,* XVI, 16.
15. St. Ignatius of Antioch, *Letter to the Philadelphians,* 4.
16. *John,* XX, 21–23.
17. *Koran,* Surah, V, 82–85.
18. *Matthew,* XVI, 17–19.
19. *Enchiridion Symbolorum,* 1825.
20. Nicolas Zernov, *The Church of the Eastern Christians,* London, 1942, p. 55.
21. Martin Luther, *Werke* (Weimar), XI, pp. 405–415.
22. Oscar Cullman, *Peter, Disciple-Apostle-Martyr,* New York, World Publishing, 1961, p. 207.
23. Carl Michalson, "Authority," in *Handbook of Christian Theology,* New York, 1962, pp. 27–28.

13. ROMAN CATHOLICISM

1. Adolph Harnack, *Das Wesen des Christentums*, Leipzig, 1933, p. 164.
2. Tacitus, *Annales*, XV, 44.
3. Pliny the Younger, *Letters*, 96, 5.
4. I Corinthians, XVI, 22; *Galatians* I, VI, 14, 17.
5. *Romans*, VIII, 35–39.
6. *Acts*, I, 21–22.
7. *Acts*, III, 6–8.
8. *Matthew*, XVI, 18; XVIII, 17.
9. *Acts*, XV, 7–11, 16–19.
10. I *Corinthians*, III, 16–17.
11. I *Peter*, I, 1.
12. *Zadokite Document*, 5.
13. *Mark* X, 4–6.
14. *Manual of Discipline for the Future Congregation of Israel*, ad finem.
15. *Ibid.*
16. St. Ireneus, *Adversus Haereses*, III, 3, 1–2.
17. *Enchiridion Symbolorum*, 54.
18. *Ibid.*, 132.
19. *Ibid.*, 469.
20. H. Finke, *Aus den Tagen Bonifaz VIII*, Munster, 1902, p. 156.
21. Abbé Englebert, *St. Francis of Assisi*, London, pp. 95–96.
22. Lecoy de la Marche, *L'esprit de nos Aieux*, Paris, p. 40.
23. H. Richard Niebuhr, *Christ and Culture*, New York, 1956, p. 130.
24. St. Thomas, *Expositio Symboli Apostolorum*, Art. 8.
25. Ferdinand Gregorovius, *Storia della Citta di Roma nel Medio Evo*, 1943, vol. XII, p. 249.
26. *Letters of St. Catherine of Siena*, New York, 1927, pp. 119, 235.
27. *Ibid.*, p. 261.
28. Mansi, vol. XXVII, col. 585, 590.
29. *Enchiridion*, 694.
30. J. Quicherat (ed.), *Proces de Condemnation et de Rehabilitation de Jeanne d'Arc*, vol. I, p. 445.
31. Ludwig Pastor, *The History of the Popes*, vol. IX, pp. 134–135.
32. *Ibid.*, p. 135.
33. Martin Luther, *Werke* (Weimar), I, p. 69.
34. *Spiritual Exercises*, First Rule for Thinking with the Church.
35. *Letters of St. Francis Xavier*, London, 1888, p. 10.
36. *Religious Education in the Schools of Canada*, 1953, p. 3.
37. John XXIII, *Osservatore Romano*, October 12, 1962.
38. St. Ignatius of Antioch, *Epistle to the Smyrneans*, 8.
39. St. Justin, *Dialogue with Trypho*, 117.
40. St. Ireneus, *Adversus Haereses*, I, 10, 2.
41. St. Robert Bellarmine, *De Ecclesia Militante*, 10.
42. *Ibid.*, 22.
43. Pius XII, *Mystici Corporis*, 17.
44. *Enchiridion*, 696.
45. *Didache* (Teaching of the Twelve Apostles), IX, 4.
46. Pius XII, *Mediator Dei*.
47. Richard Cardinal Cushing, *The Christian and the Community*, 1960, p. 15.
48. Pius XI, *Casti Connubii*, 54.
49. Paul VI, *Osservatore Romano*, September 30, 1963.

14. ISLAM

1. Surah IV, 136.
2. Surah II, 255.
3. Surah IV, 48.
4. Surah LXXIV, 31.
5. Surah I, 1.
6. Surah II, 117.
7. Surah X, 4.
8. Abdullah Yusuf Ali, *The Holy Qur-an*, New York, 1946, vol. I, p. 103.
9. Surah III, 129.
10. El-Bokhari, *Les Traditions Mussulmanes*, Paris, 1914, vol. III, pp. 278–279.
11. Surah III, 42–47, XIX, 19–22.
12. Surah XIX, 29–31.
13. Surah III, 49–52.
14. Surah III, 56–57.
15. Surah III, 3, 10, 12.
16. Surah IV, 155–158.
17. Surah XIX, 33.
18. Surah III, 59–61.

19. Surah V, 72–75.
20. Surah XXXIII, 40.
21. Surah V, 116.
22. Surah IV, 171–173.
23. Surah LXXXIV.
24. Surah XI, 119; L, 30.
25. Surah II, 190–193.
26. Surah IX, 5, 29–30.
27. Surah II, 256; V, 48; CIX, 1–6.
28. R. A. Nicholson, *Literary History of the Arabs,* Cambridge, 1930, p. 234.
29. Al-Hujwiri, *Kashf al-Mahjub,* Translated by R. A. Nicholson, n.d., p. 363.
30. Surah V, 51.
31. Surah III, 19, 85.
32. Ibn Madja, *Sunan, Hudub,* Bab. 2.
33. Statement of Moslem observers to the World Council of Churches, (Abdullah Igram,

Dean Hekim, M. Yousef Sharwarbi), 1954, private printing.
34. Abdullah Yusuf Ali, *The Holy Qur-an,* New York, 1946, vol. I, p. 145.
35. *Poems from Iqbal,* "The Way of Islam," London, 1955, p. 65.
36. *Ibid.*
37. *Constitution of Pakistan,* Part I, art. 1 (1).
38. *Ibid.,* Part III, art. 24.
39. *Ibid.,* art. 25 (1–2).
40. *Ibid.,* art. 28.
41. *Ibid.,* Part II, art. 18, 21.
42. *Ibid.,* art. 5, 13 (1).
43. *Ibid.,* art. 13 (4–5).
44. *Constitution of the Republic of Pakistan,* Part I, art. 1 (1).
45. *Ibid.,* Preamble.
46. *Ibid.,* Part X, art. 204 (1a).
47. Iqbal, *op. cit.,* pp. 42–43.
48. Surah II, 177.

15. EASTERN ORTHODOXY

1. Matthew Paris, I, p. 312.
2. *Deianiia Sviashchennago Sobora,* III, p. 83.
3. Nicholas Zernov, *The Russians and Their Church,* London, S.P.C.K., 1945, p. 163.
4. N. Orleanski, *Zakon o Religiozniykh Ob'edineniiakh,* pp. 6–12.
5. *Izvestiia,* February 4, 1945.
6. *Izvestiia,* May 12, 1945.
7. *Soviet Review.* July, 1961, p. 48.
8. *Ibid.,* p. 55.
9. M. Malinovsky, *Pravoslavonoe Dogmateskoe Bogoslovie,* 1910, p. 77.
10. *Catechismus Philaret,* Proemium.
11. August Hahn, *Bibliothek der Symbole und Glaubensregeln der alten Kirche,* Breslau, 1897, 253.
12. St. Gregory Thaumaturgus, "Expositio Fidei," *Bibliothek der Symbole* (Hahn), Breslau, 1897, p. 253.
13. Silvester Malevansky, *Opit Pravoslavvago Dogmatecheskaro Bogosloviya,* 1884, p. 62.
14. Sergius Bulgakov, *The Comforter,* Paris, 1937, p. 184.
15. Philaretus Gumilevsky, *Pravoslavnoe Dogmateskoe Bogoslovie,* Petersburg, 1882, II, p. 221.
16. Macarius Bulgakov, *Orthodox Dogmatic Theology,* Petrograd, 1883, II, p. 235.

17. Theophylact Gorskii, *Dogmas of the Orthodox Eastern Church,* Moscow, 1831, pp. 269–270.
18. Alexius Khomjakov, *L'Eglise latine et le protestantisme au point de vue de l'Eglise d'Orient,* Lausanne, 1872, p. 228.
19. N. Birbeck, *Russia and the English Church,* London, 1895, p. 94.
20. S. Bulgakov, *The Orthodox Church,* London, 1935, pp. 67, 88–89.
21. Arcudius, *De Concordia Ecclesiae Occidentalis et Orientalis,* Paris, p. 5.
22. Jerome Tarasij, *Perelom v Drevnerooskom Bogoslovie,* Warsaw, 1927, pp. 178–184.
23. Nicholas Zernov, *The Church of the Eastern Christians,* London, 1942, p. 45.
24. I. Goar, *Euchologium Gracorum,* Venice, p. 542.
25. *Ibid.*
26. Sylvester Lebedinskii, *Classic Compendium of Theology,* Moscow, 1805, p. 523.
27. Zernov, *op. cit.,* pp. 49–50.
28. I. Goar, *Euchologium,* Rome, pp. 181–204.
29. S. Bulgakov, *The Orthodox Church,* London, 1935, p. 137.
30. *Patriarch's Answer to Nonjurors,* London, 1718, p. 53.

31. "Declaration of the Orthodox Delegates Concerning the Main Theme of the Assembly," August 25, 1954, Private Printing.
32. *Longer Russian Catechism,* Moscow, p. 78.
33. *The Confession of Metrophanes Kritopoulos,* Athens, p. 345.
34. *Ibid.,* p. 353.
35. Sydney Loch, *Athos: The Holy Mountain,* London, 1957, pp. 244–248.
36. "The Confession of Dositheus" (Translated in *The Relations of the Anglican Churches with the Eastern-Orthodox,* London, 1921, p. 144).
37. F. Brightman, *Eastern Liturgies,* Oxford, pp. 386–387.

16. PROTESTANTISM

1. H. Wrampelmeyer, *Tagebuch über Dr. Martin Luther,* Halle, 1885, p. 165.
2. Luther, *Opera Latina,* VI, 8.
3. *Formula of Concord,* "De Compendiaria Regula atque Norma," 3.
4. Calvin, *Institutes of the Christian Religion,* I, 7, 4–5.
5. Luther, *Commentary on Genesis,* III, 7.
6. *Ibid.*
7. *The Augsburg Confession,* 20.
8. *Ibid.,* 18.
9. Francis Pieper, *Christian Dogmatics.* St. Louis, 1950, I, p. 555.
10. Arthur C. Piepkorn, *What the Symbolical Books of the Lutheran Church Have to Say about Worship and the Sacraments,* St. Louis, 1952, p. 30.
11. Resolution of Missouri Synod (1890), *A Century of Grace,* St. Louis, 1947, p. 207.
12. *Lutheran Hymnal,* St. Louis, p. 262.
13. *Declaration of Principles of the League for Evangelical-Catholic Reunion,* VI.
14. *Confession of Faith, Presbyterian Church U.S.A.,* XXV, 6.
15. *Ibid.,* VII, 1.
16. Karl Barth, *La Priere, d'apres les Catechismes de la Reformation,* Neuchatel (Switzerland), 1949, p. 49.
17. *Ibid.,* p. 51.
18. *Presbyterian Confession of Faith,* XXVII, 3.
19. *Baptist Church Manual,* Nashville, 1955, p. 102.
20. George Fox, *Journal,* Cambridge University Press, 1952, p. 33.
21. *Documents of the Christian Church* (H. Bettenson edit.), 1947, pp. 323–324.
22. *Statutes of the Realm,* IV, 2, pp. 841–843.
23. James T. Addison, *The Episcopal Church,* New York, 1951, p. 273.
24. *Ibid.,* p. 274.
25. *The Examiner,* December 16, 1961.
26. John Wesley, "The Character of a Methodist," *Works,* London, vol. VIII, p. 31.
27. John Wesley, "Free Grace," *Works,* vol. VII, p. 373.
28. *Methodist Discipline,* num. 86.
29. *Wesley's Prayers and Praises* (J. Alan Kay edit.), London, Epworth Press, 1958, p. 79.
30. Wesley, *Works,* vol. I, p. xxii.
31. *Methodist Discipline,* num. 2022.
32. *Acts,* II, 4.
33. *The First Assembly of the World Council of Churches, the Official Report,* New York, 1949, p. 28.
34. *Report on the Main Theme of the Second Assembly,* Geneva, 1954, p. 15.
35. *Introducing the Faith and Order Report* (Evanston), August 17, 1954.
36. *Report on Faith and Order* (Evanston), 1954, p. 3.
37. Visser 't Hooft, *The Third World Conference on Faith and Order,* London, 1953, p. 130.
38. *The Second World Council on Faith and Order,* London, 1938, p. 20.
39. Visser 't Hooft, "The Calling of the World Council of Churches," *The Ecumenical Review,* January, 1962, pp. 222–223.
40. Calvin, *Institutes,* III, 20, 1.
41. *Theological Declaration of the Synod of Barmen,* May 31, 1934.
42. Karl Barth, *Church Dogmatics,* Edinburgh, 1957, vol. II, 1, p. 173.

43. Paul Tillich, *The Protestant Era,* Chicago, 1948, pp. 162–163.
44. *Ibid.,* p. 163.
45. Reinhold Niebuhr, *Our Dependence Is Upon God* (Address at the Evanston Assembly of the World Council of Churches, 1954), Document 15-A, p. 3.

46. J. T. McNeill, *The Protestant Credo* (Vergilius Ferm, editor), New York, p. 116.
47. *The Third World Conference on Faith and Order* (Oliver S. Tomkins, editor), London, 1953, p. 20.

17. OLD CATHOLIC CHURCHES

1. Constitution, *Ad Sacram Beati Petri Cathedram,* Oct. 16, 1656.
2. J. M. Neale, *History of the So-Called Jansenist Church of Holland,* pp. 363–364.

3. Theodore Andrews, *The Polish National Church,* London, 1953, p. 90.
4. *Ibid.,* p. 91. Also Lambeth (1949) Resolution 67-b.

Note: With grateful acknowledgment, the following bibliography gives complete publishers' data on the principal sources quoted and consulted by the author.

BIBLIOGRAPHY

There is an immense literature on every aspect of the living religions of the world. The following titles are selected as most representative on the basis of scholarship and suitability for all classes of readers, including those who already have a good foundation in comparative religious culture. Except for standard source material, most of the books are recent publications or re-editions which contain more extensive bibliographies for those who wish to carry their studies further into specialized areas. *Titles marked with an asterisk are available in paperback form.* Dates of publication refer to the latest cloth-cover edition, but all the titles are either in print or easily accessible in libraries.

No effort was made to include foreign titles, both because many of the books have been translated into English and because the literature in other languages tends to be highly specialized. There are two definitive works which offer complete and up to date bibliographies in all the Indo-European languages: Maxime Gorce and Raoul Mortier, *Histoire Generale des Religions,* Aristide Quillet, Paris, 1947, in four volumes; and Kurt Galling, *Die Religionen in Geschichte und Gegenwart,* Mohr, Tubingen, 1956, in seven volumes.

The brief annotations for each title are not evaluative but merely descriptive of the contents. In the nature of things, the field of comparative religion gives the authors wide scope for interpretation according to their own religious persuasion or philosophy of life. For this reason strictly interpretative writings, which are numerous, have been omitted.

Among the higher religions, those professing monotheism are more readily treated as distinct cultural entities, whereas other religions, notably those of the Far East, tend to overlap and flow one into the other. This is reflected in their respective literatures, which are either distinctive or coalescent and more generalized.

SOURCES AND SACRED WRITINGS

Robert O. Ballou, *The Bible of the World,* New York, Viking, 1939. Handbook of 1400 pages with a wide selection of texts from the sacred books of eight living faiths. Abridged form as *The Portable World Bible.* *

A. C. Bouquet, *Sacred Books of the World,* Baltimore, Penguin, 1960. Selections arranged to show the development of religious thought. *

Lewis Browne, *The World's Great Scriptures,* New York, Macmillan, 1946. Anthology of the sacred writings of Babylonia, Egypt, India, China, Judaism, Christianity and Islam. *

William T. De Bary, *Introduction to Oriental Civilizations,* Columbia University Press, 1958 to 1960. New series of textual selections from previously unpublished writings, in three volumes, one each for the religions of China, India and Japan.

C. R. Lanman (editor), *Harvard Oriental Series,* Harvard University Press, 1895 to the present. Forty-three volumes of texts, mainly of Hindu and Buddhist sacred literature, with commentaries.

Max Muller (editor), *Sacred Books of the East,* Oxford, Clarendon, 1879–1910. Translation in fifty volumes of the sacred non-Christian books which have shaped the religion of Asia. General index in separate volume. Complements the texts in the Harvard Oriental Series.

GENERAL SURVEYS

A. C. Bouquet, *Comparative Religion,* London (Baltimore), Penguin, 1956. Readable survey covering history, thought and practice of principal faiths. *

Mircea Eliade, *Patterns in Comparative Religion,* New York, Sheed and Ward, 1958. Encyclopedic review of ancient and modern religions, classified according to basic patterns that underlie all the faiths of mankind. *

Robert E. Hume, *The World's Living Religions,* New York, Scribner's, 1959. Revision of an older work useful as reference, giving salient facts and stimulating judgments challenged by others. *

E. O. James, *Comparative Religion,* New York, Barnes and Noble, 1961. Compact analysis of the dominant issues in world religion: monism and monotheism, sin and atonement, worship and prayer. Christian appraisal. *

Joseph M. Kitagawa, *Religions of the East*, Philadelphia, Westminster, 1960. Study of Chinese religion, Hinduism, Buddhism
and Islam against the background of the Christian concept of
the Church.*

Hendrick Kraemar, *World Cultures and World Religions*, Philadelphia, Westminster, 1960. Examination of the new status of
non-Christian religions in their impact on Christianity.

Benson Y. Landis, *World Religions*, New York, Dutton, 1957. Brief
sketches of the principal beliefs of living religions. Statistical
data.*

John B. Noss, *Man's Religions*, New York, Macmillan, 1961.
Quotes freely from sacred writings and primary sources. Stress
on Indian religions and Protestantism.

Huston Smith, *The Religions of Man*, New York, Harper, 1958.
Emphasis on religious experience explained in terms of the
cultural history of the West.*

Joachim Wach, *The Comparative Study of Religions*, edited by Joseph M. Kitagawa, Columbia University Press, 1958. By the
author of the standard *Sociology of Religion*, with attention to
Christian and non-Christian types of religious experience.*

R. C. Zaehner, *The Concise Encyclopedia of Living Faiths*, New
York, Hawthorn, 1959. Fifteen contributors on as many major
religions, each a specialist in his field. Summary section in-
terprets religion in terms of Jung's depth psychology and
Hegelian idealism.

PRIMITIVE RELIGIONS

James G. Frazer, *The Golden Bough: A Study in Magic and Religion*, New York, Macmillan, 1935. Originally in twelve volumes, and later abridged to one, the *Golden Bough* seeks to
prove the linear evolution of religion from magic and of
Christianity from ancient mythologies.*

William J. Goode, *Religion Among the Primitives*, Glencoe, Ill.,
Free Press, 1951. Sociological critique of current theories on
the origin of religion. Functional approach.*

E. O. James, *Prehistoric Religion*, New York, Praeger, 1957. Factual study of earliest religious cultures: burial rituals, birth,
fertility, food supply and the ancient sky religion.

Robert H. Lowie, *Primitive Religion*, New York, Liveright, 1952.
Analysis of Crow, Ekoi, Bukaua, and Polynesian religions.
Evaluation of animism, magic and collectivist theories on reli-
gious origins.*

Bronislaw Malinowski, *Magic, Science and Religion*, New York,
Doubleday, 1960. Functionalist theory on the origins of religion, following in the tradition of Frazer.*

Paul Radin, *Primitive Religion*, New York, Dover, 1957. Reconstruction of the beliefs and religious experiences of aboriginal peoples. Highly critical of other theories. Evolutionary hypothesis of religion from animism.*

William Schmidt, *The Origin and Growth of Religion,* New York, Dial, 1935. One volume edition of the ten volume work, *Der Ursprung der Gottesidee,* challenging animist theories on the origin of religion. The most archaic cultures are shown to have a high-god pattern, with animism as a decadent development.

Edward B. Taylor, *Religion in Primitive Culture,* New York, Harper, 1958. Classic exposition of the theory that animism is the primitive culture of mankind. Sees Christianity evolving towards the age of reason without dogma.*

NON-CHRISTIAN RELIGIONS

Sydney Cave, *Living Religions of the East,* London, Duckworth, 1952. Compact and highly informative review of Hinduism, Zoroastrianism, Buddhism, the religions of China and Japan, and Islam.

Sydney Cave, *Christianity and Some Living Religions of the East,* London, Duckworth, 1944. Objective analysis of the basic principles of the main Oriental religions compared with Christianity as the fulfilment of man's religious needs.

Jacques-Albert Cuttat, *The Encounter of Religions,* New York, Desclee, 1960. Catholic evaluation of Hinduism, Buddhism and Islam, based on primary sources and directed to a deeper appreciation of Eastern religious culture.

C. N. E. Eliot, *Hinduism and Buddhism,* New York, Barnes and Noble, 1954. Three volume historical study of early Indian religion, Buddhism within and outside India, mutual influence of Eastern and Western religions, and present-day Hinduism.

Stephen Neill, *Christian Faith and Other Faiths,* London, Oxford University Press, 1961. Sympathetic Christian approach to the "coming dialogue" between Christianity and the other living faiths, notably Judaism, Islam, Hinduism and Buddhism.

George C. Ring, *Religions of the Far East,* Milwaukee, Bruce, 1950. Historical and evaluative study of the religions of China, Japan and India; also of Buddhism and Islam. Gives a Christian explanation of trends and tenets.

Arnold Toynbee, *Christianity Among the Religions of the World,* New York, Scribner's, 1957. Defends the thesis that Christians should recognize all the higher religions, especially Hinduism, Buddhism and Islam, as "revelations of what is true and right," since they also come from God."*

INDIA

Sri U. Acarya, *Tattvardhadhigama Sutra* (Sacred Books of the Jainas, II), Arrah, India; Central Jaina Publishing House, 1920. English version of some of the earliest Jain sacred literature.

A. L. Basham, *The Wonder That Was India,* New York, Evergreen, 1959. Widely read history of India, with special reference to cultural developments before the coming of the Moslems. Section on calendar, mathematics, logic and alphabet.*

Surendra N. Dasgupta, *History of Indian Philosophy,* Cambridge University Press, 1922–1955. Five volume study of the main streams of Indian thought over the centuries. Sacred texts and commentaries analyzed. Entire volume on Indian pluralism.

J. M. Dechanet, *Christian Yoga,* New York, Harper, 1959. Theory and practice of those features of Indian Yoga which the author feels can be profitably used by Christians to improve their moral life and prayer.

Mahatma K. Gandhi, *Autobiography,* Ahmedabad, 1948. Full length self appraisal of the leading figure in modern Hinduism.

Mahatma K. Gandhi, *Christian Missions, Their Place in India,* Ahmedabad, 1941. Forthright exposition of the Mahatma's critical attitude towards Christian missionary efforts.

Homer A. Jack, *The Gandhi Reader,* Indiana University Press, 1956. Twenty chapters of full-text statements by and about Gandhi on a wide range of topics, including Hinduism, Communism and Christianity.

Solange Lemâitre, *Hinduism,* New York, Hawthorn, 1959. Volume in the Twentieth Century Encyclopedia of Catholicism. Traces Hindu tradition from earliest times to the present; quotations from primary sources.

Kenneth W. Morgan, *The Religion of the Hindus,* New York, Ronald, 1953. Hindu faith and practice explained for Western readers by six Hindu scholars. Also has glossary and extension, *Selections from Hindu Sacred Writings* (130 pages), by a leading Sanskrit scholar.

Jawaharlal Nehru, *Autobiography,* London, 1953. Revealing study by the first prime minister of the Republic of India. Indispensable for a correct understanding of modern Hinduism.

Swami Prabhavananda and Christopher Isherwood, *Bhagavad-Gita,* New York, Harper, 1959. An interpretative translation of one of the major sacred writings of Hinduism. The most recent critical version is *The Bhagavadgita,* with an introductory essay, Sanskrit text, English translation and notes, by S. Radhakrishnan, New York, Harper, 1948.*

Swami Prabhavananda and Frederick Manchester, *The Upanishads*, Hollywood, Vedanta Press, 1957. Free translation of selected texts from the main philosophical scriptures of Hinduism. The standard work on the subject is *The Religion and Philosophy of the Veda and Upanishads*, in two volumes, by Arthur B. Keith, in the Harvard Oriental Series.*

Sarvepalli Radhakrishnan, *A Hindu View of Life*, New York, Macmillan, 1949. Often reprinted summary of Hindu belief by a native scholar who is well versed in Western thought.*

Sarvepalli Radhakrishnan, *A Source Book in Indian Philosophy*, Princeton University Press, 1957. Carefully selected texts covering the Vedic and Epic Periods, Orthodox and Heterodox Systems, and Contemporary Thought. Thirty pages of bibliography.*

Louis Renou, *Hinduism*, New York, Braziller, 1961. After a comprehensive introduction, the leading texts of Hindu scripture and tradition are extensively quoted, correlated and explained.*

Vincent A. Smith, *The Oxford Student's History of India*, Oxford University Press, 1951. Fifteen editions of a standard source, beginning with Ancient India and including the latest events. Religious orientation of contents.

Paul Thomas, *Epics, Myths and Legends of India*, Bombay, Taraporevala, 1949. Comprehensive survey of the sacred lore of the Hindus, Buddhists and Jains of India. Authoritative with 268 half-tone illustrations.

Ernest E. Wood, *The Glorious Presence*, London, Rider, 1952. Study of Vedanta and its relation to modern thought.

F. Zacharias, *Studies of Hinduism*, Alwaye (India), J.M. Press, 1945–1950. Five-volume appraisal by a Catholic scholar, based on primary sources.

Heinrich R. Zimmer, *Philosophies of India* (Edited by Joseph Campbell), New York, Pantheon, 1953. Scholarly commentary on Hindu, Jain, Buddhist and related systems.*

CHINA

Wing-tsit Chan, *Religious Trends in Modern China*, Columbia University Press, 1953. Up to date descriptive study.*

H. G. Creel, *Chinese Thought from Confucius to Mao Tse-Tung*, University of Chicago Press, 1953. Compact analysis, using first-hand sources.*

H. G. Creel, *Confucius: The Man and the Myth*, New York, Day, 1949. Critical yet sympathetic treatment, based on scholarly investigation.

John K. Fairbank, *Chinese Thought and Institutions*, University of Chicago Press, 1957. Gathering of studies by scholars on the inner meaning of China's culture, with special attention to its religion.

E. R. Hughes, *Chinese Philosophy in Classical Times,* London, Dent, 1942. Edited studies in Everyman's Library of the traditional and heterodox philosophical systems.

Joseph Needham and Wang Ling, *Science and Civilization in China,* Cambridge University Press, 1954. Definitive study in three volumes of Chinese scientific, cultural and religious history. Maps, illustrations and copious reference sources.

Benjamin I. Schwartz, *Chinese Communism and the Rise of Mao,* Harvard University Press, 1951. Informative essays on the sources of Communist thought in China.

Leo Sherley-Price, *Confucius and Christ,* New York, Philosophical Library, 1951. Balanced appraisal of Confucian thought and organization in the light of Christian theology.

W. E. Soothill, *The Three Religions of China,* Oxford University Press, 1951. Surveys of Confucianism, Taoism and Buddhism; comparative ideas about the Deity, world, soul, morality and ritual.

Arthur Waley, *The Analects of Confucius,* London, Allen and Unwin, 1938. English translation, with critical discussion of Confucian terminology.*

James R. Ware, *The Sayings of Confucius,* New York, New American Library, 1961. Selections from the writings of Confucius, numbered and classified.*

Liu Wu-Chi, *A Short History of Confucian Philosophy,* London, Penguin, 1955. Systematic account of Confucianism as developed by Chinese thinkers from Confucius to modern times.*

Y. C. Yang, *China's Religious Heritage,* Nashville, Abingdon, 1943. Interpretation of Chinese religion from a Christian viewpoint.

JAPAN

Masaharu Anesaki, *History of Japanese Religion,* London, 1930. Basic study by a Japanese scholar. Special attention to moral life and social customs.

C. R. Boxer, *The Christian Century in Japan,* Cambridge University Press, 1951. Documented and readable study of the century (1549–1650) when Japan first received a concentrated Christian influence.

William K. Bunce, *Religions in Japan,* Tokyo, Tuttle, 1955. Reliable and up to date account of the background and present status of Buddhism, Shinto and Christianity in Japan.*

D. C. Holtom, *The National Faith of Japan,* London, Kegan Paul, 1937. Standard authority on Shinto, dealing extensively with state and sect Shinto.

Francis J. Horner, *Case History of Japan,* New York, Sheed and

Ward, 1948. Evaluation of the religious, educational, social and political impact of various cultures (Buddhist, Shinto, Confucian and Christian) on the past history and present status of Japan.

Johannes Laures, *The Catholic Church in Japan,* Tokyo, Tuttle, 1954. Scholarly and literary account of the progress of Catholicism from its earliest beginnings to the present day.*

Carl Michalson, *Japanese Contributions to Christian Theology,* Philadelphia, Westminster, 1960. Sympathetic treatment of the religious insights furnished by the Japanese to Christian thought, mainly in Protestantism.

J. B. Pratt, *The Pilgrimage of Buddhism and a Buddhist Pilgrim,* New York, Macmillan, 1928. Survey of Buddhist movement from India to Japan. Should be read together with *Japanese Buddhism,* by Charles Eliot, which is the most authoritative study in English (London, Arnold, 1935).

George B. Sansom, *A History of Japan,* Stanford University Press, 1958, 1961. Illuminating treatment of the development of Japanese religion. First two volumes cover the periods from ancient times to 1334, and to 1615; third volume will carry the history to the present.

P. Wheeler, *Sacred Scriptures of the Japanese,* New York, Abelard, 1952. Scholarly textual compilation of sacred writings, chronologically arranged, setting forth the main currents of Japanese religious culture. With 120 pages of reference notes.

BUDDHISM

E. A. Burtt, *The Teachings of the Compassionate Buddha,* New York, New American Library, 1961. Early discourses, the Dhammapada, and later basic writings, edited with commentary.*

Edward Conze (editor), *Buddhist Texts Through the Ages,* New York, Philosophical Library, 1953. Concise and scholarly selection of texts from a broad range of Buddhist thought and history. Also the same author's *Buddhist Scriptures* (an abridgment), Baltimore, Penguin, 1960.*

Charles Eliot, *Hinduism and Buddhism,* New York, Barnes and Noble, 1954. Highly respected three-volume comparative study.

Henri de Lubac, *Aspects of Buddhism,* New York, Sheed and Ward, 1953. Sympathetic comparison of Christian and Buddhist charity, and the differences between Christ and Buddha. Complete bibliography of Buddhist writings available in English.

Richard A. Gard, *Buddhism,* New York, Braziller, 1961. Synthesis

of Buddhist history and thought, supported by extensive quotations.*

Dwight Goddard, *A Buddhist Bible*, New York, Dutton, 1952.
Anthology of texts from Pali, Sanskrit, Chinese, Tibetan and
modern sources. Many not available elsewhere in English.

Christmas Humphreys, *Buddhism*, London, Penguin, 1955. The
history, development, and present-day teaching of the various
schools of Buddhism. Author an Englishman who founded
the Buddhist Society, London.*

Kenneth W. Morgan (editor), *The Path of the Buddha: Buddhism
Interpreted by Buddhists*, New York, 1956. Eleven essays by
representative scholars, including a section on the "Unity and
Diversity of Buddhism."

T. R. V. Murti, *The Central Philosophy of Buddhism*, London,
Allen and Unwin, 1955. Hindu reconstructs the philosophical
core of Buddha's teaching by examining the various schools
in India.

Robert L. Slater, *Paradox and Nirvana*, University of Chicago
Press, 1951. Study of religious ultimates with special reference
to Burmese Buddhism.

Daisetz T. Suzuki, *The Training of the Zen Buddhist Monk*,
Kyoto, Eastern Buddhist Society, 1934. Factual explanation
of the life and practices of Zen Buddhism.

Daisetz T. Suzuki, *Essays in Zen Buddhism*, New York, Harper,
1948 to 1958. Volumes in three series giving an interpretative,
theological and historical review of Zen. Official textbooks included in contents.*

MINOR RELIGIONS OF THE EAST

J. C. Archer, *Sikhs in Relation to Hindus, Moslems, Christians and
Ahmadiyyas*, Princeton University Press, 1946. Comparative
study from a historical and doctrinal point of view. Centered
on Sikhs in India and Pakistan.

Witter Bynner, *Lao-Tzu* (Way of Life According to Lao-Tzu),
New York, Day, 1944. Biographical sketch and anthology of
poetical works of the founder of Taoism. Companion version
by R. B. Blakney, *The Way of Life: Lao Tzu*, New York, New
American Library, 1957. The latter has the poetical selections
also in paraphrase.*

M. M. Dawson, *Ethical Religion of Zoroaster*, New York, Macmillan, 1931. Defends the title of Zoroastrianism as the oldest
or at least the most accurate code of ethics. Summary analysis
of moral theory.

J. Duchesne-Guillemin, *The Western Response to Zoroaster*, Oxford University Press, 1958. Critical explanation of teaching
and its challenge to Western thought.

J. Duchesne-Guillemin, *The Hymns of Zarathustra*, London, Murray, 1952. Modern scholarly translation of the traditional hymns attributed to the founder of Zoroastrianism. Christian appraisal of the latter and its limitations.*

E. E. Herzfeld, *Zoroaster and His World*, Princeton University Press, 1947. Technical study in two volumes of the history, literature and principles of Zoroastrianism.

Jagdish C. Jain, *Life in Ancient India As Depicted in the Jain Canons*, Bombay, New Book Co., 1947. Survey of history and religion of early India as reflected in the Jain sacred writings. To be read in connection with *Outlines of Jainism*, by J. L. Jaini, Cambridge University Press, 1940.

Chimanlal J. Shah, *Jainism in North India*, London, Longmans, 1932. Documented study of Jainism from 800 B.C. to 526 A.D. Definitive work.

Khushwant Singh, *The Sikhs*, London, Allen and Unwin, 1953. Descriptive work by a prominent Sikh scholar, tracing history and teaching, practice and worship of his people. An appendix of selections from the Sikh founder.

JUDAISM

William F. Albright, *From the Stone Age to Christianity*, New York, Doubleday, 1957. Modern classic on the historical process of religion before Jewish times, under the Mosaic covenant, and into Christian times.*

American Jewish Year Book, New York, American Jewish Committee. Annual publication with timely information on American and world Judaism; status in various countries, statistics, current events, organizations, activities.

Leo Baeck, *The Essence of Judaism*, New York, Schocken, 1948. Gives the point of view of "Progressive Judaism." Guide to Rabbinical quotations and other sources.*

Salo W. Baron, *A Social and Religious History of the Jews*, Columbia University Press, 1952–1958. Present standard work in eight volumes, with extensive bibliographies, notes, and references to comparative literature.

A. Cohen, *Everyman's Talmud*, New York, Dutton, 1949. An introductory volume for the general reader.*

Isidore Epstein, *The Faith of Judaism: An Interpretation for Our Times*, London, Soncino, 1954. Presentation of the Orthodox position. Companion volume by the same author, *The Jewish Way of Life*, London, Pardes, 1946.

L. Finkelstein, *The Jews: Their History, Culture and Religion*, New York, Harper, 1955. Cross-section of Jewish thought, in two volumes, with more than thirty authors contributing.

Judah Goldin, *Living Talmud*, New York, New American Library,

1960. New translation of one of the treatises of the Talmud, with an introductory essay.*

J. Gottman, *The Philosophy of Judaism,* New York, Meridian, 1960. Systematic analysis of Jewish thought.

Arthur Hertzberg, *Judaism,* New York, Braziller, 1961. Depicts the unity of the Jewish spirit throughout the ages as a religious way of life, expressed in the words of its classic authorities.*

A. J. Heschel, *Man Is Not Alone: A Philosophy of Religion,* New York, Farrar-Strauss, 1955. Represents the mystical "neo-Hasidic" trend in modern Judaism.*

Midrash Rabbah (edited by H. F. Friedman and M. Simon), London, Soncino, 1939. Ten-volume collection of the ancient Jewish scriptural exegesis directed to discovery in the sacred text of meanings deeper than the literal.

G. F. Moore, *Judaism in the First Centuries of the Christian Era,* Harvard University Press, 1954. Standard three-volume work often reprinted, which should be read in conjunction with J. Bonsirven's *Le Judaisme Palestinien au Temps de Jesus Christ* (two volumes), Paris, Beauchesne, 1934.

L. I. Newman, *The Hasidic Anthology,* New York, Bloch, 1934. Valuable collection from the Jewish mystical writers, rarely accessible to English readers.*

Talmud (Isidore Epstein editor), London, Soncino, 1935–1948. The Babylonian Talmud in thirty-four volumes plus an index volume. Glossary, notes and introductory explanations.

The Universal Jewish Encyclopedia (Isaac Landman editor), New York, Universal Jewish Encyclopedia, 1939–1944. Ten-volume work, with reading guide and index. Should be consulted along with the older *Jewish Encyclopedia,* New York, Funk, 1916. The latter is more scholarly and fully documented.

Zohar, translated by H. Sperling and M. Simon, London, Soncino, 1931–1934. English version in five volumes of the fundamental book of Jewish Cabbalism, which is the basic source of medieval Judaic mysticism.

ISLAM

Abdullah Yusuf Ali, *The Holy Qur-an,* New York, Murray, 1946. Critical two volume edition of the Koran, in smooth translation, along with the Arabic text and extensive (verse for verse) commentary. Also one-volume form.

Tor Andrae, *Mohammed: The Man and His Faith,* London, Allen and Unwin, 1936. Widely recognized study of the life and character of the founder of Islam by a Western scholar.*

A. J. Arberry, *Revelation and Reason in Islam,* New York, Macmillan, 1957. Penetrating analysis of the tension and conflict between faith and reason in Islamic theology.

T. W. Arnold and A. Guillaume (editors), *Legacy of Islam,* Oxford, Clarendon, 1931. Documented objective essays on Hispanic Islam, Crusades, Art, Mysticism, Philosophy and Theology, Law and Science, Architecture and Medicine.

Carl Brockelmann, *History of the Islamic Peoples,* New York, Putnam, 1947. Narrative type survey of Mohammedan history, with stress on the tie-in between Islamic religion and political movements.*

Kenneth Cragg, *The Call of the Minaret,* New York, Oxford University Press, 1956. Answers the question: What are the implications of Islam for the Christian? Sympathetic study of Moslem worship and belief.*

Encyclopedia of Islam, Leyden, Brill, 1954 to present. International edition in the process of composition, with text available in English, French and German. Complements the four volume edition, 1913–1938, as a dictionary of Islamic biography, ethnology and geography. Religious history emphasized.

A. A. Fyzee, *Outlines of Mohammedan Law,* Oxford University Press, 1949. Systematic presentation of Islamic laws on marriage, property, social life.

H. A. R. Gibb, *Mohammedanism,* Oxford University Press, 1953. Compact analysis of the history, religious movements, sectarian divisions, and Islamic relations with Christianity.*

H. A. R. Gibb and H. Bowen, *Islamic Society and the West,* Oxford University Press, 1950, 1957. Projected multi-volume study of the impact of western civilization on Moslem culture in the Near East. First volume in two parts covers Islamic society in the eighteenth century.

R. Levy, *Social Structure of Islam,* Cambridge University Press, 1957. Treats grades of society, status of women and children, jurisprudence, moral customs, religious and secular law, military organization and cosmology. Exceptional bibliography.*

Kenneth W. Morgan, *Islam—The Straight Path: Islam Interpreted by Muslims,* New York, Ronald, 1958. Essays on Islamic history, faith and culture by scholars from Egypt, Iran, Turkey, Pakistan, China and Indonesia.

Shorter Encyclopedia of Islam (edited by H. A. R. Gibb and J. H. Kramers), Leyden, Brill, 1953. Condensed version of the larger encyclopedia, in about 700 pages.

Wilfred Cantwell Smith, *Islam in Modern History,* Princeton University Press, 1957. Study of the Moslems "in the turmoil of the modern world," with separate sections on Arabia, Turkey, Islamic Reformation, Pakistan and India.*

W. Montgomery Watt, *Islam and the Integration of Society,* Northwestern University Press, 1961. Scholarly appraisal of the social implications and impact of Mohammedan principles, as seen in history and projected into contemporary life.

ROMAN CATHOLICISM

Karl Adam, *The Spirit of Catholicism,* New York, Doubleday, 1962. Forceful presentation of the inner vitality of the Catholic Church, its structure and relation to other religious bodies.*

George Brantl, *Catholicism,* New York, Braziller, 1961. Concise analysis of Catholic thought and ideals, woven into the context of the Church's fundamental teachings as illustrated in representative writings.*

A Catholic Dictionary, edited by Donald Attwater, New York, Macmillan, 1958. Standard lexicon of Catholic terms, names, and personalities.*

Celestin Charlier, *The Christian Approach to the Bible,* Westminster, Md., Newman, 1959. Up to date manual on the meaning and use of the Scriptures in Catholic thought and piety.*

The Church Teaches, St. Louis, Herder, 1960. Classified collection of documents of the Church in English translation, covering all the major fields of theology, from the nature of God to eschatology.

Henri Daniel-Rops, *Jesus and His Times,* New York, Doubleday, 1960. Scholarly yet easily readable life of Christ, written in modern idiom and with special advertence to present-day Scripture thought.*

Philip Hughes, *History of the Church,* London, Sheed and Ward, 1947 to present. Three volumes to date cover: Christian origins to the Reformation. Lists, indexes and extensive bibliographies. Also by the same author, *A Popular History of the Catholic Church* (including modern times) in one volume, New York, Doubleday, 1962.*

Leo XIII, *The Church Speaks to the Modern World,* New York, Doubleday, 1961. Social teachings of Leo XIII, in lengthy quotations from encyclical letters, introduced and summarized along with the text.*

National Catholic Almanac, Paterson, N. J., St. Anthony Guild, Doubleday. Annual publication summarizing basic Catholic teaching and customs, with up to date information on events and personalities.

Joseph Pohle and Arthur Preuss, *Dogmatic Theology,* St. Louis, Herder, 1948. Treatises in Catholic dogma. Twelve volumes covering major fields: God and Trinity, Christology, Mariology, Grace and Sacraments, Eschatology.

Matthias Scheeben, *The Mysteries of Christianity,* St. Louis, Herder, 1946. Profound study of the implications and expansion of the principal mysteries of Catholicism. Dogmatic logic combined with affective piety.

Frank J. Sheed, *Theology and Sanity,* New York, Sheed and Ward,

1960. Compact explanation of the principal doctrines of the Catholic faith, examined in their dogmatic content and relevance to moral life.

George D. Smith, *The Teaching of the Catholic Church,* New York, Macmillan, 1960. Two volume summary of Catholic doctrine by recognized theologians, arranged in separate treatises, annotated, with marginal guides.

St. Thomas Aquinas, *Selected Writings* (M. C. D'Arcy, editor), London, Dent, 1939. Also *Philosophical Texts* (Thomas Gilby editor), Oxford University Press, 1951; and *Theological Texts* (*Ibid.*), 1955.* The *Summa Theologica* of St. Thomas is available in English in three volumes, New York, Benziger, 1948; and the *Summa contra Gentiles* in paperback, New York, Doubleday, 1956.

Twentieth Century Encyclopedia of Catholicism (Henri Daniel-Rops editor), New York, Hawthorn, 1958 to the present. Projected 150 title set of volumes on a wide range of subjects. Last volume in series an index and guide to the set. Translation from the French.

N. G. M. Van Doornik, S. Jelsma and A. Van de Lisdonk, *A Handbook of the Catholic Faith* (The Triptych of the Kingdom), New York, Doubleday, 1962. Comprehensive summary of the main teachings of Catholicism, with theological analysis and moral implications.*

EASTERN ORTHODOXY

Donald Attwater, *The Christian Churches of the East,* Milwaukee, Bruce, 1961. Two volumes, treating in sequence the Churches in Communion with Rome, and the Churches not in Communion with Rome. Doctrine, ritual and practice described in a historical setting.

Francis Dvornik, *The Photian Schism,* Cambridge University Press, 1938. Definitive work from the Catholic standpoint of the origins of the Eastern Schism. Based on manuscript sources and challenges prevalent notions.

Clement C. Englert, *Catholics and Orthodox—Can They Unite?,* New York, Paulist, 1961. Informative study of Orthodox teachings and practices, with a realistic appraisal of the differences and similarities between Rome and Eastern Orthodoxy.*

G. P. Fedotov, *A Treasury of Russian Spirituality,* New York, Sheed and Ward, 1948. Anthology with introductory essays of writings by and about prominent spiritual leaders of Russia up to modern times: Theodosius, Sergius, Nilus, Avvakum, Tychon, Seraphim, "The Pilgrim," John of Cronstadt and Yelchaninov.

R. M. French, *The Eastern Orthodox Church,* London, Hutchinson, 1951. Historical survey from Constantine to modern Russia; and topical analysis of Orthodox worship, monasticism, laity and current problems.

Frank Gavin, *Some Aspects of Contemporary Greek Orthodox Thought,* London, Society for the Promotion of Christian Knowledge, 1936. Orthodox dogmas analyzed from primary sources: the nature of God, Redemption, Grace, the Church and sacramental system.

P. Hammond, *The Waters of Marah,* London, Rockliff, 1956. Appraisal of the present state of the Greek Orthodox Church, against a historical background.

Archdale A. King, *The Rites of Eastern Christendom,* Vatican, Tipografia Poliglotta Vaticana, 1947. Two volume study of the ritual, text and variations among all the rites of the Eastern Churches. Standard source book.

Sydney Loch, *Athos: The Holy Mountain,* London, Lutterworth, 1957. Narrative description of the life and customs of the Orthodox monasteries on Mount Athos, drawn from personal experience.

The Orthodox Liturgy, London, Society for the Promotion of Christian Knowledge, 1954. Text of the liturgy in use by the Church of Russia, together with rubrical directions to the faithful.

Orthodox Spirituality, London, Society for the Promotion of Christian Knowledge, 1946. Written by a monk of the Eastern Church. Penetrating analysis of Orthodox asceticism and mysticism, also compared with Western traditions.

S. Runciman, *The Eastern Schism,* Oxford University Press, 1955. Traces the remote and proximate causes of the breach with Rome. Should be read in conjunction with Rene Guerdan's *Byzantium, Its Triumphs and Tragedy,* London, Allen and Unwin, 1956.*

Nicolas Zernov, *Eastern Christendom,* London, Weidenfeld and Nicolson, 1961. Comprehensive treatment of the origins and development of Eastern Orthodoxy by a writer familiar with Western thought. Primary sources used. A smaller work by the same author which treats of the unity prospects with Western Christianity is *The Church of the Eastern Christians,* London, Society for the Promotion of Christian Knowledge, 1942.

Nicolas Zernov, *The Russians and Their Church,* London, Society for the Promotion of Christian Knowledge, 1945. Historical survey from the origins of Russian Christianity to the Church's present status under Communism.

PROTESTANTISM

Karl Barth, *Church Dogmatics,* Edinburgh, Clark, 1949 to present. English translation of Barth's ten volume German work, representing the most influential Protestant writing of the century. Summarized in *Dogmatics in Outline*, New York, Harper, 1960.*

G. K. A. Bell, *Documents on Christian Unity*, Oxford University Press, 1924, 1930, 1948. Three series of collected statements illustrating the ecumenical movement. Include Protestant, Catholic and Orthodox sources.

Robert McAfee Brown, *The Spirit of Protestantism*, New York, Oxford University Press, 1961. Clear and incisive examination of the inner spirit of Protestantism: misunderstandings, catholicity, varieties, affirmations, basic problems and unsolved dilemmas.*

Herbert Butterfield, *Christianity and History*, New York, Scribner, 1950. Interpretation of historical events and movements in the light of traditional Christian principles.*

John Calvin, *Institutes of the Christian Religion*, Philadelphia, Westminster, 1961. Latest, two volume edition of Calvin's classic work, critically edited and copiously annotated.*

J. Leslie Dunstan, *Protestantism*, New York, Braziller, 1961. Closely woven texts of the Protestant tradition, quoted and explained to show the spirit of the Reformation and its perduring influence to modern times.*

Adolph Harnack, *What Is Christianity?*, New York, Harper, 1960. Analysis of the origins and development of Christianity by a dominant figure in modern liberal Protestantism. Should be read with Rudolf Bultmann's *Kerygma and Myth* (same), which follows in Harnack's tradition.*

William Hordern, *A Layman's Guide to Protestant Theology*, New York, Macmillan, 1957. Series of essays on modern Protestant theologians, with stress on the American scene.*

Winthrop S. Hudson, *American Protestantism*, University of Chicago Press, 1961. Historian's survey of the distinctive features of Protestantism in the United States, from colonial times to the present.*

Kenneth S. Latourette, *The Twentieth Century in Europe*, New York, Harper, 1961. Objective, thoroughly documented history of the Roman Catholic, Protestant and Eastern Churches in Europe since the turn of the century. Complement to the author's seven-volume work, *A History of the Expansion of Christianity*, New York, Harper, 1937–1945.

Martin Luther, *Works*, St. Louis, Concordia, 1959 to present. The projected fifty-three volume English translation of Luther's writings, edited by Jaroslav Pelikan, will cover most of his published works. Many will be available in English for the first time.

Martin E. Marty, *A Short History of Christianity*, New York, Meridian, 1959. Concise review of Christian history from the Protestant viewpoint.*

Einar Molland, *Christendom,* New York, Philosophical Library, 1959. Succinct analysis of the doctrines, constitutional forms and ways of worship of the Christian Churches, especially of those in the Protestant tradition.

Religion in American Life (James W. Smith and A. Leland Jamison editors), New York, Vail-Ballou (Princeton University Press), 1961. Four volume comprehensive review of the impact of religion on American culture. Final volume in two books is a critical bibliography of religion in American life, listing and briefly annotating several thousand titles.

R. Rouse and S. C. Neill, *A History of the Ecumenical Movement,* London, Society for the Promotion of Christian Knowledge, 1954. Definitive study of the efforts to promote Christian unity over the centuries. Exhaustive bibliography, and documented sources.

Paul Tillich, *The Protestant Era,* University of Chicago Press, 1959. Provocative exposition of the thesis that Protestantism needs a new spiritual and social reformation, with the passing of the Protestant era in its historical age.*

Cornelius Van Til, *The New Modernism,* London, Clarke, 1946. Statement of conservative Protestant theology in criticism of liberal movements in Europe and America.

World Christian Handbook (H. Wakelin Coxill and Kenneth Grubb editors), London, World Dominion Press, 1962. Issued every five years as the most comprehensive statistical report on world Protestantism available. Every denomination in every country is fully treated; names and addresses of all Protestant church agencies in the world.

Year Book of American Churches, New York, National Council of Churches. Annual publication which gives statistical and other information on all the Protestant Churches in the United States, along with summary data on other American religious bodies.

OLD CATHOLIC CHURCH MOVEMENT

Nigel Abercrombie, *The Origins of Jansenism,* Oxford, Clarendon, 1936. Studies background and development of Jansenism. Treatment historical and theological.

Theodore Andrews, *The Polish National Church,* London, Society for the Promotion of Christian Knowledge, 1953. Documented study of the origins and growth of the schism under Francis Hodur, which produced the Polish National Church in America and Europe.

Emile Caillet, *The Clue to Pascal,* London, S.C.M. Press, 1944. Sympathetic appraisal of Pascal's role in the history of Jansenism.

Ronald A. Knox, *Enthusiasm*, Oxford, Clarendon, 1957. Compre-
    hensive study, based on first-hand material, of various en-
    thusiast movements in the history of Christianity, with special
    emphasis on Jansenism and allied developments in the Old
    Catholic tradition.*
C. B. Moss, *The Old Catholic Movement*, London, Society for the
    Promotion of Christian Knowledge, 1949. Origins and history
    of the Old Catholic Churches described from the latter's stand-
    point, with references and quotations from otherwise unavail-
    able sources.

INDEX

Two forms of index are combined in the following list of terms: the *analytic* type which briefly indicates the meaning of words, or significance of persons and writings, and the *topical* kind that simply indicates on what page the term occurs.

In order to facilitate the use of the index for reference purposes, an effort was made to further classify certain leading ideas, like God and morality, and locate where they appear in the treatment of various religions.

Finally, each of the living faiths is individually indexed under many sub-headings, and thus offers a handy summary of the religion in question.

OTHER IMAGE BOOKS

THE ABORTION DECISION – Revised Edition – David Granfield

AGING: THE FULFILLMENT OF LIFE – Henri J. M. Nouwen and Walter J. Gaffney

AN AQUINAS READER – Ed., with an Intro., by Mary T. Clark

AN AUGUSTINE READER – Ed., with an Intro., by John J. O'Meara

BEING TOGETHER: OUR RELATIONSHIPS WITH OTHER PEOPLE – Marc Oraison

CATHOLIC AMERICA – John Cogley

THE CHALLENGES OF LIFE – Ignace Lepp

CHRISTIAN COMMUNITY: RESPONSE TO REALITY – Bernard J. Cooke

CHRISTIAN SACRAMENTS AND CHRISTIAN PERSONALITY – Bernard J. Cooke

THE CHURCH – Hans Küng

CITY OF GOD – St. Augustine – Ed. by Vernon J. Bourke. Intro. by Étienne Gilson

THE CONFESSIONS OF ST. AUGUSTINE – Trans., with an Intro., by John K. Ryan

CONJECTURES OF A GUILTY BYSTANDER – Thomas Merton

CONTEMPLATION IN A WORLD OF ACTION – Thomas Merton

CONTEMPLATIVE PRAYER – Thomas Merton

DARK NIGHT OF THE SOUL – St. John of the Cross. Ed. and trans. by E. Allison Peers

THE DECLINE AND FALL OF RADICAL CATHOLICISM – James Hitchcock

DIVORCE AND REMARRIAGE FOR CATHOLICS? – Stephen J. Kelleher

EVERLASTING MAN – G. K. Chesterton

EXISTENTIAL FOUNDATIONS OF PSYCHOLOGY – Adrian van Kaam

THE FOUR GOSPELS: AN INTRODUCTION (2 vols.) – Bruce Vawter, C.M.

THE FREEDOM OF SEXUAL LOVE – Joseph and Lois Bird

THE GOD OF SPACE AND TIME – Bernard J. Cooke

THE GOSPELS AND THE JESUS OF HISTORY – Xavier Léon-Dufour, S.J.

HEALTH OF MIND AND SOUL – Ignace Lepp

A HISTORY OF PHILOSOPHY: VOLUME 1 – GREECE AND ROME (2 Parts) – Frederick Copleston, S.J.

A HISTORY OF PHILOSOPHY: VOLUME 2 – MEDIAEVAL PHILOSOPHY (2 Parts) – Frederick Copleston, S.J. Part I – Augustine to Bonaventure. Part II – Albert the Great to Duns Scotus

A HISTORY OF PHILOSOPHY: VOLUME 3 – LATE MEDIAEVAL AND RENAISSANCE PHILOSOPHY (2 Parts) – Frederick Copleston, S.J. Part I – Ockham to the Speculative Mystics. Part II – The Revival of Platonism to Suárez

OTHER IMAGE BOOKS

OTHER IMAGE BOOKS

OTHER IMAGE BOOKS